Advance Praise for
Crooked Smile

"This memoir is a vivid, humanizing and tragic story of the self-destructive horrors of addiction. For anyone seeking to understand the homeless crisis gripping America's cities, Klickstein's writing is a must-read."

—LEE FANG, Journalist

"Jared hit absolute rock bottom in life but ultimately scratched and crawled his way out of hell. His story is incredibly fascinating and insanely humbling. Anyone can learn a great deal from his journey into and out of the depths."

—EDDIE BRAVO, Martial Arts Instructor, Podcaster, Comedian

"A supremely fascinating glimpse into hell."

—MATT McCUSKER, Comedian, Author, Podcaster

"Jared's life story is the wildest I've ever heard. And fortunately for us, he's an extraordinary storyteller."

—LEIGHTON WOODHOUSE, Journalist, Co-Founder of Public

"Crooked Smile provides one of the most spine-chilling accounts of homelessness and addiction, while at the same time consistently making the reader laugh."

—SAM TRIPOLI, Comedian, Podcaster

"Jared is a brave man. His story is powerful and the country would be in better shape with more people like him. Great read."

—JESSE WATTERS, Host of Jesse Watters Primetime and Co-Host of The Five

CROOKED SMILE

CROOKED SMILE

What It Took to Escape a Decade of Homelessness, Addiction, & Crime

JARED KLICKSTEIN

BOMBARDIER
BOOKS

Published by Bombardier Books
An Imprint of Post Hill Press
ISBN: 979-8-88845-252-3
ISBN (eBook): 979-8-88845-253-0

Crooked Smile:
What It Took to Escape a Decade of Homelessness, Addiction, and Crime
© 2024 by Jared Klickstein
All Rights Reserved

Cover Design by Jim Villaflores
California FB and CRooked Font by https://www.behance.net/luis_aao

Post Hill Press
New York • Nashville
posthillpress.com

Published in the United States of America
1 2 3 4 5 6 7 8 9 10

Dedicated to Neal, Suzanne, Molly, Lyle, Pierceon, Alex, Mom, Dad, and most of all, Aunt Ina and Uncle Bruce. You sacrificed so much for a scoundrel like me. And because of this, I'm a scoundrel no more.

CONTENTS

FOREWORD

By Michael Shellenberger

The only ethical response to addiction is to reduce the harms associated with it, conventional wisdom holds. We should give people with substance use disorders clean needles and a safe place to use drugs so that they don't overdose, say journalists. And they add that if addicts are caught breaking laws against public camping, open drug use, theft, and prostitution, we should offer them services, not arrest them and mandate treatment.

But Jared Klickstein argues that the conventional wisdom is wrong. This book, *Crooked Smile*, is proof of that. Had police not eventually arrested Klickstein for behaviors relating to his addiction, he would be dead today, and the memoir you are about to read would not exist.

Harm reduction advocates say Klickstein is a traitor to other people with substance use disorders, and that very few people can do what Klickstein did. Most people with substance use disorders who are arrested return to using drugs, they add. And they claim that those of us who draw attention to Klickstein's story are reinforcing a failed and oppressive war on victims of trauma, historical racism, and patriarchy.

But Klickstein is a hero, not a traitor. While it's true that many addicts relapse several times before finally quitting, the millions of people who have achieved recovery from drug addiction over a period of hundreds of years disprove the idea that Klickstein's story is rare.

While most people are able to stop using drugs on their own, addiction experts agree that some addicts—particularly those who become a threat to themselves and others—require an "intervention" in order to quit.

And when interventions by family and friends fail and addicts become homeless, it's up to the police, judges, and the criminal justice system to offer that intervention through the enforcement of laws against the antisocial behaviors that arise from addiction. That's not cruel or oppressive; it's compassionate and necessary for people to recover from their addiction and take control over their lives.

The real question is not whether many homeless addicts need an intervention but rather why progressive cities—particularly on the West Coast—have stopped them. After all, if the status quo policies of harm reduction were working, then why did the number of drug deaths rise from 20,000 in the year 2000 to 112,000 last year?

The answer frequently given is that the drug death crisis stems from the opioid epidemic of the 1990s and the introduction of fentanyl in recent years. But the courts, drug companies, and the US government restricted opioid prescriptions over a decade ago. And drug deaths were rising for fifteen years before fentanyl really hit the drug supply.

The underlying problem is the enablement of street addiction by making rehab optional, rather than mandating it as an alternative to jail or prison. This gradual shift over the last decade goes a long way toward explaining why what people misleadingly call "homelessness" got so much worse in West Coast cities.

Progressive elected officials and the NGOs who support them have, since the 1990s, opposed using the criminal justice system to impose an intervention on homeless addicts. And the main reason for this is their view that jail and prisons cause more harm than good.

But some of these complaints are misleading. Startlingly few people are ever arrested for mere drug possession, and those who police do arrest and judges do sentence to jail for possession are usually arrested for other reasons, such as illegal public camping, public defecation, or public drug use.

As such, at the heart, the harm reduction movement's opposition to imposing interventions on people like Klickstein is ideological and not based on the evidence. Indeed, the primary funder of state and local efforts to reduce consequences—including interventions by the police—and mandated rehab for homeless addicts is George Soros. And his top drug policy advisor for twenty years told me that Soros had a fundamentally libertarian view: if people wanted to do drugs, then they should.

Many of the people who enable addicts, from elected officials to the people who run county public health programs to Soros-funded drug decriminalization advocacy organizations, are motivated by a strange mixture of libertarianism and selective compassion.

Addiction enablers believe that enforcing anti-camping laws against someone who has repeatedly overdosed on fentanyl in order to mandate rehab is more oppressive than letting the person overdose again, even to the point of dying. That's because we must respect and even venerate the "bodily autonomy" of society's victims.

As such, the people accusing Klickstein of being a traitor to the cause of helping people with substance use disorders are the real traitors. If they were allies to homeless addicts, they would demand that police, judges, and criminal justice systems do what they do all over the world, from Portugal to Japan, which is to mandate rehab to those who break laws for reasons stemming from their addiction.

Klickstein's *Crooked Smile* should go a long way toward refuting what is effectively an ideology of addiction enablement and encouragement. *Crooked Smile* makes it clear that love is not all you need. Many individuals need sobriety and recovery, while all societies require law and order.

Happily, *Crooked Smile* arrives at a moment when cities and states are rethinking the laissez-faire attitudes toward drugs. In early 2024, Oregon re-criminalized drug use, San Francisco made the receipt of cash welfare dependent on passing a drug test, and New York's governor sent the national guard into the subways, in part to deal with addiction-driven crime.

Change is on the way, and *Crooked Smile* will accelerate it. We should reduce the harm of drug use without enabling it. Most importantly, when cities catch people with substance use disorders breaking laws against public camping, open drug use, theft, and prostitution, the police should arrest them and give them the option between jail and long-term treatment, not offer them services that only prolong their suffering.

PARADOXUM
(INTRODUCTION)

There's a police station on Fifth and Wall in Downtown Los Angeles where I've eaten many a baloney sandwich. Like myself, most inhabitants of Skid Row have periodically had a meal or two within its walls before getting released back into our self-imposed war. At all times the station is encompassed by countless vessels governed by drug addiction, mental illness, or both, and occasionally everyone gets a chance to go inside for a useless twenty-four-hour ceasefire. The first time I saw someone get stabbed occurred just outside the perimeter of the two-bit psych ward.

It was in the middle of the night outside the Union Rescue Mission on the north side of Fifth, where I was smoking crack not ten feet away from a woman urinating into a sewer drain. Despite her courtesy of not pissing directly on the sidewalk, the neighborhood permanently smelled like ammonia and decomposing flesh—a stench I had already grown accustomed to many months prior. As I blew out a cloud of cocaine and the sound of the woman's stream concluded, I saw two men running in my direction from the end of the block. Once ensuring that I wasn't the immediate target, I still unsheathed my knife and held it discreetly behind my forearm. When most of your peers are fighting a personalized enemy within their own minds, anyone can become a casualty, and those that aren't prepared to fight for their life—or at least another chance to get high—quickly find defeat on Skid Row.

They pushed over a man in his wheelchair and began to beat him as he floundered on the concrete. After a few moments of melee, they started to focus on the contents of his pockets while he cried out for help to the horde of surrounding fiends. We did nothing. Unable to care about anything unless it threatened our pursuit of intoxication, we observed in complete neutrality. Empathy is a handicap that hardcore addicts abandon long before they hit the gutter.

One of the attackers fished the man's wallet out of his pants, while the other probed his jacket for additional loot. The man screamed, "Please don't take my ID! I don't care about the money, just please don't take my wallet!" Once it was clear the attackers weren't going to show him any courtesies, the man began fighting back from the ground. One of the attackers then drew his blade and stabbed him several times in the midsection. It was quick and powerless and callously operational. I could hear my jugular vein pulsing as I stood motionless and watched the victim rapidly lose all vigor. The other attacker then yanked on the man's jacket, dragging him several feet in the process, before tugging it past his arms and ripping it free. After searching the interior chest pocket, he discovered the ultimate prize: a small stash of dope.

Coincidentally, a police car was now heading our way from the west, prompting one of the onlookers to yell, "*One time!*"—a street term to warn others that the cops are coming. It was one thing to remain apathetic, but to actually help the assailants was confusing to a novice cretin like myself. Little did I know that aiding the victors had a potential reward down the line, whereas helping the victim was now fruitless. With further experience on Skid Row, I would come to fully adopt such programming.

The attackers scurried away with their spoils, and the remaining onlookers darted up Wall Street out of fear of being questioned as witnesses. I followed the herd and buried myself in an alleyway. After several minutes, the few dollars I still possessed began to burn a hole in my pocket, so I walked to Sixth and San Julian the long way to avoid the crime scene. I bought some crack and immediately forgot about the most violent event I'd ever witnessed up until that point. I didn't know if the man lived, I didn't know if the attackers were caught, and I certainly didn't care. I couldn't. No amount of emotion or effort could be spared on anything but satisfying my thirst. I, like all my brethren in the final stages of addiction, had temporarily lost all agency of the human essence.

I'm not proud to share my reaction from that night, but anecdotes like this are becoming increasingly more relevant to the American conversation. The fact that I, an objectively decent person at the time of writing this, once reacted like a reptile to a disabled man getting stabbed, needs to be digested in order to properly address this epidemic. The point is that us street addicts weren't born reptiles, but when under the jurisdiction of chemical enslavement, our ability to abandon any slice of humanity that obstructs our next fix would make a lizard gasp. It's like a computer virus. Our spirit becomes detached from any moral code, and our operating system is hijacked to perform one single function: maintaining a state of inebriation at all costs. Without the natural repercussions in place for our hazardous behavior—both to ourselves and to society—overthrowing the parasite of addiction becomes nearly impossible. And yet this has become the recent strategy in most "progressive" enclaves of America.

There are warm-blooded humans trapped inside the many thousands of animated drug-corpses across this country. A small percentage of them, like my dad and I, will be lucky enough to find their way back into society. However, if we happen to reverse course away from the authorized submission to the crisis, and instead shift *all* our efforts towards the restoration of the casualties, that percentage could be much higher.

I'd be willing to bet that none of the onlookers of the stabbing that night were inherently evil, and in a sober state of mind, we would have all reacted with grave emotionality. In fact, if we had all been sober, that stabbing would have never happened. But when the solution to the current homeless and drug epidemic is essentially free-range urban farming of the mentally ill and addicted, the event that took place that night has become normal in cities like Los Angeles. When complete freedom is granted to those embattled by drug addiction and untreated mental illness, those that suffer from either are not uplifted. Addiction and sickness are. And although appeasing addiction and mental illness can sometimes appear to be the gentler route, everyone ultimately loses. Society loses, the citizenry loses, and most of all, those subjugated by these disorders lose—they are the ultimate victims. When given an inch, addiction will always take a mile, and right now it has an unprecedented army of bodies at its disposal with little to no resistance. I was one of those bodies for nearly a decade, and after many years of increasing social and state-sanctioned self-destruction, I was beyond lucky to escape with (most of) my body intact. Dozens of my friends and my own mother were less fortunate.

California, the state I was most prominently homeless in, has poured billions of dollars into "helping" over the last decade. In particular, San Francisco has made exceptional blunders. In 2021 alone, the city allocated $1.1 billion to its Department of Homelessness, and even though the department's budget has gone up 500 percent since 2016, homelessness has increased 64 percent in the same time frame[1]. The more money the state spends, the worse the problem gets, and for some reason those in power are still reluctant to listen to an actual ex-homeless junkie. Like the addicts under the spell of drugs, these politicians probably aren't evil. They simply worship at the altar of the expert class. Their logic emulates that of someone with a burst pipe that insists on hiring an irrigation policy consultant. A nobody with some lived experience and plumbing skills would have infinitely better solutions, but this would go against the orthodoxy. One must have an expensive degree, connections to the political class, or most importantly as of late, a vapid ideology of performative social justice for their voice to hold weight in the eyes of the devout. Similar issues have arisen in the private sector, with the for-profit-rehab-industrial complex. Thousands have made easy millions with the help of corrupted doctors and bureaucratic charlatans. Still, this is just a drop in the bucket compared to the amount of tax dollars laundered through sub-contracted "nonprofits" that have every incentive to fix *nothing*. The homeless-industrial complex, like the military-industrial complex, wants perpetual war. And therefore, they offer every service *but* recovery.

I was allowed to commit petty crimes with impunity, get high where I pleased, and slowly kill myself in the public square for all to see. Still, in rare moments of clarity when I desired treatment, it was almost never accessible. With the billions of dollars spent by the state during my homeless tenure, you'd think they would have built some *public* detox and rehab facilities, but they didn't. Instead, they built small batches of permanent housing for active drug addicts to die in, sanctioned open-air fentanyl markets, decriminalized nearly all antisocial behavior, and provided every amenity to help

---

1   Joaquin Palomino and Trisha Thadani, "Broken Homes," *San Francisco Chronicle*, April 26, 2022, www.sfchronicle.com/projects/2022/san-francisco-sros/.

anyone die in slow motion. This approach has been nothing less than disastrous in California, yet it continues to spread across the country. The death toll piles up as the quality of life for *everyone* in these cities declines, and untold billions are embezzled at the expense of wasted lives. *A state of perpetual war.*

During the same period, thousands of crooked for-profit rehabs cropped up and extracted unprecedented amounts of wealth out of insurance companies and naïve families. What no one seems to understand is that you can't purchase something that can't be bought. When the profit motive *doesn't* rely upon a client's success, and permissiveness is granted to ensure the client remains a paying customer, it's difficult for recovery to be the intended goal. There's simply more money to be made from *failure*. Like those that profit off the "homeless business" in California, this is the covert mantra of an industry built on the maintenance of suffering.

After long waiting periods, I managed to get into one of the few public detoxes in Los Angeles County a handful of times, but I always left early on my own accord. When given the choice, my addiction always chose for me in this terminal stage. I'd voluntarily go back to the streets where I was given meals around the clock, cell phones, opportunities for housing, tents, food stamps, cash relief, and a general lack of consequences for my vagrancy, which I'm not complaining about. All those things are helpful to a *genuine* homeless person that's down on their luck. However, they aren't helpful to a drug addict that happens to be homeless, which is fast becoming the majority of homeless people in our country's urban centers. As it turns out, the only thing that's helpful to a severe drug addict is to help them get off drugs. And if they don't want help, the most helpful thing you can do is to incentivize them to change their mind—be it through consequences or rewards. But when the infrastructure for public treatment doesn't exist, and the political and social apparatus thinks its fashionably humane to give you just enough rope to hang yourself with, it's extremely hard for a street addict to ever desire change. By the time I truly wanted it, the best option I had was a long-term jail sentence. It's not the ideal solution, nor is it even a *good* solution in most cases, and frankly it's disgusting that it was the best solution I had available. And although it most certainly saved my life, those that still suffer out on the streets in active addiction deserve a more comprehensive route.

After my last stint in jail, I never got physically addicted to heroin again, but the mental obsession remained. I relapsed a few times after getting out, all of which were short bursts of bad decisions with ethereal consequences. Sometimes an addict needs an experience so traumatic that they finally wise up and devote themselves entirely to staying clean *for good*. These kinds of addicts, in my opinion, are the lucky ones. With the increasing negligence that this disaster is being handled with, I honestly believe I would have died in recent years had one of these experiences not happened to me. An addict of my variety seems to require such a phenomenon within the current broken system. I simply didn't have the inner resolve to overcome addiction until I saw a true horror—an act of carnage so reprehensible that it surpassed the boundaries of most imaginations. I needed an event that bordered on otherworldly, and not just a simple stabbing. I'd end up seeing plenty of those throughout my years of depravity, and not one of them would even move the needle.

I will be called a communist for the preceding paragraphs by some. Others will call me a fascist. But the bottom line is that both Stalin and Hitler would have sent our nation's homeless drug addicts to the death camps long ago. Obviously I don't subscribe to either of these ideologies, but dullards tend to froth at the mouth to label anything they don't understand as extreme. To their dismay, this is not a political issue. It's a human issue. Hell, it's a national crisis that doesn't fit anywhere within a simple political compass. And if we stay on this path of total mismanagement, most, if not all, Americans will endure its wrath in some capacity.

To understand how I arrived at such a conclusion, one must first understand my total experience. A journey that begins with a childhood marred by my parents' heroin addictions and ends with me waking up in a stranger's bathtub with a missing body part. Shortly after, I intentionally overdosed in a public bathroom not far from where I witnessed my first stabbing. Today I'm grateful for the fact that someone found my dead body in time for paramedics to revive me, as are many of my loved ones. But this wasn't always the case. Sometimes the worst thing that has ever happened to you turns into the only thing that could have saved your life. This was the catalyst that *shouldn't* have been needed for me to recover, and if we readjust our approach and consider the points made in this book, many thousands could avoid the same hellish path. We could achieve something, dare I say, *truly* progressive.

I've been sober for a number of years now, but more importantly, I've been restored of the human essence. I'm pleased with who I am, I accept who I was, and I couldn't have done it without thoroughly utilizing the nightmare. Change the formula, and you can manipulate the outcome of most variables. Statistically I should be dead or spending the rest of my life in prison, and most would say I didn't have much of a shot given my traumatic upbringing. I would have agreed a few years ago, but nowadays I consider it my greatest asset. Had my life been a cakewalk, I would most certainly not have found the need to write this book. And had I still wound up a heroin addict, a life of comfort would have only been a hindrance. You see, no one ever got coddled into putting down the needle. Luckily for me, the universe was able to crush me into submission when there was finally nothing left to get in its way.

The first incarnation of this book was a suicide letter of sorts. Many drafts later, it's now a lengthy celebration of a once beautifully tragic life. Hopefully for the reader, it's an education on the mind of a drug addict, what worked and what didn't work to encourage a change in my behavior, and at the very least, mildly entertaining. Most of us are acquainted with someone who has been afflicted by opiate addiction, but if you aren't, here's your opportunity to get to know a real bastard of the utmost hopeless variety. Those that know me today would say that I'm quite the opposite now. Here's what happened.

CHAPTER 1

JEWISH WHITE TRASH

Outside a snow-covered duplex in Worcester, Massachusetts, I witnessed my father do a backflip on a sled in the winter of 1997. Shawn Michaels held the WWF championship belt at the time, but for a brief moment, Dad was the real champion in my eyes. I, along with my cousins Joshua and Victor, had built up a natural bump in the landscape with snow and created a launch pad at the bottom of a small bunny hill in their backyard. The three of us were reunited once again, as we were every Christmas since I could remember.

Although Dad was usually pretty composed on his normal regimen of heroin and cocaine, the Christmas spirit had encouraged him to drink a bit more than usual, which inspired this act of bravery. He stumbled over to us kids, snatched my disc-shaped sled, and positioned himself at the starting line. Sitting cross-legged, he began his descent towards the jump and rapidly gained speed. Somehow, possibly due to his limber intoxication, he managed to complete a full backwards revolution in the air before crashing and eating shit into the landing patch.

I'm almost certain this happened. The memory is extremely vivid; however, it doesn't seem plausible. And although Dad can halfway corroborate it, I also question it because this period of my life is bowed with confusion. Joshua and Victor were Puerto Rican and looked quite different than me, but we were blood-related cousins. Their grandmother, Helen, was also my grandmother, although I already had two other grandmothers, so I didn't understand how this could be. Lastly, we were Jewish, so why were we celebrating Christmas with a seemingly Christian branch of relatives? The answer was that this was my *secret* family that couldn't be acknowledged all year, until Christmas time approached, and we took our annual trip to Worcester.

I'd eventually learn that my mother was adopted, and a few years before I was born, she had reunited with her birth family. They were all located in Worcester, so every year, unbeknownst to my Boston family, we'd take the fifty-mile trip out west and celebrate Christmas. Under no circumstances could this *ever* be discussed with the Boston family, who were under the impression that every Christmas we took a vacation somewhere else.

Although I looked forward to our Christmas trip every year, it aroused an identity crisis within me at a young age. Who was I? I felt out of place in Worcester—not completely a part of the family, given that I didn't see or speak to them fifty-one weeks out of the year. They were a unit plagued with alcoholism, addiction, and poverty, but they were wholly connected. Christmas dinner was complete with inside jokes, stories about people I'd never met, and a warmth that I wasn't completely attached to.

On the other hand, I couldn't feel comfortable around my Boston family either, seeing that I was in on my mother's dark secret. Was I even Jewish anymore? Did it matter? Getting bullied at school by the other Jewish kids for being "poor white trash" only added to my disorientation. I was forever an outsider, at least in my own head, and used whatever evidence I could tack together to support this notion. I utilized it as an excuse until I was nearly thirty to wreak absolute havoc.

Mom, who suffered from the same affliction tenfold, didn't survive it. She died with a needle in her arm about six years after my dad's infamous backflip. I tried to let it kill me for about a decade, and despite welcoming death at every moment, I seemingly emerged the victor. I'm no stronger or better than her, I was just lucky enough to hit the zenith of my savagery before a flatline.

The complexity of addiction is that the more experience you have with it, the more baffling it becomes. While still in chains, an indentured mind *alone* cannot outmaneuver its master, so once you surrender to the fact that you've lost all sovereignty, you finally have a chance in hell of overcoming it. The coin toss for most of us, especially heroin addicts, is between reaching this conclusion and an untimely death.

I was different in that my parents were heroin addicts. Although us kids didn't completely understand this detail, it was obvious to me that my home life was atypical. My clothes were dirtier, my social skills were less refined, and I needed a way to relieve stress from day one of kindergarten.

Pretending to get caught in between a set of French doors and scream-ing comically, I managed to get a rise out of a few kids at school that, prior to this event, regularly ignored me. I felt high from their approval. From an early age I learned that making people laugh, especially at the cost of my own dignity, could provide a rush of endorphins and numb the pain for a brief moment. It would remain my greatest tool until I discovered alcohol at age fourteen, and then heroin five years after that. Alcohol made me feel like I fit in, while heroin made me feel like I didn't exist. This cured every-thing. For without an identity, there was nowhere for the shame to roost.

I used heroin, along with a variety of other drugs, for a decade. Its drop in effectiveness correlated with an increase in consequences. Chronic homelessness, violence, lengthy jail sentences, and ultimately acts of irre-deemable self-mutilation became unavoidable, while heroin's ability to placate lost all potency. I still couldn't stop. Not until I woke up in that bloody bathtub did I understand that there would never be a compromise. Horrific repercussions, shame, and the blessing of having nothing left to enable my brutality led to my complete submission. I then became honest, open-minded, and willing to reboot my psyche, defragment my mind, and reinstall the software. Given the extremity of my strife, one would probably imagine that this should have come quicker, but like others that come from morbid roots, I was willing to fight (myself) to the death for far too long.

When I was maybe eight or nine, I asked my dad about my great-grand-father's family in Ukraine. Were they farmers? Blacksmiths? I was curious what they did for work before my ancestors came to America. Dad told me that they owned a mill that processed flour to make bread. I thought that was pretty neat. I always pictured this huge barn with nineteenth-century machinery in it and dozens of employees scampering around and doing all kinds of odd jobs around the mill. I imagined a giant silo to the left of the barn, where my family would store the already-processed flour to make room on the production floor for more wheat. Maybe my distant relatives still owned the mill, I always thought, and one day I would venture out to meet them.

When I was nineteen, I saved up a few grand from selling Oxycontin and bought a plane ticket to Europe. I figured while I was over on that side of the planet, I might as well make a quick stop in Ukraine and see the Klickstein flour mill.

Excited, I called Dad and asked him if he could give me any information on how to get the address. He couldn't compute my question. I said that I wanted to go to Ukraine and find the Klickstein mill, meet our family, and see how the business was holding up. After having a good laugh, he told me there was a misunderstanding in regard to my lineage. In actuality, my great-great grandfather had two flat rocks that he'd grind wheat into flour with. When he was killed in the pogroms at the turn of the century, his son (my great-grandfather) escaped and left behind the two rocks. That was the fucking mill.

This distorted my perception of familial identity, a shallow concept to begin with. But having been raised in a quintessentially broken home, it had provided me with some amount of inherited self-worth. My particular offshoot of the Klickstein clan was clearly a human dumpster fire, but with inspiration of one day seeing the family mill in all its glory, I thought maybe my junkie parents were just a deviation from an otherwise reputable gene pool.

I'm older now, and not so black and white in my thinking, but when Dad told me about those two rocks, I couldn't help but lose a little bit of hope. Having drug-addicted parents was a never-ending source of shame and self-hatred, so this ancestral clarification instilled in me the belief that I was inherently destined to fail. Impending alcoholism, drug addiction, mental instability, trouble with the law, suicidal thoughts, and an early grave were simply *expected*. To put it more lightly, the practice of positive thinking was completely foreign to me from birth.

I pretty much always dwelled in the negative during large portions of my young life, which is a place no child should have any reason to find themselves. So why did I? Maybe the answer was in my genetic code. Maybe I had the imperfect balance of Jewish neuroticism and Irish guilt.

I was born in Boston, Massachusetts. So was my father and his father too. According to my dad, My great-grandfather Hyman, born somewhere in what is now Ukraine, was an alcoholic that painted houses for a meager living. Because of all the lead paint he'd been exposed to for decades, he suffered from painful neurological damage, hence the penchant for liquor. Other family members have now told me that he wasn't an alcoholic, and given my dad's tendency to sometimes warp reality, their version of family history is probably more trustworthy. Regardless, not much is known about any of the Klicksteins that came before Hyman. Like most people of this earth, we were likely peasants going back millennia.

We're Jewish; that much we know. I'm ethnically Jewish on my father's side. My mother was adopted by Jews (and ironically raised much more adherent to the religion than my father), but on account of her blood, she would be considered impure by the more devout. She was born Irish-Catholic but raised in the Jewish faith, yet she had to have an "official conversion" before her wedding by order of the rabbi. My dad, who was about as Gentile as they come, was technically a Jew by blood, and thus didn't have to jump through any similar hoops.

I was raised Jewish in a cultural sense, although in terms of the religion we were completely non-observant. This isn't to say that we didn't celebrate any holidays, but our observance of such traditions was not religiously focused. Discussion of God or the bible was almost non-existent. The plight of the Jews, especially my dad's personal experience with antisemitic ball-breaking, occasionally was. Being a Jewish carpenter, and a superior one at that, wasn't always easy in an Irish-dominated union.

"It's not easy bein' the only fahkin' Jew in the union, you understand that, Jared?" he warned in his strong working-class Boston accent. "You'ah not gonna have to go through any of that when you grow up, though. You'ah gonna go to college, become a doctah, something like that. Whatevah yah want, but yah ain't gonna work with yah hands like me." He'd say this sometimes as I took his boots off after he got home from work. I'd often do this when he got home, when every day he'd take a ritualistic thirty-minute nap inspired by a long day's work and a fading heroin high.

My grandfather on my dad's side was born with nothing, got drafted during World War II, and eventually achieved the lower-middle-class American dream. He was part of the appropriately named "Greatest Generation." After the war he married my grandmother, worked as an autobody man, and had my Aunt Ina three years before my dad was born. Grandpa also took advantage of the GI bill and bought a little house for a decent price outside of Boston. It was in a veterans' project development called Oak Hill Park, and it eventually became the house that I grew up in. A lot of pain would occur in that house, and nearly a million dollars' worth of crack cocaine would be smoked within its walls. My mother would eventually die from a heroin overdose in my bedroom.

By the mid-sixties, a lot of World War II veterans had full-grown sons, and the government apparently thought it was about time to send them to war too. My dad's friends' older brothers started coming home from Vietnam, where most of them had acquired full-blown heroin addictions, crippling mental illness, and necklaces comprised of ears cut off the corpses of Vietnamese soldiers. These were the ones lucky enough to come back alive.

In fact, most of them died within a few years of returning to the States. Some overdosed, some shot themselves in the head, some wound up doing life in prison, and a couple managed to live a decent life. When Dad was finally drafted in '71, he simply didn't go. He was a "draft dodger" until amnesty was declared almost ten years later. But he still managed to get addicted to heroin and completely lose his mind. It just took him a few decades longer.

Dad told me about the first time he tried it. There were a lot of disabled vets returning to his neighborhood, and he and his friends would help them run errands for tips. One day, Dad went to the grocery store for a vet who'd lost his legs, and when he returned, the vet offered him a little snort of heroin.

Did it really happen like that? Maybe. Sounds like an odd way to discover the most addictive drug on the planet, but Dad always stressed to me that no one knew what they were getting themselves into back then, drugwise. His parents refused to teach him about sex, let alone the ins and outs of narcotics. This cute anecdote could have been an attempt to romanticize his first encounter with the drug that would ultimately destroy his life, as us heroin addicts like to do. We love to exaggerate the days of innocence and black out the years of horror.

Although Dad and I both turned out to be heroin addicts, our journeys with the drug couldn't be any more different. All heroin addicts share a bond, in that we can relate to each other on a spiritual level of suffering. We know what it's like to shoot dope, get strung out, start getting sick when you don't have it, decide to quit, throw up and want to die for days, get some of your health back, and repeat it over and over again. Heroin destroyed both of our lives, but for some reason, it destroyed mine a lot quicker. In fact, my largest prior resentment against my dad was that he got to get high for decades without many consequences. His life was a success on paper for nearly half a century, all while maintaining an off-and-on-again habit. He got married, excelled in his career, had a son, and never missed a bill, all the while having fun and getting high. Until it all came crashing down.

Of course, for a real drug addict, getting high doesn't stay fun, and it certainly didn't stay fun for him. It might be exciting, but it's usually accompanied by massive amounts of loss and pain—sooner rather than later. Heroin addiction can turn a happy life into a life not worth living faster than most vices, and although most addicts come to acknowledge this, we still can't fucking stop.

Dad started using heroin when he was around thirteen years old and cleaned up when he was fifty-eight. That time frame should speak for itself. He used it off and on in a somewhat manageable fashion for many years, which is relatively unheard of in the opiate world. Unlike most heroin addicts, he didn't experience any significant consequences until he was in his mid-forties, all of which I had a front-row seat to.

I, on the other hand, tried heroin for the first time at nineteen, and by twenty-two I was living in a tent on Skid Row. The window of "getting high and having fun with no pain" was much smaller for me than it was for Dad, although we both ended up losing everything all the same.

Some would prefer a quick defeat over a prolonged fight, and I would have to agree. I fucked up early enough that I got a second chance at life, whereas Dad just got a second chance to stay alive. I envy his journey as much as he despises it, and despite everything that happened he has undoubtedly been a good father. I love him more than anything in this world and can't thank him enough for everything happening exactly the way it did. As I like to say, and he hates to hear, in the end it all worked out.

My mother was born to a Hungarian immigrant and a homeless Irish alcoholic. They named her Debbie Murphy. Her mother's name was Helenka Kociban, and her father's first name is still unknown. After giving a few of her kids up for adoption, Helenka (who went by Helen) later harassed the adoptive parents in an attempt to extort money. She would come around and threaten to tell her birth children that she was their real mother if the adoptive parents didn't pay her off. Helen's threats were empty, however, and she left my mother and her adoptive parents alone after several attempts.

One Christmas when we were visiting Worcester, I heard Helen randomly spout to my aunt Denise, "I was born in Poland!" Denise was the one child Helen had kept, so she had the authority to quickly shut this claim down. A few months later, I was in a car with Mom and my grandparents, and the memory popped into my head for no apparent reason, so I said, "Hey Mom, remember when Helen said she was born in Poland?" Mom shot me a look of rage that I'll never forget, as Grandma asked, "Who's Helen?" This was the biggest mistake I'd ever committed, and Mom would never forgive me for bringing up a member of the secret family in front of my grandparents. She scolded me when we got home and nearly struck me for making such an error.

Back in 1950, Helen and a different Irish drunkard had a son. They put him up for adoption and insisted that he be adopted by a well-to-do Jewish family. A suitable couple was found, who named him Stephan. This is my blood uncle, who I've only met a handful of times. Stephan's adoptive parents were quite wealthy, and thus Helen's extortion plan was successfully carried out.

In 1953, Helen gave birth to my mother by way of Mr. Murphy. Once again, she insisted her baby be adopted by a Jewish family, and again her wish was granted. The adoptive couple, Belle and Al Tabachnick, were my real grandparents. They practically raised me just as much as my mom and dad, and as their first grandchild, they absolutely adored me.

They were Jewish, working-class, and both worked various jobs within the garment industry when Mom was growing up. The offspring of immigrants from Ukraine, they lived in a multi-family house in Mattapan along with extended relatives. After failing to conceive a child, they adopted my mother and changed her name to Jane, but just a year later they successfully got pregnant and had my Uncle Neal. Eventually they bought their own house in Newton and had my Aunt Debbie shortly after.

Mom did not look like the rest of her family. According to her, she had a lot of aunts, uncles, and cousins who knew that she was adopted and treated her so. Mom looked Irish, and everyone around her looked Jewish, which left her feeling unaccepted her entire life. Most of the adults knew she was adopted, all the while she was completely unaware. With no explanation for why she looked different and was largely ignored in comparison to the other kids, she felt like an outcast. Belle and Al loved her and treated her just the same as their other kids, but the aunts, uncles, cousins, and grandparents were another story. According to her, Yiddish was often used to disguise their discussions when she was within earshot.

Regardless of whether Mom's take on her childhood was distorted, in the end it doesn't matter. The number one customer of any drug addict's sales pitch is the drug addict themselves. She suffered heavily from a crisis of identity, whether she manufactured it herself or not, and things got drastically more complicated once her biological brother contacted her in the mid-eighties.

Stephan grew up wealthy, and when he finally desired to find his biological family, he could afford to hire a private investigator. He quickly discovered that my mother was his sister. The unbelievable part was that they already knew each other. They not only went to high school together, but had regularly bumped shoulders within the same social circle. Fortunately, they were only friends and nothing more. When Dad received a call from Stephan in 1985, he assumed that it was concerning something benign like a wedding invite. It wasn't, and it would change the trajectory of all our lives.

After the infamous phone call, Mom slowly got reacquainted with her birth family, and the tradition of going to Worcester for Christmas was born. However, Mom was crushed by the guilt of "cheating" on her adoptive parents, hence every Christmas trip that we took to Worcester was kept secret. Not only did she feel guilt for seeing her biological family, but more so because she visited them to celebrate a Christian holiday. Belle and Al were relatively observant of the Jewish faith, leaving Mom completely guilt-stricken and spiritually lost. Her whole life she felt like she had to fight to be accepted as a Jew, and here she was running off in secret to celebrate Christmas. For all I know, Belle and Al wouldn't have minded this at all, but to Mom, it was the greatest sin she could ever commit.

Mom was also raped when she was eight. I was about the same age when she told me. I don't know the gritty details, nor would I need to, but she told me that it was the father of one of the other kids that she carpooled with. She made sure that I understood that she was not molested; she was *raped*. Why she would tell her young son this, I still don't know. Always cautious about my interaction with strangers, she might have been trying to instill an awareness of predators. Either way, she needed me to know the severity of what happened to her. Dad was always convinced that the rape wasn't a false memory, despite other family members insisting that it would have been near impossible. The man in question was never known to have access to Mom unchaperoned by Uncle Neal, and his own children have stated that they never noticed a single inkling of pedophiliac behavior. This of course doesn't negate her claim, but by the time the family got wind of the accusations, she was already deep into drug abuse. So I must begrudgingly sympathize with those who have trouble believing her.

Eventually she would be diagnosed as schizophrenic, which only further undermined her credibility. However, anyone smoking as much crack as she was would have had a hard time not receiving a similar diagnosis. I've been labeled everything under the sun at one time or another.

Sometimes the truth is far simpler than any doctor can drum up: we're fucking high on drugs. The drive to overdiagnose and overmedicate often results in disaster, but it certainly feeds the ego of the professional class. It's also a typical practice at a lot of for-profit rehabs. Overmedicate the clients so they don't make too much of a fuss and don't want to leave, so that insurance can continue to get billed for $1500 a day. Easy money.

It's a bad time in cultural terms to be calling into question a woman's allegations of rape, and rightfully so. But although there's little evidence to support her claim, I still believe her. I believe that she may have been raped because she wasn't Jewish by blood. Out of the many kids amongst the social circle of Jewish parents, my mother was the only non-Jew at birth. Because of this, it's possible the man viewed raping her as less of a crime. Other family members now also consider it a possibility.

The trauma of this rape, along with the denial by her family, was catastrophic. Heroin, unlike therapy, offers an immediate, short-term solution, because it allows you to forget about anything for six to twelve hours. It's not a sustainable solution, but it works so fucking well at first that it's nearly impossible to consider an alternative. It will always eventually kill you, but if the pain it creates doesn't outweigh the pain it numbs, quitting is beyond difficult. For Mom, the pain that it numbed was simply too great. Dad and I were more fortunate.

My parents grew up within a few miles of each other and attended the same high school. Like Dad, Mom came up during the sixties, and she got high like most of the kids of that era. She lived in a nicer (more Jewish) neighborhood than Dad, although his family was slightly better off. The only reason her parents even let her date my dad was because he was Jewish. Entering his neighborhood, let alone dating someone from it, was normally forbidden. Knowing her parents would never allow her to date a non-Jew, her desire for a "bad boy" was satisfied by finding the worst-behaved Jew at school. This happened to be my dad, who was the only Jewish kid in his circle of criminals and degenerates.

Their first date consisted of joyriding in a stolen car. Because of stories like this, I wonder sometimes if my dad corrupted my mom. Other times I wonder if it was the other way around. This kind of question shouldn't matter. Rarely is it appropriate to blame someone for the actions of another, and in my parents' case, it's no different. Neither of them introduced heroin to the other, but that's insignificant; both seemed to have had a genetic disposition for mayhem.

She didn't become a full-blown junkie until she was in her forties. Throughout the years she had dabbled, but cocaine, weed, and alcohol were her primary drugs of choice in her youth. Maybe she partied a little more than the average person, but nothing close to what we would now consider hardcore abuse. On the other hand, my father had an on-and-off relationship with heroin that he (mostly) hid from her successfully. He always went to work and paid the bills, and therefore was able to keep it discreet and under control. In fact, he was able to hide it from everyone, and could seemingly start and stop using with some ease.

After Uncle Stephan reached out to her in 1985, Mom's drug use intensified to the point that she had a miscarriage in 1987. As her familial identity blurred into obscurity, her drug use increased until she got pregnant with me. Her life then reverted back to semi-manageable for several years until I was about three, when Uncle Stephan, who had his own struggles with heroin, became homeless and moved in with us temporarily. Mom finally had a chance to bond with her biological brother and attempt to figure out who she really was. She never got a complete answer, but she certainly figured out that she loved heroin. She loved what it did for her, most notably the fact that it made such a question irrelevant. Sometimes it starts with how good it makes you feel, because it undoubtedly feels better than anything humanly possible, but in the end its only about what it can make you *not* feel. This is why we can stop from time to time, but most of us can't seem to figure out how to stay stopped. This is our true dilemma.

Whether it was the layer of grief that constantly poked through her fragile smile, or the manic impulsivity that gave me some of my greatest childhood memories, I was vaguely aware that something wasn't right with my mother. She was broken, and I knew it from far too early of an age. Getting woken up at three in the morning on a school night to go get pancakes is fun, but looking back, it wasn't the behavior of a stable person. She was lively, protective, and above all else gave me security in knowing that I was treasured. There was a tremendous amount of love in my house during my formative years. Love not only between my parents and me, but also between my mother and my father.

Had I not gotten that experience prior to their downfall with addiction, I'd probably be a few steps closer to sociopathy. I consider myself privileged for the fact that I got those first few years of unadulterated homelife. Normality, or something close enough to it, defined my first couple years of memories.

I was not a crack baby, although some have rightfully made assumptions. No offense to people born addicted to crack cocaine. I've known many former crack babies in adulthood that were of the highest human caliber. Humans, as we learn and forget time and time again, are much more resilient than we sometimes give ourselves credit for. Mom hadn't yet tried crack at the time of her pregnancy, and although she wasn't a stranger to narcotics, she remained completely sober while I was in the womb (as far as I know). According to Dad, this is true, and at this point he has no reason to lie about it.

My parents were working class, whatever that means. My dad put on work boots every morning, and although he may have made nearly as much money as many white-collar professionals, we were working class by societal definitions. From my earliest days, he would show me his boots and his calloused hands while explaining, "I'm a blue-collah worker, Jared, which means I get paid to work with my hands. When you grow up, you're gonna be a white-collah worker, like your Uncle Neal."

He was a carpenter, but not just any carpenter. Despite whatever bias you would rightfully think I have, the man was a blue-collar genius. He could make anything and everything out of wood. Two-story radial banisters, ball-and-claw-legged bureaus, thirty-foot oval conference tables, you name it. More importantly I got to see all of this being done, which clinched my fascination and complete reverence for him at an early age. For fun he would take apart motors and put them back together, and although he wasn't formally educated, he was of high mechanical and verbal intelligence.

He wasn't a large man but had a coarse look to him that made it obvious he wasn't a doctor or a lawyer. The only Jew in his entire union of over five hundred men, this wasn't obvious to anyone until his last name was revealed. He'd tell me that when anyone would find out he was Jewish they'd ask him if his father owned the company. He'd laugh, tell them no, and then say that he was the only Jewish carpenter besides Jesus himself. He took a lot of shit at work from his mostly Irish and Italian coworkers, but he had the social skills and sense of humor to not only avoid most conflicts, but to also command respect from most everyone. Being a mainstay of working-class Boston culture, ethnic humor was completely normalized.

Coworkers would come over for beers, call my dad a cheap kike for having Budweiser instead of Guinness, and he'd say, "Yeah, well maybe you dumb Irish bastards could retire before you're eighty if you knew a thing or two about being a tightwad like me!" and they'd all have a good laugh. I remember hearing that conversation at an early age and being shocked. Prejudice, which I understood to be wrong, was being thrown around our living room and laughed about. Later I would learn that, whether I liked it or not, this was how some people joked around, and I would eventually have to know how to handle it. Using a combination of self-deprecation and wit, Dad knew how to flip the script, which was something I'd inherit from him and would heavily utilize later in life, especially in jail.

A larger aspect about growing up in the nineties, for me personally, was the assumption that things would always be OK. What I mean is that life was only going to get better and never worse in America. Back then it was just expected that you moseyed through adolescence, went to college, and whether you worked hard or not, you would end up with a 401K and a three-bedroom house in the suburbs. Class mobility was tangible because America was surging. This wasn't stated directly; it merely filled the social and economic atmosphere of the era. Life was good, the internet boom was just getting ramped up, and an everlasting source of American prosperity was assumed for the Millennial generation. The country's global dominance was settled, imminent war seemed like a thing of the past, and we had faith in our institutions once again. An oncoming opioid crisis that would destroy hundreds of thousands of American lives, all the while being enabled by the pharmaceutical industry and the US government, seemed like something only your conspiracy theorist uncle could make up. And that was just the tip of the iceberg considering its evolution into the current fentanyl epidemic.

Mom and Dad owned a house outright before I was even born on an inflated working-class income. Although Dad made decent money in the union, he also participated in a bit of drug trafficking that made this easier to achieve. He didn't want me to have to rely on illegal activity to make a good living like himself, so from kindergarten on I was told that I'd be required to go to college. Uncle Neal, the only person in my family to really do something with his life, made it through law school and escaped the working class. I was to be like him in every which way. In the nineties it was assumed that going to college would guarantee you a lucrative white-collar career, and as we know now, it's a bit more complicated than that. Sure, a college degree can certainly help one attain class mobility, but it turns out that it actually matters what you get that degree in. Who would have thought?

I now have friends with engineering degrees who are making less than my dad did thirty years ago as a blue-collar worker, and the way things are going, they may never be able to afford a home in the same city that they grew up in. Maybe the boomers collectively overshot the mark. Or maybe the Millennials are a bunch of entitled good-for-nothings. Maybe our parents had an artificially inflated standard of living that no generation will ever see again. I wouldn't know; I'm not an economist. I majored in European history and dropped out to pursue homelessness.

Drug use in the household during my early years in West Roxbury was kept at a semi-recreational level. Because of this, my life until we moved to Oak Hill Park is filled with mostly positive memories. Mom cooking me dinner while watching *Full House* with her on the kitchen TV, Dad taking me to watch local high school baseball games, and the both of them showering me with love were regular occurrences. Sure, Mom was damaged, and it rubbed off on my still-forming personality, but I never witnessed anything traumatic during this period.

When I was seven, we moved out of West Roxbury and into the Newton neighborhood of Oak Hill Park. Dad bought the house he had grown up in from Grandpa. Amongst the friends that I would make on my block I was known as a "rich kid," whereas at school I was one of the "poor kids" in comparison to those from other parts of Newton. In actuality, none of us kids really knew anything about our parents' financial standings. However, we were aware of the class differences between the neighborhoods that we came from. A lot of the dads on my street came home around four o'clock and took their Carhartt jackets off, whereas a few streets over the dads came home around six-thirty wearing a button-down shirt with a blazer. That much we knew.

As things progressed and Dad's drug trafficking got more lucrative through the nineties, my parents wound up with a seemingly endless supply of cash that had no way of being laundered. It could be cautiously spent on assets, or easily spent on untraceable goods like drugs. Moving back to the old neighborhood, where Dad's drug pals still lived in their parents' basements, would only contribute to them spending the money on the latter.

Right before I started first grade, Grandpa decided to move to Florida and sell us the house so I could go to a better school in Newton. The decision to move had been made with only my interest in mind, but ultimately it proved to be catastrophic to my homelife. The childhood buddies of my dad became frequent guests in our new home, and within months, Dad was completely strung out. By second grade Mom was too, and by the time I turned ten, our home had been transformed into a fully dysfunctional crack house.

The memories of my mother from this time are mostly suppressed or wiped off the hard drive, but the ones that manage to ominously linger are difficult to think about. Various snapshots of her nodding out in social settings plague my mental image of her, with her signature drooping bottom lip and folding spine most prominent. Whether washing the dishes or driving me to school, she was usually less than fully conscious. "Fender benders" became a near-weekly occurrence. The person I had once felt most safe around became an absolute threat to my wellbeing, given the amount of car accidents and dangerous situations she was regularly involved in. Although I feared getting in the car with her, this was not the crux of what affected me. It was her mental absence that crushed me nearly beyond repair. It wasn't that the last few years I got to interact with the person who created me were frightening, it was that they were empty. She was a shell of a human that swung like a pendulum between nodding out of consciousness and erratic, crack-induced paranoia. She would have been better described as a bad roommate than my actual mother.

Dad absolutely abhorred this behavior. He would scream at her, then scream at me for laughing at the sight of her half asleep, mumbling in junkie tongues. I knew that it wasn't normal, and I also knew that it shouldn't have been conventionally humorous, but laughter as a coping mechanism was more manageable sometimes than bearing the horror of what was actually happening. It tortured Dad to watch his son laugh at the sight of his own mother slowly killing herself, but he had no other option. There was no way to explain the gravity of the situation to a nine-year-old.

Mom didn't handle heroin very well. Some heroin addicts can semi-function when they get high, and others can barely keep their eyes open. Dad could get high and go to work with minimal issues, but more importantly, he could mostly keep it a secret from the public. Mom, on the other hand, couldn't keep it secret from anyone within eyesight. I take more after my dad in this area; however, with heroin now extinct and replaced by fentanyl, neither of us could use without being completely incapacitated in today's age.

Dad and I might have been able to handle our heroin better than Mom, but there was one major problem that we all would come to suffer from: we couldn't use heroin without eventually smoking crack. Once that ingredient is added to any junkie's diet, everything's off the table. Heroin may be mine and my dad's drug of choice, and it's always been the first drug we both run to when we decide to implode our lives, but within minutes of doing our first shot, we always find ourselves hankering for a hit of something else. This wasn't the case for Dad spanning decades, and it wasn't always the case for me, but at some point, it seemed to become irreversible for the both of us.

Addiction only moves in one direction: the wrong one, and there's never any backtracking. Once you smoke heroin, you don't want to snort oxy anymore. Once you shoot heroin, you don't want to smoke it anymore. The nail in the coffin is when you finally mix heroin and cocaine at the same time, and you can't really think about anything else from that day forth. Something about this combination somehow ruins both drugs on their own.

This is what happened to my parents one day in 1998, when my mom's friend from the methadone clinic showed her how to cook and smoke crack. She liked it. She liked it so much that she brought some home to share with Dad, and to no one's surprise, he happened to like it too. It immediately changed my entire life trajectory.

It was around the time I turned nine years old that my parents started smoking substantial amounts of crack, and with their newfound hobby, they also began to go without sleep for many days at a time. This secondary symptom of stimulant abuse was possibly more destructive than the crack itself, and it led to a drastic mental unraveling of all of us, me included.

Screaming matches became daily, sometimes getting violent, all over what seemed to be figments of cocaine-induced hallucinations. There had been little love in the home for several years already, but once the cocaine took over, an ungodly level of neglect replaced any sense of affection. With minimal supervision, complete lack of order, and even less of a grip on reality, my parents had essentially left me to raise myself.

I didn't shower, I didn't wear clean clothes, and a homecooked meal from Mom would never be experienced again. Strange acquaintances of my parents now regularly lurked around the house, and periods of time would pass where one of my parents (usually Mom) would disappear for days. This was when she started getting arrested. Unsurprisingly, this was also when social services started snooping around to get a feel of my wellbeing.

Every month or so they would come and interview me about my homelife, and I would lie to them about the current state of affairs. I'd say that Mom cooked me breakfast every morning, and that when I rode my bike Dad made sure I wore a helmet. This is what my parents told me to say, and although it wasn't true, my parents thought they had my best interest in mind. Like most addicts, they wanted to sweep everything under the rug with the hope that they'd get their act together (somehow) before it all came crumbling down. They took care of me the best they could, given the horrific states of their addictions, and even though there wasn't much parenting going on by then, I knew their love for me hadn't simply vanished.

But it was temporarily consumed by *something*—something a child could never put their finger on. I recognized that the culprit of this issue was out of their control, but I was just too young to understand the concept of drugs. So regardless of now being unfit, these two sick individuals had created me, nursed me, held me in their arms, and provided me with my first sense of protection. As indisposed as they had become, I was willing to lie for them in an act of what I thought was protecting the three of us. Things hadn't gotten bad enough yet to tell the truth, but they would.

My out-of-town family would call and ask things like if Dad was diagnosed with cancer and keeping it a secret, or if Mom was taking any psychiatric medication. Like any child in fear of being removed from their home,

it was only natural for me to defend my parents and protect the reality from being exposed. "No, everything's fine," I would say when Uncle Neal or Aunt Ina, my dad's sister, called the house. They'd ask why I sounded so despondent and sad, and I would repeat the line until their suspicions were kept at bay. I said the same line to my teachers, my neighbors, and anyone else that happened to ask, and although it was obvious that it wasn't so, there wasn't much anyone could do about it. I wasn't getting physically abused, and I stayed fed for the most part, so all anyone could do was wait for the inevitable to occur.

The trauma of my confusion surrounding my parents' issues was just as damaging as the actual neglect. Had they been straight alcoholics, the source of their condition would have been much more obvious, but they managed to keep their drug use and paraphernalia out of sight. I'd ask my mother why life had changed so dramatically in the home and always got vague explanations of menopause, depression, or looming divorce. These were heavy subjects to introduce into a child's mind, and even though they were conceivable excuses, I was never persuaded.

To quell my curiosity, I began peeping through their belongings and the pockets in their clothes to find an answer. Other than a few hidden packs of cigarettes and stashes of cash, I found nothing of interest. I did, however, pick up a smoking and stealing habit out of the ordeal. This further pushed me towards the group of outcasts in the neighborhood, and I began spending most of my free time in the woods with the other unsupervised children of degenerates.

By sixth grade I was missing school regularly, barely passing any of my classes, and utterly incapable of establishing healthy friendships. I was a feral animal amongst an entire school of relatively normal children. I got along with the delinquents in my neighborhood because I always had cigarettes, but these were mostly older kids that bullied me more times than not.

My only real friend was one of the Russians named Oleg, who was several years younger than me, but our bond over WWF wrestling superseded any age gap. Oleg's parents were immigrants who both worked multiple jobs, and therefore he didn't have much more supervision than me. Both of us being embarrassed about the homes we came from allowed us to trust one another, and even though none of my classmates would have been caught dead coming over to my house to hang out, Oleg was the only kid I was comfortable with seeing its tragic state. We were shunned by our classmates for the most part, which only furthered our social ineptitude, but we found solace in our dream of becoming WWF stars. With our entrance music picked out and special moves choreographed, we spent much of our free time obsessing over the idea of being someone else: professional wrestlers, complete with made-up backstories and different names than the ones our parents gave us. We were full-grown men with muscles, heroic athleticism, and charismatic stage presence. We were everything we weren't, every day after school in my backyard.

Oleg's hoodlum of an older brother, Dima, introduced me to weed and alcohol sometime in the sixth grade, and by "introduced me" I mean he forced me to get high with him in his garage. After several of these incidents, I became more than willing to participate.

Although I couldn't manage to ever get thoroughly stoned, I liked it because it won the approval of Dima. After a few weeks of smoking weed with him, a lightbulb went off in my head: maybe my parents were smoking weed, and that's why their behavior had changed so dramatically over the past few years.

My dad had begun spending much of his time in the basement as of late and had told me I absolutely wasn't allowed to go down there. In the basement were tons of tools and old woodworking machinery, making it too dangerous of a place for me to play around in. After my epiphany, I worked up the courage to go down there and look around for any weed paraphernalia, and not to my surprise, I found an odd-looking pipe hidden in a cinder block. Whatever it was resembled something you'd smoke weed out of, so I was convinced that the mystery had been solved.

Little did I know that what I had found was actually a *crack* pipe, but regardless, I was on the right track. This idea was 100 percent confirmed the following weekend when I caught a glimpse of Mom hitting a similar pipe in the car while I was inside Blockbuster picking out a movie. I peered through the Blockbuster window into Mom's Chrysler, where I saw her illuminated face behind the glow of a hot crack pipe and thought, "Man, I guess my parents are stoners. That's kinda cool."

The summer of 2001 was more traumatic for me than anything I'd eventually endure on my own accord. The depths of barbarity I witnessed in those several months not only haunt my daily thoughts, but also nearly every single one of my dreams to this day. No matter the tone, my dreams often conclude with some abstract construction of memories from that short time frame. At the very least I find myself in that house at some point during most of my slumbers. As far as nightmares go, I can't think of a single one I've had in the past twenty years that didn't end in that basement. Sometimes I'll get a big whiff of mildew and crack smoke before catching a glimpse of Mom crouched behind the water heater. These kinds of nightmares are few and far between these days, but when I was still using, they were a constant. I couldn't help but wonder whether she was trying to warn me from the grave.

This period was especially horrifying because I was on summer vacation from school, forcing me to see the uncensored version of my parents' twenty-four seven debauchery. This was when it became fully apparent, even to a twelve-year-old, that they were quickly approaching death. Although I don't know the exact numbers, Dad couldn't have weighed more than a hundred twenty pounds, and Mom was without a doubt less than ninety. At this point they were in isolation for nearly every hour of the day, unless it was to sneak out of the house and buy more drugs.

Mom would lock herself in the master bedroom, and Dad would spend every moment from when he got home until he left to go back to work in the morning sealed in the basement woodshop. To prevent anyone from interrupting him—both real and imagined—he drilled wooden planks across the basement door to cinch himself in. Deeply paranoid, this pattern of barricading himself inside his own private dungeon happened like clockwork as the sun set, and every time the sun would come up, I would wake to the sound of reversing screws.

Somehow, he still managed to get to work most days, but quite often he was getting sent home early. Looking back, it's clear that he was in no position to be employed, let alone operate the vehicle he drove to work every day. With his arms covered in track marks and small abscesses, it's surprising that he was even allowed in the workshop. Maybe his boss, Artie, was in a similar state of denial as my young self, along with certain family members, or maybe he had become irreplaceable. To this day he assures me his work was of the finest caliber, even during this last chapter of his employability. That's hard to believe given that he looked like he lived at a POW camp.

My snooping continued through the summer and led me to find syringes and burnt spoons hidden around the house, yet I still managed to suppress the recognition of what was truly happening. It was only after later seeing a picture of my parents from that summer (which my aunt took to keep a record of their demise), that I was finally able to perceive the true terror. They were ghosts: lifeless and covered with bruised needle marks all over their arms and legs, comatosely staring a hundred miles beyond the camera.

However removed from reality they may have been, they were still mildly aware of the trauma they were putting me through. They were burdened with constant guilt, which I took advantage of in the form of calculated manipulation. This began a lifelong pattern. All I wanted was normality, but knowing that was no longer an option, I squeezed whatever I could out of them. This mostly came in the form of them letting me keep any pet I came across.

By that summer, the house was teeming with half-domesticated animals and the scattered feces that went along with their lack of care: seventeen guinea pigs, three ferrets, and an untrained Belgian sheepdog. These animals, like me, were neglected and maladjusted, and therefore the main source of comfort I found within the home. We were all filthy, antisocial, barely toilet-trained, and destined to die in a cage. We held each other together.

In an act of rarity, after weeks of requests, Mom took me and the dog to a park that summer. I was able to take the dog to the park on my own, but what I really wanted was time with my mother. I hadn't had any in what felt like many years. I knew it was all going to come crashing down soon and wanted to get one last moment of joy with her before whatever impending doom was carried out. This could have ranged from getting taken away by the authorities to one of my parents suddenly overdosing, but either way, I knew something terrible was imminent.

On that day, she was to fulfill her promise of taking me and the dog to the park—which she did—but before we even got out of the car, she looked me dead in the eyes and said, "Jared, I'm sorry, honey, but I forgot something at home. We can come right back after I grab it."

Knowing damn well that she didn't forget anything at all, but rather couldn't go twenty minutes without taking a hit, I cried. She cried too, and despite both of us indirectly acknowledging we knew exactly what was really going on, she drove the car home and locked herself in the bedroom.

Although quaint in comparison to some of the more shocking things I witnessed that summer, this was the saddest moment of my childhood. Probably the saddest moment of my life, and the last vivid memory I have of my mother. The pure powerlessness of her being unable to spend a moment with her child because drugs had superseded the most basic form of parental love will forever haunt me.

One night in a fit of oddity, Dad unscrewed himself from the basement hours before his regular schedule and woke me up. Confused, I began to ask what this was about before being interrupted and told to stay quiet.

While another firearm was clenched in one hand, he used the other to hand me a gun. In a state of unbridled paranoia, he quietly explained that there were people spying on us from outside, and that I would have to help him figure out who they were. I was to cover him if bullets started flying. He insisted that it was most likely a government agency behind this, so calling the police wasn't a viable solution.

Even at twelve years old, I knew that this was a complete delusion, but I complied anyway and circled the house several times. After all, father-son bonding time was sparse as of late. After entertaining his fantasy for ten minutes or so, I halfway convinced him that they must have retreated. I then returned to bed and left my deranged father alone, staggering around our backyard with a loaded weapon. This soon became a regular occurrence, and I always participated despite knowing it wasn't real, let alone healthy. I longed for my father and had to take what I could get, even if it meant participating in his crack-induced hallucinations.

I was embarrassed for my parents to find out that I was aware of what was going on. I became their enabler. I not only put up with their psychosis, but I actually utilized it to garner much-needed attention. Dad would film his closet with a camcorder for hours, one night swearing that there was some kind of demon living in it, another night it would be a dragon. When he would ask me to watch what he had recorded to verify, I would happily oblige. This had become my version of playing catch. I was old enough to know that I should have contacted someone for help—that my parents' health was in jeopardy—but I also knew that there was a risk of getting taken away, so I stayed quiet. I didn't want them to go to jail, and I didn't want to go into foster care, so I did everything I could to preserve the nightmare.

Aunt Debbie had been engaged to get married, and our house happened to be a central location to hold a family get-together. None of my family had seen my parents in over a year, and they had no clue about the depths they had sunken to in recent months. They were each smoking about a thousand dollars' worth of crack a day, along with a few hundred dollars' worth of heroin, which was an intense amount of drugs to be doing at a typical shooting gallery, let alone a bridal shower.

Dad had been laid off at the beginning of August for crashing into his boss's Mercedes in the shop parking lot, which proved to be the tipping point at which his work would no longer enable him. Unfortunately, he had a plentiful amount of cash left from his prior drug dealing, so losing his job didn't hinder his ability to afford an ungodly habit. In fact, it just gave him a lot more time to get even more fucked up.

Nonetheless, my parents agreed to host the engagement party. Instead of coming clean right there and then to avoid the oncoming disaster, they did what any drug addict would do and kicked the can down the road. Addicts have the remarkable ability to live in the moment to a fault. If a problem can be postponed, even if the consequences will grow tenfold, an addict will always do so. Addiction has an impressive lack of foresight.

Upon my extended family's arrival in Boston, I made the decision to inform them of what was going on. I figured my parents' decrepit state would speak for itself, but either way I decided that I was going to give my family the whole story. Whether my aunts and uncles were aware of my parents' addiction prior to this is up for debate—they knew my parents liked to party—but the level of severity they'd reached over the past year was incapable of being hidden.

After being questioned about the state of their physical appearances, my parents denied absolutely everything. It wasn't until I pulled Uncle Neal aside and told him my version of the truth: my parents were on some kind of drugs, and although the extent of what a twelve-year-old could possibly figure out was faint, I assured him that they were on the brink of death.

After hours of deliberation and the aid of my testimony, my parents gave in and came clean to the family. Within twenty-four hours, a plan was devised: I would go live with Aunt Ina in California for a month while my parents went to rehab, and then I would return to Boston and everything would go back to normal.

My family honestly believed this was possible. Remember: they had no understanding or experience with drug addiction, so like any normal humans, they figured that this was how it worked. Twenty-eight days in rehab and you're good to go. Maybe it would have worked for my parents this way, but we'll never know—because shortly after the plan was created, they managed to get arrested.

Because Aunt Ina was now staying at the house and taking care of me, my parents felt the need to get high elsewhere. A few days before they were scheduled to go to rehab, they managed to get caught smoking crack in a parking lot and resisted arrest. This really spoiled the whole "twenty-eight days in a fancy rehab and then happily ever after" thing we were all hoping for, but honestly, that probably wouldn't have been enough time for them to even thoroughly detox. The only thing that would have fixed them at that point was probably prison or a year-long program out in the middle of nowhere, neither of which would happen. They would make bail and be right back at it within a week with absolutely nothing to slow them down.

No one knows how to throw a wrench in the gears at the worst possible time better than two drug addicts in love. For some reason, it's significantly worse than anything a drug addict can do solo. When it comes to making someone act in their own worst interest, drugs are the only thing on this earth more powerful than love. Combine the two, and you get the most potent recipe for self-sabotage known to mankind. My family would come to learn this the hard way over the next two years.

CHAPTER 2

DOMESTICATION

People who aren't experienced with addiction often fail to wrap their heads around how truly difficult it is to get sober on your own accord. I know a lady who smoked crack throughout all nine months of her pregnancy, and when her water broke inside of her crack dealer's house, she sat outside on the curb with a pipe in her mouth until an ambulance arrived. Just because you know you absolutely need to stop in order to save your own life, or even your baby's life, it simply doesn't matter. We're hogtied and locked in the trunk while our addiction sits behind the wheel. It often gets to a place where being temporarily forced into submission would be in our best interest, and until we are, we're merely vessels of lethal consumption.

At the age of twelve in late August of 2001, Aunt Ina and I flew from Boston to San Francisco, about two weeks before 9/11. I mention this because ever since I've perverted the catastrophe as a demarcation between my parents and me. This is just as nonsensical as it is egocentric, but you must understand that this tragedy coincided with the most traumatic experience of my childhood.

Self-obsessively, like any drug addict in the making, I took the world-changing event personally, and adopted its margin in time as my own. There were the good times before, and then the bad times after. Just like those that thought everything in this country was just fine until September 11, I was equally delusional about my docket. The times with my parents had been good, the times with my aunt and uncle would be bad, and there was no changing my mind until I found myself slowly dying in the gutter seventeen years later.

Global historic events aside, I didn't handle the transition to California well. Despite being told that this change would be short term (everyone assumed my parents would get their act together after their arrest and probation), I was completely dispirited and refused to accept Aunt Ina and Uncle Bruce as temporary parental figures. Aunt Ina didn't have any children, and my uncle's daughters from a previous marriage were well into adulthood, so their quaint middle-aged lives were suddenly shattered by a twelve-year-old feral child. I don't mean to downplay their monumental sacrifice. I'm simply stating that, understandably, no party was excited about the situation. After all, it was deeply traumatizing for them as well, which I never took into consideration until years after our eventual schism.

I was supposed to enter seventh grade that year. School started shortly after my arrival, but I refused to attend for the first several weeks because I saw no point to it. I figured my parents would be out of jail shortly, and we would chalk this all up as a mistake; everything would simply return to the way it had been before my parents started smoking crack. All they needed was to sit in jail for a little bit, dry out, and realize that they shouldn't get high anymore, right? Certainly, no parent could go on with this kind of behavior after experiencing the consequence of losing a child.

This is what I believed, as many family members of drug addicts do as well. I can't tell you how many young women I've sat and got high with in my adulthood that were one dirty urine test away from losing custody of their kids, and yet the needle still finds a way into their veins. Quadruple that number and you wouldn't even be close to the amount of men I've known who haven't seen their children in years as a result of getting high. It didn't slow them down a bit.

Having a decent amount of dirty money left in the reserve, my parents were able to hire a good lawyer (unfortunately), and neither of them having a serious prior criminal record also played in their favor. Because of this, they got released from jail with nothing more than informal probation. In my opinion, there shouldn't be a punishment for using drugs in your own home if it's not endangering anyone else. But smoking crack in public, combined with the fact that my parents' addictions were ruining the life of their child, should have been enough for them to get mandated to a long-term program. Instead, they were sent back to their drug den and required to pay a fine. During their brief time in jail, they missed the check-in for the rehab my family had set up, and with getting to rehab now in their own hands, they of course couldn't defy their addictions.

Yet we all still hoped that this slap on the wrist would inspire them to get clean, but now with my full comprehension of addiction, I understand why it didn't. On the contrary, the fact that I was now out of the picture and their bad behavior wasn't met with any life-saving consequences, they were finally allowed to utilize 100 percent of their effort towards getting high. This in combination with the $600,000 in cash Dad had in the basement was not a winning combo for good behavior. When they ran out of that in about fourteen months, they at last agreed to start a methadone maintenance program. However, this really had no lasting positive effect on reducing their drug intake. It merely became just another variable in the cocktail of destruction, and my mother would be dead shortly after.

Aunt Ina and Uncle Bruce were pretty well-off and lived in a little town called Piedmont, which was the inverse of whatever idea you would have about Oakland. Piedmont was less than five miles from some of the worst neighborhoods in California, despite having few residents that didn't live in million-dollar homes. Back in Boston I hadn't been raised in a poor neighborhood per se, but it was a completely different socio-economic level in comparison to my new stomping grounds.

Regardless of the class differences, people in California seemed to be more friendly. In fact, the first thing I told my aunt that I noticed about California was that the people were "nicer than they were in Boston." They were polite, calm, approachable, and for lack of a better term, meek. Unlike the adults that I was used to, the ones in California were delicate, uncalloused, and open-minded. This general pleasantness seems to be a Northern California trait, and not just constricted to middle-upper-class towns like Piedmont. Boston has a terrible reputation for not only being racist but, more definitively, filled to the brim with complete assholes. So much so that the white people there don't even like other types of white people. Everyone's a Guinea asshole, an Irish fuck, a Portuguese prick, or a Russian bastard. It's a culture of open hostility, which sounds terrible, but in some ways it's less sinister than the façade that Northern California desperately tries to keep afloat.

The Bay Area was the polar opposite of Boston *in attitude*. Although socially abrasive and rough around the edges, Boston is a city that's always been defined by its flourishing working-class. On the other hand, the Bay Area is tolerant and soft to the touch, but underneath its mask of progressivism is nothing more than a playground for millionaires. Most inhabitants either inherit immense wealth, make six figures and can afford to rent their own apartment, or live in squalor. The haves and the have-nots are essentially living on two different planets within the same thirty-mile radius. More definitively, the gap between the moderately rich and the devastatingly poor is despicable for a place that smugly prides itself on being the shepherd of modern egalitarianism. I will always love the Bay Area and call it my home, despite the unravelling dystopia that it's become in certain areas, and beyond its never-ending ignorance and inability to see itself in the mirror, it remains one of my favorite places—mostly because of the weather, but also because of its (sadly, rapidly depleting) charm.

I'd spend my adolescent years in the region with Gavin Newsom at the helm of San Francisco's downfall, arguably once the most enlightened city in America. In time his desire shifted towards the entire state, and he handed the torch to other mayors, like London Breed, who have thoroughly followed in his footsteps. We're currently on the verge of legislative-assisted suicide not being a winning strategy at the polls, so of course both have finally begun to change their tune. But I'll never forget when a few years ago Newsom said, "Clean and sober is the biggest damn mistake this country ever made," while addressing the homelessness and addiction crisis. A bold statement for *anyone* to make, overlooking other "mistakes" such as slavery or the internment of Japanese citizens to name a couple. But for the governor of a state that can't stop throwing gasoline on the fire of both epidemics, it's absolutely repulsive that he said this. Meanwhile the working class has all but disappeared into the dregs of paycheck-to-paycheck scarcity, the radical ideologues are endlessly indulged over the well-being of the struggling majority, and the uber-wealthy remain content and protected in their sandbox. That's the legacy I watched play out as I spent my formative years in the Bay Area, culminating with the absolute failure in which they've addressed the homelessness and addiction crises.

To be fair, most of the issues I've just mentioned are nationally congru-ent, although California most certainly takes the lead. With the arbitrary hurdles to build much-needed housing and the artificially high cost of liv-ing, there's no doubt this, too, has some effect on homelessness. However, it's the failed policies that incentivize drug abuse that have turned it into a mecca for antisocial behavior. Homeless addicts from all over make their way to California to take advantage of theses "benefits," and along with the rejection of recovery and general order, the problem has become disturb-ingly palpable. I assure you it was nothing like this twenty years ago. The foundation for this catastrophe was still just getting poured.

After several months in Piedmont, I managed to make a few friends and appear to be a mildly normal seventh grader. How did this happen? I'll mostly give credit to my extended family that did everything in their power to give me a new and improved life. Most children of drug addicts aren't as lucky as me, in that I had a family that was loving and financially secure enough to ground me with a sense of normalcy. It was far from perfect, and knowing that my parents were killing themselves three thousand miles away didn't make anything easier, but I can assure you that if it wasn't for my aunts and uncles, I would be a permanent savage. Aunt Ina quickly whipped me into shape and taught me how to be remotely human that first year.

She was perhaps one of the most fascinating people I've ever encoun-tered, and it would be an understatement to say I took every moment I had with her for granted. She was a hippie-turned-entrepreneur with an endless amount of wisdom and cultural insight. If only I could have appreciated her the way I do now, maybe I would have only caused half the damage. I imagine it's hard to forgive when you sacrificed everything for someone and got nothing but rejection and contempt in return. This, unfortunately, was the extent of our entire relationship.

Along with her intrigue was her sheer brilliance. The woman knew everything, and although our relationship was rocky at best, she made sure to expose me to as much knowledge as possible. Museums, books, food, art, music, foreign countries, you name it. In the matter of a few years, I went from white trash pseudo-crack baby to a cultured highbrow. From showing me the Velvet Underground on vinyl to Kurt Vonnegut on paper, *Waiting for Godot* to the Aztec pyramids, my aunt introduced the world to me. In exchange, I showed not an ounce of gratitude because I couldn't disassociate her from the separation between my parents and me.

Unlike my parents, Aunt Ina and Uncle Bruce were well read, formally educated, and on the periphery of Bay Area high society. Not that my parents were dumb in any way, but they were certainly of a different social order. This, of course, wasn't the issue at hand when it came to my parents' faults. Had they nipped their addictions in the bud and gone on to raise me in my adolescent years, I'm sure they would have done a fine job. For class and education level are in no way a correlating factor when it comes to parental skills, in my opinion. In fact, it could be argued that such things actually detract from the authenticity of a child's upbringing and human experience.

It wasn't the sudden difference in class that changed my odds, but rather the fact that my Aunt Ina and Uncle Bruce filled a parental void and took a vested interest in my future. Unappreciative in the moment, I despised my exposure to such social cultivation. In recent years, I've finally recognized how truly fortunate I was. From teaching me about general hygiene to taking me to the palace at Versailles, I was transformed from a guaranteed statistic to someone with, at the very least, a chance in hell to one day prosper. Despite a decade of self-led circumvention, that chance in hell eventually caught a spark, thanks to the foundation that Aunt Ina and Uncle Bruce laid. I wouldn't be a fraction of the person I am today without the sacrifice of my aunt and uncle, and because of this, the greatest atrocity I've ever committed was my lack of gratitude for them in the moment.

The day before I graduated eighth grade, Mom bought her last bag of heroin. She overdosed in my childhood bedroom and didn't hit the ground loud enough to jostle my father awake. Eventually he found her, far past the window of revival, and has since never been able to forgive himself.

I've never blamed him or held any resentment against him for her death; I've always understood that it was completely out of his control. He, on the other hand, has had a much more arduous journey with his role in the event. He will most likely never forgive himself.

Although Mom's death was not entirely unexpected by the adults in my family after a year and a half of my parents' roguery, I was slightly caught off guard by what most children would consider the worst day of their life. Part of me had held onto the idea that one day my parents would get their act together and I'd go home and finish high school in Boston. Those with a more objective take on my parents' condition knew that a positive outcome wasn't likely.

Upon hearing the news, I didn't react much. In fact, I didn't react much for the entire first few years. By some people's standards, I still haven't given an adequate emotional response to my own mother's death, but others would say that I've expressed it thoroughly via ten years of self-destruction. I would never blame Mom's passing for my subsequent antisocial behavior, but I can wholeheartedly say that it didn't help keep me on the straight and narrow. Despicably, I utilized the event for a long time to excuse myself from giving a fuck about anything. That's probably not what she would have wanted, and fortunately, I figured this out before accidently following in her footsteps.

One of my first thoughts after Mom died was that I could now get away with a lot more under my aunt and uncle. No one wants to punish a kid whose mom just passed. To be specific, I thought about how much I could drink and smoke weed that summer, because Aunt Ina had been on my case about not getting high since taking me in. A shameful first thought after your mother dies, no doubt, but the seed had already been planted. Getting inebriated had officially surpassed every other thing of importance in my life—including whether or not my mom was in the ground. Her death was tragic, sure, but as long as it didn't get in the way of my using, I didn't see it as something to get overly emotional about. This kind of response is what makes me a drug addict. And the shame that comes with recognizing this cold-blooded reaction a few years later only refined it.

I didn't cry for about a year after it happened. I didn't cry about anything. I surely didn't cry at her funeral and was much more concerned about getting home to California and enjoying a summer of drunken adolescence. I felt I deserved to permanently check out from reality. When they lowered the casket into the ground, the rabbi handed me a shovel and asked me to start burying my mother in front of everyone, as is Jewish tradition. I felt nothing: completely dissociated with a look of composure on my face as many onlookers watched with tears in their eyes. I felt less than most anyone at the funeral, because I didn't even feel bored. With a bird's-eye view, I floated above my own body and watched the dirt hit the lid of her coffin with disinterest.

I shoveled dirt into her grave for several minutes before handing the shovel off to Dad, who was freshly entrenched within a complete nervous breakdown. He was also incredibly drunk—to the point that he doesn't remember a single detail of that day. In fact, he doesn't remember much of the rest of the decade. As it was pointed out to me years later, during one of my many "my mom died, don't you understand!" tirades directed towards my father, a mutual friend said, "You think your mom dying is hard? You knew her for fourteen years. Your father knew her for damn near forty. They built their entire life around one another, and somehow, he's managed to grow the fuck up and stop getting high. It's about time you do the same, don't you think?" That would end up being one of the most powerful "light switch" moments of my young adulthood.

Dad most certainly didn't take the death of Mom well—understandably. For many years after that day, I only saw him a handful of times, most of which occurred in the visiting rooms of mental institutions, rehabs, hospitals, and jails. With limited understanding of the issue, Aunt Ina thought that moving him out to Oakland to be closer to family would slow him down. On the contrary, his cross-country move provided no mitigation. When these places had had enough of him, he lived on the streets, where Aunt Ina would eventually find him and take me to say a brief hello.

That summer flew by, with nothing relevant happening other than my increased appreciation for alcohol. My thoughts were centered on developing my social life, figuring out how to talk to girls, and the arch stone that joined the two: hard liquor. The anticipation of weekend drunkenness was what propelled me to experience most joy during the school week.

While I was having fun in the salad days of substance abuse, Dad could absolutely not stop drinking himself into oblivion and shooting heroin. He couldn't go a week without getting kicked out of a crack house, let alone a sober living. Having been in the carpenters' union for nearly twenty-five years, his monthly pension deposits made it all the more difficult for my aunt to corral his drug use. She eventually established power of attorney over his finances, but what she would soon learn was that a real drug addict will go to any lengths to get high. Dad, like me and most of the others that have similar tales of moral decay, would always find a way. Like most children of alcoholics and drug addicts, I knew nothing (yet) of this neurological dilemma, and therefore assumed that my dad simply didn't love me. This in turn fed my desire to check out from reality, and so began the toddler stage of my own affliction with substance abuse.

Like in Boston, I was different in Piedmont. Many of my friends lived in mansions, belonged to country clubs, and came from healthy, intact families. I didn't. Instead of being bullied for such a thing, I was more so obsessed over and respected. Being alright at sports and physically maturing faster than most kids aided in this. I was the "mysterious bad kid from Boston" with a checkered past, present, and future. Combined with my aunt teaching me how to brush my teeth and change my underwear, this made for an opportunity to become relatively popular. However, I still couldn't function socially and not want to crawl out of my own skin. Weed helped with this at first, but it couldn't quiet my mind quite like alcohol. My ability to not only obtain it but to also consume it with impunity garnered me a reputation that I took pride in. It made me feel like I fit in as the guy that didn't fit in.

My alcohol consumption would soon become purely economical. I wanted to get drunk as easy and as quickly as possible, so through trial and error, I devised a system that allowed me to achieve this. It was a simple equation. Beer was delicious and socially acceptable amongst my adolescent cohorts, but it took too much time and effort to get me where I wanted to go. I could drink half a pint of whisky in two minutes, creep into the right amount of emotional suppression, then keep it alive by sipping a few beers. When my buzz started to fade a few hours later, I could chug the second half of my pint and go back to casual beer drinking like a normal teenager experimenting with alcohol. This kind of booze math is not something you ever want to catch yourself doing because it may mean that you're an alcoholic. It certainly doesn't lead to a prosperous outcome if you find yourself doing it at fourteen years of age.

One additional perk of hard liquor was that it was covert. You could drink it quickly and carry it around in your jacket pocket. My social circle would often only want to drink if someone's parents were out of town or going to be away from home for several hours. They were "social drinkers" and saw no point in drinking if there wasn't going to be a party of some sort. This was nonsense to me. Who needs to drink in a house when you could easily drink in a park, a schoolyard, or even the public bathroom of a shopping center? These guidelines are what separated the well-adjusted casual partiers from the broken souls that I attracted.

The two groups intermingled, but only a few dedicated youngsters drank the way I did. We drank at every opportunity that we could, sacrificed our education, experienced consequences with the law, and spent our teenage years slowly dismantling our foundation for a bright future. Some of us escaped the cycle during college. Some of us found harder drugs and had a few wild years before managing to tone it down. Others eventually got DUIs and figured it was time to grow up and become productive members of society. Not me. My ship had been taking in water since the day it set sail, and by the time I found myself engulfed by the waves, my best thinking got me nothing but a lungful of saltwater.

By my sophomore year in high school, alcohol's ability to quiet my mind began to fade, and I sank into a deep depression over my mother's death. I informed Aunt Ina, who was relieved to see that I had finally displayed an inkling of grief. Being handed the reins of a family destroyed by addiction, she managed everything as well as any human possibly could, but nothing could prepare her for the absolute mess that dropped into her lap. I found relief in disassociation via drugs and alcohol. My aunt didn't have the luxury of having a penchant for substance abuse, so quick and hollow coping wasn't an option for her. How she got through those years without murdering me I will never comprehend.

One late Friday night I came home after a night of partying, and she insisted on smelling my breath. Caught red-handed, I admitted to drinking, and she told me that I wasn't like the other kids. They could drink and party, but most of them probably wouldn't end up becoming alcoholics. Aunt Ina then told me that I, contrary to most other people, had a genetic disposition because of my parents. I was heartbroken. Not because she told me this, but because I knew it was right. By fifteen years old, I already couldn't imagine a life without using alcohol as a crutch. In an attempt to convince her to let me keep drinking, I explained that for me, alcohol was medicinal. When I used that word, she cringed as she couldn't help but tear up. It cured every ailment I had, from stomach pains to social anxiety, but most importantly, I explained, was that when I was drunk, I didn't have to know who I was. The trauma of my childhood temporarily didn't exist, and I was artificially normal for a segment of time. This was the moment that she knew there wasn't much she could do for me, so she wiped away her tears, hugged me, and said that it was time to see a professional.

Although her decision to bring me to a psychiatrist was sensible, it wouldn't end up doing much in the way of alleviating my hopeless state. Shortly after being prescribed Zoloft from a doctor with a Zoloft calendar and a Zoloft clipboard, mild relief became apparent—mostly because I discovered that mixing alcohol and Zoloft induced a more anesthetized state. I wonder what else Zoloft gave him to prescribe a child that medication within ten minutes of meeting them? Providing some amount of therapy would have possibly been more helpful, but that would have required work. "Why work when you can just give someone pills?" seems to be the mantra of the mental health crisis in America, and this is probably a large component of why we're failing at addressing it. Regardless, I liked the way drinking on Zoloft made me feel, so I desired to stay medicated. Teenage life, although foggy now, became halfway manageable. Still, this combo had me feeling unfocused come Monday morning, so I diagnosed myself with ADD. To no one's surprise, the "doctor" agreed, and I left his office with an Adderall prescription not ten minutes after my proposal. This didn't help much, but it certainly prepped my neurochemistry for an oncoming meth addiction a few years later. Who would have thought?

Mind you, I mostly enjoyed my adolescent years. Had I not had easy access to alcohol and drugs, this wouldn't have been the case. In fact, I may have very well wound up hanging from a makeshift noose in my closet.

I was on several high school sports teams, had plenty of friends (mostly drinking associates), and played multiple instruments in a few local bands. The only reason I was able to remotely function and achieve social success was possibly *because* of drugs and alcohol. They may have saved my life from teenage suicide. Of course, they would eventually stop working, but in my early years of youth, they played an integral role in muting the deadly inner monologue.

Despite my troubles with alcohol and loathsome behavior, I did alright in school. Once my drinking habits were intractable, Aunt Ina made it clear that as long as I kept my grades up, I at least had a chance of not getting kicked out of the house. She, along with extended family, instilled the importance of education in me and made it clear that going to college wasn't up for debate. Maybe it would even be an opportunity to "find my true self" and mature away from bad behavior, they thought. Worst-case scenario, I'd be a drunken loser with a degree, which, let's face it, is slightly better than being a drunken loser without one.

I got accepted to UC Davis, UC Santa Barbara, and UC Santa Cruz. Davis and Santa Barbara were superior schools academically, so someone that cared about their future would have chosen between those two. Santa Cruz had little scholastic prestige, and a far more depraved reputation as a drug-littered party school. I made my decision accordingly.

Sure, I had a passive dream of one day attending law school and being like Uncle Neal, but my desire to start a band and surround myself with a more "creative" student body trumped any realistic investment in my future. In reality I just wanted to party and get by without having to try too hard. I ended up developing a habit that would require a lot more effort than anything school could ever throw at me, though. As it would turn out, maintaining a heroin addiction wouldn't be a cakewalk.

CHAPTER 3

PICKLED SLUG

The University of California, Santa Cruz is a sister school to UCLA and UC Berkeley, but it's more like an adopted sister with a learning disability than an actual blood relative. It's a strange place partly because of its position within the state, and I'd come to learn that it was a major stop on the drug-trafficking route from Mexico up to Northern California. Despite being littered with insufferable aging hippies and Arc'teryx-wearing tech millionaires, it's one of the most beautiful places I've ever seen. The campus may be unrivaled in its redwood-studded splendor.

I hated it, but then again, I would have hated anything. It just wasn't my kind of place, I convinced myself, as I struggled the whole time that I was there trying to artificially adjust who I was to make more sense of it. I have no desire to ever return, out of fear of replayed tragedies and beach-themed meth flashbacks, but nevertheless, Santa Cruz is charming to those who have not experienced its gruesome underbelly.

Nineteen kids from my high school went to UC Santa Cruz, which was a school of about seventeen thousand undergrads. I didn't like my room-mates—or to put it honestly, I was too socially inept to accept people I refused to get to know before I judged them. Within the first month, I pur-chased an air mattress and moved into a dorm room occupied by a couple of high school friends, Kevin and Peter. Being too anxious to handle any amount of social discomfort, I embedded myself within the lives of people I already knew. My other friends, Alex and Mark, were in the dorm building next door, making my non-sanctioned move even more justified. I knew it would be easier to hang out with people who were already accustomed to my transgressions than to figure out how to not be an asshole.

UC Santa Cruz was known as a stoner school in a stoner town, and it was, but within a few months of my freshman year, kids in my dorm were smoking black tar heroin. Sure, weed was a big part of the local culture, but we'd come to find out that the whole town was saturated with any drug you could name, and that beneath the pasture of hippies and beach bums was a bedrock composed of heroin and crystal meth. The town was flooded with high-quality tar directly from the cartel, causing an epidemic that preceded other parts of the country by a few years. While places like Florida and the Midwest were still plagued by Oxycontin, Santa Cruz, and the West Coast in general, spearheaded the transition from prescription opiates to heroin in the late aughts.

Unlike a substantial amount of my social circle, I didn't touch heroin my freshman year. After all, as a child I saw firsthand its capacity for destruction. I knew heroin was something to stay away from, but I had no fucking clue what Oxycontin was. Like I stated earlier, Oxycontin was already losing popularity in California at this time, but access to the overly prescribed painkiller was still plentiful in those days. Upon seeing other kids taking it at college parties, I grew very curious. It was a pill—it was medicine, like an aspirin or Tylenol or a blood thinner. That might be a stretch, but we can all agree that Oxycontin looks more like aspirin than a needle full of dope. Using this thought process, I concluded that oxy was one of the safest drugs I could possibly take, given that it was approved by the FDA. If you research the purpose of Oxycontin's creation, you'll find out that it was marketed as a *non-habit-forming* replacement for traditional opiate-based painkillers. Doesn't that sound like the perfect recreational drug? All the high that an opiate can offer without the horrific physical addiction. A literal miracle. Unfortunately, like millions of other Americans over the past few decades, I would come to find out that this wasn't exactly accurate.

After nearly a year of watching my classmates intermittently smoke heroin, I caved the summer before sophomore year. For some it had become a problem already that they were good at hiding, and others successfully got high here and there without forming a habit. My friend Adam offered me some in the living room of our off-campus housing, and like all the other times it was offered to me, I pictured my mother's dead body collapsed in my childhood bedroom. For some reason that day, I finally tried it. I figured I'd squash the hype and cross it off the checklist. I was strong enough to handle it, I thought, which was odd because I was scared of literally everything else in life: what I looked like, what I sounded like, what people thought of me, what people didn't think about me, you name it. The inner workings of my mind were defined by self-centered fear. Heroin, I would come to learn, negated all of this.

Like some first-time experiences with other drugs, I didn't feel much from the couple of hits that Adam gave me. Maybe I smoked it wrong or maybe it wasn't very good shit, but either way, I didn't have an immediate attraction to the drug upon trying it. I pretty much stayed away from it for a few months after that. I preferred oxy, simply because the first time I tried it, it worked perfectly. Oxy was simple, socially acceptable, and you didn't have to smoke it off aluminum foil like some "strung-out junkie." You just swallowed a pill like a law-abiding citizen and all your problems drifted away.

As my recreational oxy use started to gain steam, I managed to acquire my first girlfriend. Through a Craigslist ad that Kevin and I had posted sophomore year looking for a third roommate, a fellow student named Melissa responded, and after meeting one another, she agreed to move in. I liked her right away, but dating a roommate was out of the question, so I proceeded to be myself around her as opposed to pretending to be someone I thought she'd be attracted to. This, for the first time in my life, invoked a genuine romantic connection (by accident). We began dating within a few months of her moving in, and for once I felt like I was skimming the membrane of normality. I was nearly a typical young man with the ability to establish a relationship beyond a drunken one-night stand. This was all I needed to convince myself I had a shot at life. If I could get a nice girl like Melissa to love me, then I was worth something. I then based my self-worth entirely upon this fact, which although unhealthy in the long run, worked in the moment. Things were on the up-and-up, I was happy, and my mangled relationship with Aunt Ina even saw some progress.

I started to get dull pains in my gums before my twentieth birthday and was told that I would need to get my wisdom teeth surgically removed. The operation occurred some weeks later, and I was given a bottle of ten-milligram Percocet for the pain. I lied to my aunt and uncle and told them I had only been prescribed ibuprofen from the doctor. Uncle Bruce, sympathetic to how swollen my face was, wrote me a prescription for Vicodin.

Despite the nearly non-existent relationship between my uncle and me (entirely due to my stubbornness), from that day forth I thought he was pretty damn cool. I took both the Percocet and Vicodin, along with a few oxys I'd acquired through other means, for about three weeks straight. When I started running low, I panicked—both mentally and physically—and this is when the forbidden line had been crossed. I was pickled.

I had never taken painkillers daily for that length of time before, and when I finally ran out, I felt the symptoms of minor physical withdrawal: insomnia, restlessness, and mild anxiety. More debilitating was the fact that I was no longer high. Being exposed to this experience—a prolonged daily intake of opiates—I now knew that I never wanted to live a day in which opiates weren't in my bloodstream. They were the true panacea that surpassed any of my prior cures.

Of what, you ask? Name anything you want, any problem in the world, and I'll tell you that opiates can cure it. You have a cramp in your neck? Opiates will cure that. Your mother died when you were fourteen and you never processed it in a healthy manner? Opiates will cure that too. There's nothing they wouldn't fix for me, and there was nothing that was going to change my mind about the necessity of having them.

Melissa knew something was wrong, but she had no clue that it had anything to do with the pills. The two of us (along with Kevin) had been dabbling with oxys since the beginning of the school year. However, after my surgery I was no longer dabbling. I was *needing*.

I made some phone calls to pill-heads I knew and learned about a connection for thirty-milligram Roxicodone (generic Oxycontin) up in Oakland, from my high school friend's sister, Maggie. Maggie lived by the West Oakland BART station with her mom, who had gotten shot earlier in the year as an innocent bystander in a gang-related incident. As tragic as this was, a lifetime prescription for Roxys was the goldmine she needed to make a decent living while permanently disabled.

Nowadays you couldn't find an authentic thirty-milligram Roxicodone if you hired a private detective. However, if you threw a rock in San

Francisco, you could hit someone selling or smoking a fake one. Although it would have the markings of a real Roxy, these deadly pills are nothing more than lactose powder and fentanyl. Back in 2008 it was a different story. This was the golden era, when the skies were still practically raining down opioids on unsuspecting victims of the pharmaceutical industry, and Maggie would sell me individual Roxys for ten dollars each. I eventually got Maggie to sell me a hundred Roxys at a time for four hundred bucks, and then would go back down to Santa Cruz where I could sell them for fifteen or twenty dollars apiece. I wasn't a big-time drug dealer by any measure—nor did I desire to become one—I was simply trying to get my medicine for free.

This worked for several months. Until it didn't. Maggie could no longer meet my demand, and I had to find larger, more dangerous connections.

For those that are not familiar with the early days of Oxycontin—meaning the drug's entire existence up until about 2012—the following information should be helpful. Oxycontin is a medication produced by an American pharmaceutical company called Purdue Pharma. Although marketed as a safer alternative than mainstay narcotics for pain management, Oxycontin can just as easily be snorted, smoked, or injected as it can be swallowed in its intended fashion. Oxycontin is a brand name, and the active ingredient of this pain killer is called oxycodone. Chemically speaking, oxycodone is nothing less than a more refined form of heroin. An oxycodone user's tolerance will skyrocket in comparison to that of a heroin user, and the withdrawals from oxy are typically just as bad, if not worse. Regardless of the immense dangers of oxycodone abuse, there was no attempt to create a "tamper-proof" version of the drug until tens of thousands had already died, and many more had spiraled into utter despair. It's one of the largest crimes ever committed against the American people by a corporation with the blessing of the government—namely the FDA. To date, no one involved has been held criminally accountable. Like most crimes against humanity committed by a corporation or our own government, no one actually went to jail, but we did get a few decent mini-series about it years later. This seems to be the truest form of American justice. Hundreds of thousands of lives ruined, but at least we got to witness a killer performance by Michael Keaton.

Kevin and I used to split one Roxy and be obliterated until we fell asleep. Within a few months of daily use, the two of us were each smoking or snorting twenty of them a day. This had gotten out of control in every possible way, but what irked us most was the financial component. As our forefathers had done before us, we knew exactly what we had to do. No, not quit.

We needed heroin. It was common knowledge that heroin was cheaper, got you higher, and in some places like Santa Cruz, it was easier to find than any pill.

I knew that my friend Molly—one of the people that this book is dedicated to—would be able to help us out. Molly had already gotten deep into heroin use the previous year and had ended up getting kicked out of school. She was living with her parents in Southern California, running the streets of LA and wasting away, so she would have to help us find dope remotely.

I called Molly and gave her the spiel. Because Molly's a decent human being, she was reluctant to offer help. Like a good junkie, I hit her in the weak spot, by describing my exaggerated withdrawal symptoms. I told her that I was hopeless, dopesick, and had scoured the streets looking for oxy to no avail. Every junkie—whether in active addiction or recovery—is sympathetic to one of their own in withdrawals, so with the right amount of manipulation, I got her to budge. I was expecting her to give me a phone number to call, but instead she asked me to grab a pen and paper to take down directions.

Around dusk Kevin and I drove up Highway Nine to the two-mile marker, just like Molly had dictated. She said there would be a shoulder in the road about a hundred feet past the marker, and that there was a dirt path that formed into the wooded area from the center of the clearing. We pulled up to the shoulder, parked the car, and spotted a path. It led up an ivy-covered hill, and after hiking for a few minutes, the path fed out to a train track. We took a right, heading north alongside the tracks, and started to blink our flashlight on and off, like Molly had instructed. According to her, a small Mexican man would either pop out of the trees or message us back with his flashlight if he was further north than usual. It was like we were in a fairy tale, tracking down a goblin to barter for treasure—except instead of treasure it was heroin, and instead of a goblin it was a guy named

Pedro. We finally saw a blinking light about thirty feet ahead of us, which completely expunged our anxiety.

"Holy shit, this actually worked. I can't fucking believe it!" I was overjoyed. Not just because we found the connect, but because of the adventure that came with it. Frankly, early addiction can be quite fun, and some of the situations you get yourself in are a high in themselves. It's naughty. It's mischievous and still has some romance. It's a dark secret that you can only cherish with a select few. Deep down you know you're hurtling towards absolute tragedy, but you can't help but relish in the prospect of hazard during initial launch.

Pedro yelled out to us, and we assured him that we came in peace. He sold us a gram of heroin, gave us his number, and told us to call him next time we planned on making the hike back to give him forewarning.

When you picture someone doing heroin, you might think of a homeless man covered in sores with a needle in his arm. All my life I assumed this was the inevitable fate of a heroin injector, and naturally I was turned off by the thought of ever sticking anything in my vein. It was depraved. When I found out in college that you could smoke heroin off aluminum foil, this changed my perception. Heroin, when consumed any way other than with a needle, seemed on par with snorting a few lines of cocaine. Not entirely innocent, but at the same time, not earth-shattering.

Although the same drug is entering your system, lies must be told to oneself when trying to soften the blow of reality. A drug addict sets boundaries for themselves, and when the necessity to cross those boundaries arrives due to the worsening of their addiction, they will fabricate any delusion to convince themself that the boundary needs to be broken. Heroin was generally verboten in my eyes, but when that boundary was infringing on my need to get high the way I wanted to get high, I convinced myself that using needles was the real issue at hand. This phenomenon repeats itself until you find yourself using the side mirror of a parked car to shoot a speedball into your neck.

A year went by of nonstop use. Kevin couldn't handle the spiral and transferred to NYU for his junior year. Melissa and I were still in love, I guess, but the relationship was contaminated. We became a junkie couple. We didn't shower much, wash our clothes, or eat anything close to a normal diet. We sat in our room, chain-smoked cigarettes, nodded out, had awful, anti-climactic sex, and rotted away. We only left the apartment to occasionally attend class or buy dope.

After the cash from selling all our possessions ran out, I got a job at 7-Eleven just to help support both of our habits. Middlemanning coke to fellow students brought in some cash, but Melissa also shoplifted and babysat to keep us high. Our relationship had a foundation in innocence, but now we had come to associate everything about one another with heroin, similarly to my parents. I obsessed over this fact as if it were inherently bestowed upon me. We tried to stop numerous times, but you can't just quit heroin while you're a full-time student, unless you intend on taking a leave of absence. Doing so would sound the alarms and raise suspicion from our families. You need a good two weeks of bed rest to really get through the withdrawals, and that wasn't possible during the school year without failing our classes. This is assuming we could actually go two weeks without getting high, which even if given the opportunity, we couldn't.

The truth was that it wouldn't be possible for me to quit on my own accord no matter what the circumstances were for many years. Back in my college days, however, I was still fully convinced that I was merely *physically* addicted. If only I could be locked in a room for a few weeks and complete the withdrawal process, I'd never touch the stuff again, but despite the many golden opportunities I would eventually have—including medical detox—I would find myself voluntarily jumping back to the same old hell. So fast do we forget. Sure, the physical addiction to opiates is vicious, but the mental obsession that lingers once it's been eradicated from your system is what's truly sinister. This is what makes us—when temporarily sober—pick up a bag of dope and think that somehow this time might be different.

When Melissa's father finally came down to rescue her a few months before graduation, she left to attend a residential rehab program. She had finished her school credits a semester early by attending summer courses, so she was able to leave with no scholastic consequences. She also left her '92 Acura Integra behind, and after making me return my key to her before she left, it was expected that it would sit safely in our driveway. Being the well prepared, yet absolute piece of shit that I was, I had foreseen something like this eventually happening and made a copy of my key months prior. Hugo—my cartel-affiliated drug dealer at the time—had repeatedly offered me a job, and with Melissa out of the picture, it seemed about time to take him up on the opportunity. The gig was driving around Santa Cruz and dropping off heroin to waiting customers, which was just as easy as it was dangerous. Melissa had been opposed to this because she had an ounce of sense, but more specifically, she was the rightful owner of the vehicle and didn't want to lose it.

My shift was from 9:00 AM to 3:00 PM, and my job duties were simple: customers would call Hugo and tell him where they were, and then he would tell me where to meet them over a walkie-talkie. I was given $120 per six-hour shift, along with a thirty-minute lunch break and money for gas. I could take my pay in cash or the equivalency in heroin—one and a half grams. Absolutely stellar gig for a junkie.

Easiness aside, this job had one crucial stipulation. Hugo knew I was a junkie, and he knew that junkies had the tendency to fall asleep behind the wheel, so he could only trust me if he could assure that I'd stay alert. To prevent this issue, he required his drivers to snort a line of meth at the beginning of every shift. I would have to get to his house right before 9:00 AM every morning to pick up the product—which was rationed out into forty-dollar half-gram bags—and after snorting a line of meth, I would then be allowed to start the workday. I had never done meth prior to working for Hugo; in fact, I was wholeheartedly against using a drug like that, but I needed this opportunity for steady income. Once again, a boundary would have to be crossed, and like every prior boundary and every boundary to come, my new justification would be accepted rather quickly.

At the time, crystal meth was considered the lowest of the low in my opinion. To me, there was no drug that was more dangerous or repulsive. Basing my opinion solely on what I'd seen from anti-drug commercials, I knew nothing factual about meth to back this up. As it turned out, those commercials were pretty spot on. The only positive review I'd ever heard was from a cousin a few years back, however, this may have been because he was broke at the time, and was trying to convince me to buy us some. Not a solid source.

I always heard awful things about people *smoking* meth; I'd seen the horrific pictures of meth users with dirty pipes twirling between their lips. I shared my concerns with Hugo, and he emphasized the lack of harm when *snorting* crystal meth. Hugo wasn't a doctor, nor was he a pharmacist, but after that brief conversation, I was compelled to believe him. Snorting was the *manageable* way to get high on crystal meth. No different than popping an Adderall before a midterm, I convinced myself.

At the beginning of my first shift, Hugo—a five-foot-nothing man shaped like a kiwi—chopped me up my first line. I noticed instantly that snorting meth was very painful, and as the seconds passed, the pain only worsened—the opposite of cocaine. There was absolutely no numbing sensation as it dripped from my sinus cavities to the back of my throat, which allowed me to interpret its entire palette of flavors. Ajax dissolved in lemon juice, along with other treats found under the kitchen sink, immediately came to mind.

The uncompromising pain in my face dissipated after a long sixty seconds, making way for an angelic hum that crawled down my temples and landed in my gut. After a lifetime of persistent lag, my nervous system felt like it was finally operating at full capacity—ultimate tranquility combined with an updated processor. A crystal meth high doesn't begin at a hundred miles an hour, it savors the acceleration. It's a smooth and refined ride that leaves your brain feeling like it was sautéed in oil as opposed to boiled in water. A class act straight out of the gate, meth can retain its elegance for hours, sometimes even days. It's not until you've been awake for a week that the swanky fellow you thought you'd become is chased off by a mumbling lunatic, set on crippling your reality until it resembles a windowless prison cell; no sound can be heard other than that of a broken record repeating fragments of various schizophrenic delusions. In simpler terms, it's much more complex than your standard rendezvous with cocaine.

I took a real liking to meth right off the bat. It was the inverse of heroin; the hasty yin to heroin's lethargic yang. Heroin addiction a la carte had grown far too tedious, and meth appeared to be the perfect ingredient to spice things up. With heroin alone, the same tape plays over and over until months flash by without leaving a single footprint of stimulation. When you throw crystal meth into the mix, every moment has potential for memory-making. I've had certain weeks on meth that could be turned into an entire series of graphic novels. The stories just end up writing themselves when you put yourself in a near-death situation on a daily basis. I'm not saying that heroin doesn't get you into some deadly predicaments, but a junkie will only risk his life to obtain more heroin. A tweaker, on the other hand, could risk his life over a cool stick that he found. Meth just seems to attract death like a magnet.

The job was going great, I was keeping my heroin habit afloat, and Hugo was giving me free meth every morning. Although under the impression that I'd never do crystal in my life before I took the job, I began requesting part of my take-home pay in speed before the end of the week. A few days after that, I broke Hugo's cardinal rule by acquiring my first meth pipe, and with that first hit I passed the point of no return.

Unsurprisingly, there were issues with me graduating. Sure, I turned in my fifty-page senior thesis of meth gibberish, but even if I hadn't gotten an F on it, it still wouldn't have been enough to get a passing grade after not showing up the entire semester. Despite not completing my major and failing all my other classes, UC Santa Cruz allowed me to walk with my graduating class. This was under an agreement that I would stay for summer school and fall quarter to make up my required credits, which was a kind gesture, but I would, of course, not uphold my end of the bargain.

Aunt Ina drove down to Santa Cruz for my graduation, as well as my Uncle Neal, who drove up from Los Angeles. I was a wreck, and my family had their suspicions, but after some devious convincing on my part, they chalked it up to stress from my "breakup" with Melissa. Somewhere inside I was heartbroken, but my new cocktail of drugs was distracting me entirely from my feelings about it. Still, the breakup was the perfect excuse to explain my erratic behavior, weight loss, and scholastic troubles.

Melissa was also back in town to attend graduation, and unfortunately for me, she needed her car back. Her parents wouldn't even let me see her, which I thought was ruthless at the time, but now understand that they did the right thing. In fact, I'd end up never seeing her again, and she would end up getting off heroin forever and living a prosperous life. I commend her parents for protecting her from me.

They requested that I not be at the house when they came by to pick up the car. I obeyed but found myself in quite the quandary. Not having a car was going to put a damper on my career aspirations with Hugo, so I needed to convince my aunt to let me borrow hers for the summer.

She knew that I would need to stay in Santa Cruz for the summer session to make up missing credits, which she was disappointed about, but knew that there was no other solution if I were to graduate in a timely fashion. I manufactured a lie about the limited summer bus schedule and eventually got her to agree to lend me her second car. She took me back to Piedmont where she gave me money for June's rent and the keys to her '91 Toyota Corolla station wagon. None of that money would end up being spent on rent, the Corolla would not be used even once to get to class, and unbeknownst to either of us, that would be the last we spoke in person for twelve years. I was an absolute bastard that summer.

Hugo got wise to my erratic behavior on meth and gave me my first verbal warning. I assured him that I wasn't smoking the stuff—only snorting it like company policy stated—but he was no amateur. My paranoid rants over the walkie-talkie started to become more frequent, and when I accused him of cutting the dope he was paying me with, he kindly asked me to "clock out" for the last time. To this day, this was the only job that I've ever been fired from. Usually, I have a knack for quitting just before the hammer drops, but Hugo was too on the ball. Plus, I had become completely delusional at that point and was much more concerned with the imagined people following me than retaining steady employment. I wasn't happy about losing the job, but in my shattered mind, there were bigger issues at play.

When you get high on meth and stay awake for days on end, you start hearing voices. In my case, the voices that I always heard were realistic. They were the voices of my roommates, my neighbors, and sure, the occasional conversation with "God," but most of what I heard was people that I cared about saying negative things about me: my friends saying that they didn't like me anymore, my neighbor telling his wife that he was going to call the police on me, or my roommates plotting to kick me out of the house. Although this sounds rather tame for your typical drug hallucination, it thoroughly distressed all my (remaining) personal relationships and magnified my sense of alienation. My neighbor, who I used to chat with regularly, now avoided me at all costs due to my new habit of dementedly staring at him through my rumpled blinds. My close friends, who I now texted daily accusing them of spying on me through my window, couldn't deal with my madness anymore. Meth was what caused me to lose what little sense I had left of belonging anywhere.

My already short list of acquaintances dwindled down to zero, so I started a quest to find new friends—friends that shared the same hobbies as me, like smoking meth. Due to my falling out with Hugo, I started buying drugs from a new dealer that went by the name of G, and we hit it off from the start. We met through a junkie friend at a Taco Bell parking lot, where G rolled up to my vehicle on a Mongoose BMX. He was without a car, and I was without a friend, so naturally we formed a semi-professional relationship almost immediately.

After hanging out a bit, mostly just helping G run errands in exchange for dope, I discovered that he was quite enlightened for a crystal meth dealer. We liked some of the same movies, books, and music and could hold a higher level of conversation than what was possible with Hugo. I found out that G was temporarily living in another customer's garage, so I offered to let him stay with me in my bedroom. I was still living with college housemates, some of which had been close friends of mine since freshman year, but everyone was in the process of moving out. It was already mid-June, so with our lease ending at the end of the month, I figured nobody would mind a short-term visitor.

Despite their initial protest, my roommates failed in their attempt to stop me. They knew that the lease was up in a matter of weeks, and frankly, they probably felt uncomfortable arguing with me about anything. Between my meth psychosis and lack of hygiene, interacting with me on any level was not for the faint of heart. G, who shared my lack of empathy and meth-induced repugnance, set up shop in my room and introduced me to his circle of customers and colleagues.

In the days leading up to July, I came up with what I thought was a wonderful idea: not moving out once the lease was up. Given that my portion of June's rent was already nearly a month late, this would be an exceptionally ballsy move. Some tweaker the night prior was yammering about squatters' rights and how in California it's the law that you don't *have* to move out of your house once your lease is up. Now this particular tweaker didn't strike me as a law student, but I figured that he might have had a history of actually getting away with this. Instead of verifying, I made the assumption and committed to the plan. Up until the second week of July, it worked flawlessly.

Then the police came. My landlord had been calling me nonstop, but I assumed he would stop by in person before he called the authorities. I hadn't slept since June, so my judgment wasn't quite up to par. After getting formally evicted, I packed my car—or to be more accurate, Aunt Ina's car—with my essential belongings and left everything else behind. I didn't know where I was going, but I knew that wherever it was, I probably wasn't going to need a dresser.

On that glorious day, my extensive career of homelessness had sprung. Not yet would I experience true homelessness—the literal absence of all shelter—but rather I started my journey with training wheels. You can't learn to walk before you crawl, and in this metaphor, by crawling I mean living in a water-tight vehicle. Houseless is really the correct term for such a predicament, for one is not truly homeless unless one fears when it rains, in my opinion. That's the graduate school of destitution, whereas having a car to sleep in is still kindergarten.

I continued to tag around with G and help him sell dope, in exchange for getting free drugs and companionship. When one is completely broken, they'll latch onto anyone willing to associate. We had nowhere to sleep comfortably anymore, but then again, we hadn't slept much since we'd met each other. Roaming the streets of Santa Cruz at all hours of the night, G introduced me to most staples of tweakerdom: breaking into cars, picking through dumpsters, stealing bikes, and falsely suspecting one another of plotting murder.

During this early period of my love affair with meth, I developed the adverse habit of fictive speculation. No matter who I was with or what we were doing, I always ended up thinking that someone was trying to kill me. This didn't always sit well with G and his cohorts, but my value as someone with a vehicle encouraged them to accept it. After all, they were guilty of the same thing on occasion. However, I was the most novice and, therefore, was still adjusting to a life of constant hallucination.

One specific example that sticks out is when G played the song "Guilty Conscience" on his phone through my car stereo. Despite being extremely familiar with the song, every lyric that I heard coming through the speakers didn't match up with my memory. Giving it a closer listen, I discovered that every line was a specific reference to my own personal murder. I accused G and the others of downloading the instrumental track of the song, and then using a production program to record their own verses over the track, rapping as if they were Eminem about how they were going to torture me until I died. This was impossible, given that none of us had access to electricity, let alone a music studio, but still, I couldn't deny what I was hearing.

I slammed the brakes in the middle of an intersection and ripped the auxiliary cord out of the tape deck. After pulling over and having a mental breakdown for a few minutes, G and his friends were able to calm me down and bring me back to Earth. It's not easy accepting that what you hear with your own ears may only be a product of your own imagination, and for some, this revelation never comes. Fortunately, after months of training, I would eventually be able to free myself from these auditory hallucinations. In the course of time they couldn't trick me anymore, and once I saw through the façade of my own fabricated reality, they faded into obscurity. The visual and mental hallucinations would persist, however, no matter how hard I tried to overcome them. What can I say, you'd be a fool to think you could tame meth outright. Many who have tried are living under a freeway overpass at this very moment, screaming in horror at things that don't even exist.

About a week after the "Guilty Conscience" event, G confessed his love for me. Alone in the car, he shed several tears while explaining that our friendship had inspired strong sexual and emotional feelings. This was extremely unexpected. G not only had the persona of a machismo thug, but he always made an effort, uncomfortably so, to express interest in his female customers. However, none of these expressions were ever acted upon to my knowledge, and looking back, I realized that his uber-heterosexuality had always felt a bit forced. He was perhaps a closeted man, who felt that he needed to hide his orientation in order to maintain a tough persona. To this day I'm still not sure, nor would I ever judge him for being gay. The issue was that he had fallen in love with me (for some reason), and the feeling wasn't mutual. Despite being the kind of guy that could move past something like this, I wasn't sure if G was. I was correct. In a fit of anger, he told me I'd have to "get on my knees and work for it" if I ever wanted a bag of dope from him again, which I didn't take kindly to. We parted ways, never to see each other again, but I'd find out years later that he got clean in prison and lives a normal life today.

Without G by my side, I'd learn quickly that being alone while homeless made the whole ordeal much more tangible. When in a painful situation, we drug addicts seek to numb, not only by way of chemicals but also through any remnant of a human connection. Sometimes this is expressed through screaming at strangers on the sidewalk, but for the more fortunate who haven't completely lost their marbles yet, we seek anyone willing to accompany us on a shared downward spiral.

Ben—a sociopath that I'd met through G—liked to get high the way I liked to get high and seemed like a good candidate to become my new junkie partner. I sought him out, moved him into my car, and we teamed up to tackle our common goal of suppressing our tragic realities. He even let me tag along on a few home invasions—which felt a bit above my pay grade. I knew breaking into houses was not exactly petty theft, but I wasn't aware that it could be a fifteen-year prison sentence if you got caught. I'm beyond blessed that I never got arrested during that brief crime spree, or else I'd be writing this in a prison cell. Perhaps that's what I deserve.

One time we had been awake for nearly five days when we got our hands on some very potent heroin. I, still being a smoker, brought the lighter to the foil and inhaled a plume of smoke that tasted like red wine and dirt. Never had I tasted heroin so earthy, as if it had come straight off the poppy from the soils of Afghanistan. As wonderful as this sounds, it wasn't a great combination with not having slept for many a day, and I ended up getting higher than I intended to.

Normally there's no such thing as "higher than I intended to," but in this case I was driving a car that I wished to keep from ending up wrapped around a tree. My heroin nod crept slowly until it caused me to fall out of consciousness (Hugo's caution was valid), and I slipped into a state of sleep while traveling thirty miles per hour. Deep in slumber, my mind stayed vacant only for a moment until I was awoken by my collision with a parked Lexus.

Lucky for Ben and me—two men that had no value for their own lives—we had our seatbelts buckled for some odd reason. Both cars were totaled, but our worthless lives were not. My car was filled to the brim with drug paraphernalia, so I had no desire to interact with the police, although this would become unavoidable if I didn't disappear immediately. Despite being smashed to hell and no longer able to make much of a left turn, this wasn't enough to hold me back from fleeing the scene. After all, I wasn't about to have my house impounded. We continued on for several weeks, only able to make right turns, until an event would cause us to lose the car and we'd both graduate to true homelessness.

We used to occasionally buy heroin from this guy named Steve. That's what he said his name was, but it definitely wasn't his real name. He only spoke Spanish, and you never had to call him. You just had to drive about a mile and a half up the Pacific Coast Highway and park across the road from a strawberry stand. There you would find a sand path that led down to the beach, and if the sun was still up, Steve would always be standing in a rocky alcove about fifty feet from the water.

If he recognized you, you would tell him how much heroin you wanted to buy, then he would walk over to a rock in the sand where he kept a box full of dope buried underneath. It wasn't very good dope, but everyone else was out and he was our only option. As a heroin addict, you always have to keep two or three dealers at a time, because sometimes one runs out and the other won't answer the phone. That's when you need a Steve.

Ben and I were on our way to meet him when cop lights appeared in my rear-view mirror. I was being pulled over for the first time in my life. Relieved that we were merely on our way to purchase heroin and not in possession of it yet, I steered my way over to the breakdown lane and waited for the officer to approach the thrashed vehicle.

"What happened to your car?" the cop asked as I cranked my window down.

"Oh, you mean the front? *Um*, the damage in the front, yeah, I hit a telephone pole, Officer. She still drives fine, though," I replied.

"Alright, we'll get to that, but first—you're Jared Klickstein?" He asked, somehow knowing my name before seeing my ID. Unless you're a celebrity, that's never a good sign.

"Wait, what? That's crazy!" Befuddled, I looked over to Ben, who looked like he'd seen a ghost. "I mean, yes, that's me, but what's going on? How do you know that?"

"Is this your vehicle, Jared?"

"What, this…this vehicle, yes, well, no, not technically, but…my aunt, she—"

"Because it's been reported stolen by its owner, and she's standing by my cruiser. Can you look in your rear-view mirror and tell me if that's your aunt?"

I was in shock. I gazed up at the mirror and saw Aunt Ina visibly upset, even from thirty feet away.

"Yeah…." I took a moment to absorb the gravity of the situation. "That's her. I don't know how the hell, what the hell is goin' on, but you gotta… Officer, you gotta listen to me because I didn't steal this car, she let me *borrow* it. And yes, I forgot to return it, or respond to my aunt's messages, but life gets pretty complicated sometimes and—"

"Alright, this is what's gonna happen. You and your friend are gonna vacate the vehicle and empty it of all your belongings. Then you're gonna walk about a hundred feet up the road, and not make eye contact with your aunt while she gets in the car and drives away. And by the looks of it, she's probably gonna have to take it straight to a garage. You're lucky, though, she said as long as she gets the car back with no fuss, she won't press charges. You follow all that?"

"Yeah, but…can I just talk to her for a minute? I really need to talk to her, man, can I just—"

"No. She made it very clear she *doesn't* want to talk, or even make eye contact with you." I was speechless as he continued, "So start gettin' your shit out of the car. And maybe think about gettin' off the dope too. You've got your aunt worried sick."

Ben and I emptied the car of our few belongings, hiked a minute on foot up the road, and watched from a distance as Aunt Ina made a lopsided U-turn in the burgundy station wagon. Deep down I did love my aunt, despite never showing it once, and this made for an anguished relationship from day one. I had been a rotten, untamed animal of a child, thrown into her arms out of nowhere, and this final act of desecration really put the nail in the coffin. I was never a good nephew. Not once. Nor did I *ever* show a drop of gratitude for the sacrifice she made by taking me in. She wasn't perfect, but who could be in a situation like that? With years of mental torture under her belt from my attitude and behavior, this final event would be the conclusion of our relationship; my biggest regret until the day I die. There's no bigger crime I've ever committed than the way I treated the woman that saved my life.

I felt awful about what I had put her through just then, yet my concern for getting dope outweighed any feelings of remorse. I was starting to feel dopesick, and we were still a good half mile away from the beach where Steve was, so the reality of destroying my relationship with Aunt Ina was unable to be absorbed. When you need heroin, nothing else can permeate.

We trekked down PCH until we reached Steve, bought our dope, and got high—all before we had a single concern about the fact that we no longer had a vehicle. My Santa Cruz run had tuckered out. Ben and I walked back to town and parted ways for good.

After a week or so of stealing bikes to finance my habit and sleeping by the river, I'd grown too lonely in my homelessness and got ahold of Uncle Neal. Having expressed his suspicions of my drug use at my graduation ceremony a few months back, I figured I could come clean to him and ask for some help. I told him that I had a drug problem—although I downplayed it by saying I was only using Vicodin—and that I needed to go to rehab. Did I *want* to go to rehab? Certainly not, but I also didn't want to be homeless in Santa Cruz anymore. I was far from mastering the twenty-four seven hustle of a street junkie and had simply ran out of gas for the time being.

Neal loved me deeply, and although he hadn't adopted me like my dad's sister after shit hit the fan in Boston, he was my main father figure throughout my time in California. He and his wife (Aunt Suzanne) had me stay with them every few months in LA for a long weekend, as well as every summer since I'd moved in with Aunt Ina and Uncle Bruce. We were extremely close, and when I explained my dire situation, he couldn't help but weep over the phone. I was the offspring of his sister—his sibling who was no longer alive due to the very affliction I now had. And like his sister, I manipulated my family members to do what I wanted them to do—and in this case, I wanted my uncle to provide me an opportunity that I would undoubtedly squander. He purchased me a bus ticket and told me he'd give me one chance.

Most people have not smoked crystal meth in the bathroom of a moving Greyhound bus, but it's safe to say that most bathrooms on Greyhound buses have had crystal meth smoked in them. The bathroom on the bus that I took that night to Los Angeles was no exception to this rule. In fact, I probably wasn't the only person that smoked meth in the bathroom during that very ride. This is the nature of long-distance bus travel. If you prefer to use a bathroom during your travels that doesn't smell like meth smoke, I would advise you to stick to airplanes—but even then, no form of transportation is guaranteed to be free of such behavior.

The Los Angeles Greyhound station is on East Seventh Street and Alameda, right on the border of downtown and Skid Row. It would become a familiar neighborhood a few weeks after my arrival. I called Uncle Neal and asked him to pick me up, but he was at work and told me that I would have to take the city bus to his office. "How dare he!" I thought. I in no way recognized, let alone cared about, how this was affecting him, and couldn't let go of the fact that I wasn't being catered to.

Blinded by my youthful impotence, I believed none of this was my fault, specifically because I was the victim of a troubled childhood and bad genetics. "How dare they!"—this would be my battle cry for many a troubled year to come. A battle with no one other than the voice in my own head. "This is not how you treat a wounded animal" and other such nonsense. I would eventually come to find out that this attitude would only get me deeper in the hole of degeneracy, but by then I'd already have dug myself to the other side of the earth. Obsessing over my own so-called victimhood had always been on my "greatest hits" of selfish thought patterns, and until it alienated me from every single person that ever loved me, I ran around that maze until I had exhausted every path. Maybe I had a predisposition to addiction. And maybe I didn't have the greatest childhood. Maybe my mom wasn't supposed to die and I wasn't supposed to get prescribed Percocet after my wisdom teeth were pulled. None of it matters now. Self-pity and what-ifs never got anyone out of a coffin.

My uncle was expecting his slightly disheveled "Vicodin"-addicted nephew, and therefore felt comfortable with me showing up at his place of work. He was a lawyer at a reputable law firm in West LA who had trusted me when I told him that I was in a presentable condition. I wasn't lying when I told him this; I really believed I looked just one notch below normal. Being thirty pounds underweight and not having showered or washed my clothes in many weeks, however, I was closer to one notch above dead. Clothing and stench aside, my grooming was also not up to par. My hair was lacquered in a summer's worth of meth sweat, which was accompanied by a strip of pubic hair above my upper lip. I had shaved at the Greyhound station and on a whim decided to keep my premature mustache to look more orderly. It didn't work.

Upon my embarrassing arrival at his office, he dragged me to his car immediately, somehow avoided homicide, and drove me directly to his house. The first thing he said to me in the car was that I looked just like my mother, followed by several minutes of tears. What may have been the saddest thing anyone had ever said to me flew right over my head. The falsity of the Vicodin story was immediate, so I explained my version of reality—which only heightened my resemblance to Mom.

Completely absent was my recognition of the magnitude of my problem, and therefore my plan of detoxing myself on my uncle's couch was not met with enthusiasm. I told him that I had brought a bag of methadone pills with me, and that this would all be over in a week if he would just let me sweat it out in his living room.

"Jared…I don't even want to let you into my house, let alone have you kick drugs in front of my children. Are you fucking insane? One of my kids could get ahold of the methadone and die, this is ridiculous!"

"Neal, come on. You're not going to let me into your house? What am I, some kind of animal?" I snarled. "What the fuck did I even come down here for, I mean, I know you have a family—they're my family too! I love them and would never put them in danger. Besides, this could be a good opportunity for me to get to know my little cousins better."

"Jared, your cousins are old enough now that they ask questions. You wouldn't know; you've put zero effort into visiting them the past few years. They aren't babies anymore…. What do you think I'm gonna do, let their long-lost, meth-addicted cousin babysit? You're out of your fuckin' mind."

Who wants a junkie in their house, let alone around their children? He knew that I was around junkies when I was growing up, and look how the fuck I turned out. I attempted several more times to convince him he was blowing this out of proportion, but my attempt at manipulation was no match for his instinct to protect his family.

We agreed that he would take me to his house under the agreement that I would have a plan within twenty-four hours. Once there, we verified that my university health insurance was active for a few more months. I found a detox in Pasadena, and the plan was that while I was there, Aunt Suzanne and Uncle Neal would find an inpatient rehab that my insurance would cover as well.

Everyone was satisfied—especially me, who honestly believed that I would soon wake from this nightmare. All I would have to do was detox, go to rehab, get cured, never use heroin or meth again, and go back to the normal life of a college student. Simple. The physical addiction to heroin was my only issue, I believed. Once busted free from that ball and chain, this horrific chapter in my life would finally come to an end. Addiction will always weaponize the naïveté of those it holds captive.

I would later find out, repeatedly, that breaking the physical addiction to heroin was actually the *easiest* part of the whole deal. That's not to downplay the most brutal discomfort and pain I've ever gone through (many a time), but at least you know that the *physical* pain eventually ends. It will always go away with time. However, the mind that continually gets you into this mess is the true menace. Short of a lobotomy, there isn't a simple solution to this aspect of addiction. The fix, often spiritual in some capacity, requires daily maintenance, and most don't become willing until after immense repercussions.

The "coming to" after a few weeks of physical misery is what really hurts; waking up and realizing you're still…you. That's the real gripe about cleaning up: you figure out that using drugs didn't turn you into a fucked-up person; it's that you used the drugs to shield yourself from the fact that you're so fucked up.

Too bad it would take me a decade of increasing consequences to iron that wrinkle out. Sometimes the weight of reality has to be sitting on your sternum before you can get a proper look at it.

I entered my first medial detox with a bag of methadone, a few dozen Ritalin, and a little bit of weed carefully tucked under my scrotum in case they searched me. They didn't. This was what I would later find out to be one of the "fancy" places. Health insurance is a hell of a thing. Unlike every future state-run detox I would attempt to beg myself into, this place cost (my insurance) about five grand a day. They want that sweet insurance cash, so why would they risk having to kick you out by searching you for illegal drugs? This is a major problem with private rehabilitation. Don't get me wrong, I'm a believer in competition and profit-motive driving innovation in nearly all sectors, but drug treatment isn't one of them. Unless a facility doesn't get paid until the patient is successfully clean for a segment of time *after* completion, there's little drive to deliver a successful product. They get paid astronomical rates inflated by insurance without having to deliver *any* results. That's a broken system. And with a new private rehab popping up every day in places like California and Florida, they begin competing to retain clientele by way of leniency and amenities as opposed to therapeutic services that work. The government doesn't seem to do anything better than the private sector, except lose money. But for this one thing and one thing only, that might actually be an asset.

The detox had great food, semi-private rooms, cable TV, loads of Valium, and nurses that were essentially servants. They offered me sixteen milligrams of Subutex my first day and would "step me down" one milligram a day until I hit eight. Then they'd keep me on eight milligrams for the remaining six days until they cut me loose with essentially zero detoxification having occurred. Sure, I would have fourteen days of not using heroin under my belt, but taking that much Subutex for two weeks would just replace one physically addictive drug for the other. For those not well versed in opiate detox protocol, this was not a viable solution, but it does keep people doped up enough to stay for the entire two weeks. This way detox facilities ensure that they can get every dollar out of your insurance. If they detoxed you properly and made you feel the inevitable pain, most patients would leave early and thus not "pay" for the whole stay. Another *major* flaw in the private detox industry.

Contrary to my initial reaction, detox was turning out to be rather fun. Everyone that I befriended had snuck some amount of drugs in, making it feel more like a supervised dope house than an actual medical facility. One girl was even having her friend come at night and throw bags of heroin over the fence of the outside smoking area. Lucky for me I had plenty of Ritalin to trade.

Ashley, the girl who was getting heroin delivered, was a mildly attractive broken pixie type. Short hair, skinny frame, and skin the color of spoiled cream, Ashley was the epitome of suburban junkie trash. Nevertheless, I thought she was cute, and when she told me that her dad was a wealthy pushover, I "fell in love."

At the end of my two-week stint, the doctor told me I was ready to move on to my next step of the scam. Given that I hadn't experienced a single withdrawal symptom during my entire stay, I certainly wasn't ready for residential rehab, but I'd have to make do. Unbeknownst to him, I had either used heroin or methadone on each day I was there, but even if I had followed his protocol, I wouldn't have been much better off. The real pain hadn't even started yet—this, I was somewhat aware of—but I had nowhere else to go. Aunt Suzanne found a rehab through my insurance where I would have to kick cold turkey.

The rehab arranged for my transportation from the detox, but I was adamant about handling this myself. The slim chance that I could find a way to get high one last time was enough for me to pass up a free ride and make the ten-mile trek on my own.

Minutes before I was to be released from detox, I went through an exit interview conducted by a doctor. He brought me into a private room, sat me down, and joined me after he placed his wallet and car keys on the table. He asked me several questions regarding my symptoms, went through the motions, and concluded that I was fit for release. I would still need to sign some paperwork—which he forgot at the nurse's station—so he left the room and told me that he would be back shortly.

Once he was gone, my sticky fingers made their way over to his wallet, which had four crisp twenty-dollar bills. I put forty in my pocket and forty back in the wallet, just in case he gave it a quick scan after he walked back in. When he returned, he actually made a comment about leaving his wallet and car keys behind, implying sarcastically that he was lucky that I didn't run off with his car. I chuckled nervously, and then urged him to expedite my discharge so I could move on to my "next chapter in recovery."

When the security guard opened the door to release me, Ashley came out of the woodwork and sprinted past the both of us. I didn't know if she liked me, or if she was just excited about the forty dollars I told her I had stolen, but either way, I guess we were an item now. That's just how junkie love works.

I didn't want to show up too late to the rehab, not out of fear of them caring—I knew they wouldn't give a shit as long as they could bill my insurance for the day, but out of fear that word would get back to my aunt and uncle. Because of the time constraint, Ashley suggested we take the subway to Skid Row. She assured me that we would be guaranteed to find dope immediately, which I took with a grain of salt, but I wound up being proven wrong upon our arrival.

Many cities across the nation claim to have their own "Skid Row" section of town, but I'm confident in saying that there's no slum in America that compares to that of Downtown Los Angeles. It's a futuristic time capsule of a post-apocalyptic city crammed into ten square blocks. Imagine what the Great Depression might have looked like in the middle of a metropolitan area, and then add monthly Social Security checks and grade A narcotics. This was Skid Row. All the characters looked similar to those of *Mad Max* if only they had been fighting over crack cocaine instead of gasoline. An estimated ten thousand people lived in this tiny, unmanaged sector, which was validated by the clusters of half-dead human traffic, streams of sewage, and the persistent stench of crowded death.

It was absolutely terrifying seeing it all for the first time, but despite the hysteria and several threats of violence we received, it turned out to be the most reliable place to buy drugs that I'd ever seen. Acquiring heroin is not easy in most cities; you usually need to know people and establish a solid connection if you want consistent access to good product. Cold copping in most cities can result in getting robbed, sold fake dope, or even getting arrested, before ever actually getting your hands on some decent heroin.

Not on LA's Skid Row. The quality isn't the best, but it's good enough, and dealers often argue with each other and fight for your business. It was an open-air free market where you could buy dope, a syringe, crack cocaine, a pipe, lighter, cigarette, and even a Shasta Cola, all from the same person. It was junkie heaven.

Ashley and I got high, took the train back to Pasadena, and we said our goodbyes. She was off to do God knows what on her father's dime, and I was to begin my lackluster attempt at recovery. The rehab where I was going to spend the next fourteen days was at a palatial Victorian house close to Downtown Pasadena in the San Gabriel Valley. This was an upscale place, complete with yoga classes, trips to the beach, and a personal chef that cooked for the forty or so men that lived there. The staff meant well, but business was business, and when there's millions to be milked from insurance companies, lines get blurry. Can you blame them? It's not like the rehabs are directly robbing their clients—only the few that pay out of pocket—they're only robbing the insurance companies blind, who are no less guilty of the same crime against their own policy holders. Most of the time, unfortunately, it's just one big game of fuckery. A lot of rehabs have good intentions, but good intentions are hard to maintain when there's that much money on the line. Do they save lives? Yes. Have some of them been guilty of enabling addicts all the way to their deathbeds? Yes. Is addiction a nearly incomprehensible human condition that we've barely scratched the surface of understanding how to treat? Yes. All three things can be true at the same time.

The most important thing that rehabs do are separate you from drugs for a period of time and provide you with some human connection. Like

I stated before, drugs can obviously infiltrate rehabs just like they do jails, but typically, they're much more difficult to obtain in both places than on the streets. If you're in treatment long enough and remain close after you depart, they can sometimes provide clients with a sense of community—another key factor in fighting addiction. Rehabs also introduce clientele to the lifelong communities of twelve-step programs, which are free, but aren't always easy to get involved in on your own without a rehab to essentially force you at first. Are these services worth thousands of dollars a day? Of course not. And do a lot of private rehabs employ nefarious doctors that overdiagnose and overmedicate? Yes. But even so, plenty of people do turn their lives around at private rehabs, even the fancy ones like the one I went to.

My university insurance would only cover fourteen days of inpatient rehab, as opposed to the typical twenty-eight, and subsidized this with covering up to three months of "intensive outpatient care." This meant that I would be on lockdown at the rehab for two weeks, then be transferred to the sober living section of the facility, where I would be free to come and go as I pleased as long as I attended my "treatment" sessions. What this meant to me was that I was going to stay completely sober for two weeks, and then be able to do whatever the fuck I wanted to do as long as I showed face and kept up appearances. I lasted about a month before getting kicked out for my fifth dirty urine test.

I was drifting nowhere, not staying sober, and knew that this day was going to eventually come. Uncle Neal had already gotten word that I had tested dirty several times, so he had written me off for good. Apparently when he said I had one chance, he meant it, and rightfully so. Leeching off my family any further was out of the cards, so I had to come up with a plan.

Several of my rehab brethren pitched in and gave me a couple packs of cigarettes and about sixty dollars to help with whatever bad decisions were in my immediate future.

We were all caught up on the news cycle—there's a lot of watching TV at rehab, which had been dominated by the budding civil unrest occurring across the country. What I'm referring to was the Occupy Wall Street movement, which was an organized reaction towards the 2009 bank bailouts and the widening gap between the rich and poor. New York City was obviously where this movement kicked off, but other cities—most notably Los Angeles—followed shortly after. One of my rehab friends suggested that I take the train downtown and live at the Occupy LA protest until I managed to figure out a better long-term plan. My first stop was obviously going to get high, so a "better long-term plan" wasn't in the cards. Still, showing up to this protest seemed like the most logical step for me. It also didn't hurt that Occupy LA was only about ten blocks west from Skid Row, where I planned on immediately spending that sixty dollars on drugs.

CHAPTER 4

SKID ROW ROUND ONE

In early autumn of 2011, the haphazard offshoot of Occupy Wall Street took form in Los Angeles. The economy was in shambles, college graduates felt disenfranchised and lied to about the value of their education, class mobility had all but disappeared, and the uneven distribution of wealth had reached proportions that left even conservatives feeling uneasy. We all know the story, and frankly it depresses me to dwell on it or take a legitimate stance, because like most of the others at Occupy LA, I had no rational solution. I was just there to party and take advantage of others, just like our technocratic and corporate overlords. A lot of the participants meant well. However, most didn't have a fucking clue about anything, me included.

I couldn't have cared less about the military-industrial complex or whose pockets the 2009 government bailout money fell into, because I was a two-dimensional being: a reptile in a hoodie with nothing unique about me other than my Social Security number. Being a homeless drug addict meant I was free from any introspective worries about my place within a broken system. Some would say that's part of the appeal. People flocked from all over Southern California to express their frustrations, while I showed up for nothing else but to get a free sleeping bag. After all, I was on drugs, which despite their many drawbacks, do wonders in their ability to drown out national current events. Unless it got in the way of me being able to get high, I wasn't concerned in the slightest. Political matters are the last thing on the mind of someone who starts violently dry heaving if they go twelve hours without a gram of heroin. Ironically, most of the country's foreign policy of the last decade had only resulted in cheaper, higher-quality dope on the streets. If I had the mental capability to put together this notion back in 2011, my politics would have probably made

John Bolton flinch. I would have been a "one-issue voter," alright. Invade any country with the right climate for poppy cultivation and you would have had my support.

I showed up to Occupy LA with a trash bag full of clothes and a half gram of crystal meth—a winning combination in attracting fellow shit-bags. A group of bums from Texas welcomed me at the sight of my luggage, inviting me to camp with them once they found out I had some speed. We smoked some crystal, exchanged a few half-truths, then they gave me the rundown on Occupy. They had been there for about a week and had acquired a few tents and some other supplies along the way. Apparently, college kids would arrive with fancy gear, and depending on what would happen first, they would either get sick of sleeping outside or get robbed of all their belongings.

These bums were gutter punks from Texas. A gutter punk is one of those homeless kids you see downtown, wearing a jean jacket vest with patches all over it and usually accompanied by a canine of some sort. Essentially, they're suburban white kids who think they're misunderstood by society because they heard about it in a NOFX song when they were twelve years old. Once they're not allowed to sleep on their parents' couch anymore, they run away and travel by train to waste away somewhere else. Not a fun bunch usually. Quite boring and no drive to commit real crimes. Gutter punks slink around town and get high when they can on what they can. These guys were no different, and the next day they invited me to take the train to Hollywood with them to beg for change on the boulevard.

I'd never begged for change before—which they called spanging—and after several hours of laying in front of a Popeye's Chicken with a cardboard sign, I wasn't much satisfied with the gig. We called it quits once we had about eight dollars in loose change, which was enough for them to get a gram of mid-quality weed and be satisfied. Pathetic.

I broke off from the group the second we got back to downtown to figure out how I was going to get my fix. Flustered, I jogged to Skid Row and traded my iPod for a couple bags of dope. A more concrete system of steady income would have to be established if I were to stay afloat, because spanging for hours to split eight dollars amongst four bums wasn't going to cut it. Although I needed comradery and protection, joining this crew and becoming a gutter punk wasn't sustainable for the habit I desired.

The encampment adjacent to the punks was made up of five Latino men, each with their own personal tent. This was a rarity, as most people I had encountered were sharing tents with multiple others. All five of the men typically had their shirts off, revealing a collection of prison tattoos, which indicated that they were most likely gang members. Stereotypes aside, they didn't look like they were at Occupy to protest income inequality. They looked like they were there to sell drugs and get high, and although I looked much different than them, our objectives were much more in line than that of the gutter punks and me. One of the Texans told me that although the Latinos weren't very friendly, they did sell some good crystal.

I got my hands on an HP laptop later that day—I don't remember how, but I'm sure it wasn't kosher—and I inquired to one of my Mexican neighbors if they were interested in purchasing it. I had to get my foot in the door somehow. My new acquaintance introduced himself as Youngster. Standing no more than five foot three, Youngster was built like an English Bulldog and had his last name tattooed across his shoulders: "Morales" in faded green block lettering.

He asked me where I got the laptop from, and hoping to impress him, I quickly announced that I stole it. Youngster smirked and told me he didn't think a clean-cut white boy like myself would be a thief.

Youngster took me down to Fifth and Los Angeles Street, where he introduced me to some folks that paid cash for stolen goods. They ran a taco shop that did in fact sell food, but it was more so just a front for a fence operation. They gave me fifty dollars for the laptop—quite generous for a street price, probably due to the fact that I was with Youngster.

He wanted to wait until we got back to Occupy to spend the money on dope, to ensure that I bought it from his crew. I agreed to this and assured him I'd break him off for his troubles, but I insisted that we buy a small bag and take a few blasts before we hit the road. Youngster paused, then nodded in half-agreement.

I bought a dime from the Paisas up the block, tossed a shard in my pipe, and took a hit within my sweatshirt to guard against the wind.

"My boy, you can't wait ten minutes 'til we get back before you start hittin' that?" Youngster joked.

"Naw, I can't, man, I'm not patient when it comes to this shit," I replied as smoke billowed out through the fabric around my torso.

"Damn, this foo shot the fuck out, huh?! I can relate, my boy," Youngster exclaimed as he motioned for me to pass the pipe his way.

As we finished up the bowl and started on our return, Youngster and I began to make each other laugh and talk about dope. I could tell that he was a fiend just like me, not just a drug user or even an abuser, but an absolute degenerate.

People like us, well, we get high rain or shine, January or July. We find a way to quiet the mind no matter what because there's simply no other option once we're running. We don't settle for a different drug other than the drug of our choice, and the thought, "Well, there's always tomorrow," has never run through our heads when it comes to getting fucked up.

After blowing out his hit, Youngster took a seat down on the curb and said, "Hey, my boy, listen…. I usually shoot up. I don't smoke it anymore, doesn't really do it for me, you feel me? You mind if I do a little shot right quick?"

"Yeah, no problem," I took a seat next to him, "I just like to smoke it, but I get it, you gotta do it the way you like to do it."

"Exactly. I like to shoot it, you like to smoke it…for now. Shit, I remember those days, doggy!" Youngster grinned.

I handed him a small shard of crystal—about a tenth of a gram—as he pulled his works out of his pocket with his other hand. He ran over to rummage for an empty bottle of water in the gutter and used the cap to mix up the crystal with the few drops that were left. He then picked up a cigarette butt off the crusty sidewalk and tore a little piece of the filter off to throw in the cap. Sticking the tip of his needle in the now-soaked piece of amber cigarette filter, he sucked it dry by drawing the plunger up on the syringe. With his adrenaline already pumping in anticipation, he quickly found a plump vein in his left arm, poked it, and then pulled the trigger.

Gnarly. Completely unsanitary. Junkiedom of the highest order. Surely, I would never do something so foul in my addiction, but I was yet to break many boundaries, some a whole lot worse.

I couldn't help but feel nauseated yet completely enthralled at the same time. Based on the deep cough and subsequent drool slipping out of Youngster's bottom lip, it appeared that he was having quite the reaction. With a smile so repugnant it could nearly make you gag, Youngster had returned to his little piece of heaven with the push of a button. It was tragically beautiful, watching someone do something so disgusting yet that provided them with the highest level of synthetic joy. Deep down I knew I was looking in the mirror.

"That's that shit!" He lurched his soulless gaze in my direction once again, "You were right, my boy. I'm fuckin' glad we didn't wait."

On our walk home, I asked Youngster where he was from, and I found out that he was raised in Boyle Heights. I told him that I was from Oakland, and since he had forgotten my name, he told me that Oakland was what he would call me. That was my moniker at Occupy from then on out.

I would have preferred a better nickname—one that more smoothly slipped off the tongue—but I couldn't think of anything on the spot, and "Jared" wasn't going to do me any favors on Skid Row. Truly, I was just happy to have any nickname at all. A nickname meant you had friends—that you were a part of a group. Maybe I would find mine in Youngster and his crew. It was a long shot, given that I was white and not a former gang member, but with Youngster's approval and christened nickname, I knew I had a chance.

Back at his camp, he introduced me to the rest of the guys. There was Boxer, Shadow, Chinola, and Smiley. Boxer and Shadow were apparently brothers, Chinola didn't speak a word of English and looked twenty years older than everybody else, and Smiley, well, he smiled a lot. Unsurprisingly, they weren't excited to meet me at all. If anything, they were skeptical about whether I was a cop or not. Youngster assured them that I was legit and told them I was going to stay in his tent until I managed to get my hands on my own. Given the comments I heard from under their breaths, this seemed to evoke suspicions of gay activity. Maybe their suspicions were correct. Youngster never gave off that vibe to me, but after my experience with G up in Santa Cruz, nothing like that would ever surprise me again.

I was scared, massively uncomfortable, and had come to realize that homelessness was not something you could take half measures with. This lifestyle required constant effort and adaptability to survive. Some kids wind up in the same position as I did but have an eventual saving grace by contacting a worried parent. This was not going to be the case for me. The only family left that would entertain a phone call with me was Dad, whose status was completely unknown. For all I knew, he didn't even have a phone to be answered, and perhaps he was homeless himself. If I were to have any semblance of family, it wasn't going to come from anyone related to me. It would have to be made with fellow homeless.

I wasn't very street smart (yet), and I wasn't tough at all, but I knew that Youngster and my soon-to-be other friends were. My plan was to somehow grab onto their coattails and hitch a ride through Skid Row until I figured out how to fend for myself. They were Mexican—gang affiliated to a certain extent—and knew how to conduct themselves in this environment. They had all done time in jail or prison, been on and off the streets for years, and had given up all hope of ever leaving the streets for good. I was white—which was typically a handicap on Skid Row—but more importantly, I was meek. Both physically timid and spiritually (somewhat) innocent, I looked like the kind of person that would get torn to pieces in such a place. On the other hand, I had no police record, knew how to talk myself out of trouble, and had an immaculate ability to slip under the radar and thieve. I knew I was going to need these guys to ensure my literal survival, and in order to retain their friendship/protection, I would have to prove to them that our relationship would be mutually beneficial. Fortunately for me, my ability to steal, gather supplies, and solicit customers for the dope they were selling quickly convinced them that I was worth keeping around. We grew tight, and once the riot police came in and finally disbanded Occupy for good, we stuck together as we moved our base of operations. For me, Occupy was just boot camp, and seven blocks due south was the war that I'd been training for.

Youngster and Smiley disappeared after Occupy was bulldozed. No one was certain where they went, but the other guys assured me that homeless comrades disappearing from time to time was to be expected when living on the streets. No one paid an ounce of attention to it.

Chinola, Boxer, Shadow, and I remained together at the new camp we had established on the side of a freeway onramp. We each had our own tent, setting them up in a row behind a guardrail and some trees that kept us hidden from the 101 traffic. We chose this spot off the beaten path in order to establish a somewhat permanent site, but were still just a few blocks from Skid Row proper. This was back in the old days when you really couldn't leave a tent pitched on Skid Row (or anywhere in LA, for that matter) past sunrise in most parts without the cops threatening to arrest you if you didn't break it down. There were a few back lanes on Skid Row, like Crocker Street, where you could keep a tent pitched for longer, but eventually the cops would always do a sweep at some point. These areas were pretty territorial, but along the main drag of San Pedro Street, spots were more up for grabs. Still, we wanted to be camped next to each other, and the odds of us finding enough available space down there were slim.

Nowadays every major city in California is littered with permanent tents, some complete with electricity, second stories, and furniture. This was nearly nonexistent in 2011, which made for a much different atmosphere upon my return to Skid Row in 2015. The second they gave us an inch just a few years later, we took a whole yard and planted our tent poles in for good. Giving leniency to a homeless drug addict is like trying to negotiate the borders of your home with a cockroach. I hate to speak about my own kind in such a crude manner, but when under the spell of drugs, we have almost no ability to compromise. Maybe our flagrant selfishness is justified, after all, life isn't easy sleeping outside. And when the homeless numbers are through the roof, you can't exactly outlaw it without providing an alternative solution. Instead of doing so, places like California seemed to have just decriminalized open drug use and vagrancy, which to me is the more heartless route. It also requires the least amount of effort from anyone in charge, which I suspect is why this path was chosen. It's so much easier to keep promising the fairy tale of "permanent housing for all" instead of having to actually build shelters, rehabs, and mental health centers—that would require actual work beyond flapping your gums for years on end. Those with lifelong careers of broken promises, for the time being, seem to still win elections. But eventually we'll find out how much worse it has to get before that no longer works.

The holiday season had begun, and I started to make quick and easy money by way of deceit. With emotions running high and heartstrings suspended just waiting to be yanked, I grasped at every opportunity. I would take the five-minute stroll to Union Station—the main subway hub of Los Angeles—up to twenty times a day, perfecting the art of defrauding people of their hard-earned money. It proved to be much quicker and easier than thieving. To the best of my knowledge, it also wasn't illegal. I would wash up in the bathroom, contort myself into anything that was remotely presentable, and craft the perfect presentation for a sob story. People regularly handed me cash—and not just dollar bills, but fives, tens, twenties, gift cards, sandwiches, clothing, cigarettes—all sorts of things that I could convert into money for dope.

My standard pitch was that I had come down to LA to participate in the Occupy movement, and now that it was over, I needed to get back home. Given that I had run out of money—and it was getting close to Thanksgiving—I desperately needed to take a break from "fighting for the working class" to see my loved ones. Grandma's famous stuffing was only a seventy-dollar train ticket away, I would tell them. It didn't work every time, but it certainly worked enough. Over the few months that I did this, I'd estimate that about twenty times someone took me to the ATM and gave me eighty dollars to cover the whole train ticket and a warm meal. It was not quite evil, but it wasn't far off. At the very least, it was brazen dishonesty in its purest form. Still young and innocent looking, and always a good talker, I could pull this off at age twenty-two. A few years later I'd lose all ability.

One of my victims was a middle-aged woman who had apparently just won $10,000 off a scratcher a few weeks prior. She walked me over to the ATM, withdrew $300, and handed me the largest wad of cash I'd held in years. She said she would have given me more, but $300 was her daily withdrawal limit. My jaw remained dropped for the duration of my sprint towards Sixth and San Pedro. An eight ball of meth and several grams of heroin later, I found myself blacked out on the streets of East Hollywood, miles away from Skid Row.

Coming back to consciousness several days later, I wound up at the doorstep of a small home, attempting to twist open the knob of the front door. Not the safest activity to wake up to. Someone opened the door and chased me off, as I noticed with each weighted step my chin was in a great deal of pain. Pus oozed from a golf-ball-sized abscess protruding from the lower part of my face.

This was my introduction to a vast history of blacking out and waking up with near-lethal staph infections. Two awkward bus rides later, I was at the county hospital, where they kept me overnight to administer intravenous antibiotics. Little did I know that this would now become a regular part of my drug-addled routine.

Once the inflammation went down the following day, they sent me "home" with a bottle of antibiotics and some ibuprofen. After tossing the medication in the trash, I quickly made my way back downtown to purchase enough heroin to guide me into a gentle comedown. The boys were glad to see me—mostly because I had leftover crystal meth—but also because I had arrived with a king's feast worth of Mexican cuisine. A briefly unattended El Pollo Loco delivery bike had come into my path at some point during my return, and I wasn't one to turn down an easy opportunity.

After a twenty-four-hour nap, I bought an army green BMX bicycle for eight dollars off a crackhead named Walter. I needed a bike because my feet were starting to disintegrate, and the delivery bike I had stolen was much too cumbersome to ride with ease. I gave it to Shadow so he could try to trade it for some dope. Meth dehydrates your body, which not only causes you to sweat profusely, but also turns your feet into an anatomical water tap. Gravity causes a lot of the hydration in your body to exit through your feet when meth is introduced into the system. After being awake for three days and having walked twenty or so miles, the soles of your feet look and feel like water-bogged sheets of lasagna noodles. Not only is this repugnant, but it's extremely painful. I've called it quits before and toppled over into a bush for a few days until the skin beneath my feet hardened up and created semi-functional pads to walk upon. This often works to some degree, but you don't always have a few days to spare—especially if you're a heroin addict that constantly needs to stave off withdrawals. Being very much physically addicted, at the bare minimum I needed at least twenty dollars' worth of heroin every day just to not shit myself. If I wanted to actually get high and enjoy myself for twelve hours, I'd need to spend about eighty dollars. This need to constantly hustle up money to make sure I had my next dose didn't jive well with work-related injuries, so I had no choice but to invest in a proper bike to spare my feet from total destruction.

This is the side of homelessness that sometimes goes unnoticed. Sure, there's the obvious downsides—like having to sleep outside and eating primarily out of a trash can—but the immense side effects to your health from living this sort of life aren't always as apparent. One bad night of rain could lead to months of foot rot. One too many months of foot rot could lead to a bone infection. One too many weeks of a bone infection could lead to an amputation, and so on.

I began to grow apart from Boxer, Shadow, and Chinola. Although they had spent much more time on the street than me, their earnings said otherwise. It's possible they had a smaller appetite than me for getting high—they were only addicted to meth and not heroin, but more than likely they were just exhausted from years of getting beat down by the concrete. Unlike them, I was still in the honeymoon phase of gutter life, with a pinch of innocence left on my face that made my swindling more fruitful. They grew to resent my exuberance, and I was blind to the fact that I would one day share their aged fatigue.

Humans are social creatures—even those of us enslaved by chemicals—that develop extremely strong bonds when they share distress such as homelessness. We once shared that bond, but as my sanity faded with increased meth use, I started to sense ostracization from the group. This interpretation of our social interactions could have been muddled by hallucinations, but whether or not my suspicions matched up with reality, I felt more comfortable as a lone ranger. I pretty much gave up on sleeping for the rest of the month and told Shadow he could use my tent for storage.

Although my judgment and memory were cloudy during my time on Skid Row, I managed to avoid violence for the most part. I've since realized that this is one of my innate gifts. I could be blessed, or maybe I have the natural ability at defusing tension; I'm not sure, but I've met many people—especially suburban white kids like myself—who got their jaw broken and everything stolen from them within minutes of their first time being in the area. I'm not large by any means, nor am I particularly intimidating on any level. By some people's standards, I could have still passed for a teenager well into my mid-twenties. In simpler terms, I'm not the kind of person that would normally command any amount of respect on Skid Row. I'm not saying I didn't experience violence, but the amount seems to be dwarfed by the stories that I've heard from other transients. During this initial 2011 stretch on Skid Row, I was attacked only about a dozen times, all resulting in rapid de-escalation and no significant injuries. I was successfully strong-armed only once, and beat another man half to death with a chain and padlock who had attempted to steal my heroin. I only strong-armed one person during that run, and given that he was black-out drunk, it didn't require much effort.

One night in mid-December, I was riding my bike across the intersection of Seventh and Crocker when I came upon a parked car with its lights on. It looked like a newer car—maybe a BMW that was just a few years old—but regardless of what year or model it was, the important thing was that it looked out of place.

I rolled by slowly on my BMX so I could peek through the passenger window, where I saw a young kid passed out at the wheel. He was wearing a plain black shirt that was completely unbuttoned, revealing a wifebeater that looked damp with sweat. I assumed he had come downtown to go clubbing, and in the midst of trying to get home after boozing too hard, he pulled over to sleep some of his drunk off. It was a smart move as opposed to driving home wasted, but unfortunately, he made three heartbreaking mistakes: one, he could not have chosen a more sadistic block in Los Angeles County to take a nap; two, he left his lights on—thus drawing attention to his vehicle from any doped-up lurker on the prowl; and three, he left his fucking doors unlocked.

I knew my bike would probably get stolen if I left it on the sidewalk while I hopped in this kid's car, but I was willing to lose it in exchange for whatever valuables I found in his pockets. He appeared dead to the world, and I figured I could fish some cash out of his jeans without waking him up, but I had my knife in my hand just in case.

The block wasn't dead; there were a dozen or so people within a shouting distance, as well as two police cruisers parked with their lights on about two blocks west. I couldn't believe that no one else had jumped on this gold mine of an opportunity yet. I laid my bike down about five feet from the car and gingerly opened the passenger door.

"Heyyy eyyyyahwahhh…" he moaned as the interior lights flicked on and I crept onto the passenger seat. He reacted to my entry but showed no signs of full consciousness.

I pulled the passenger door tight up to the frame of the car, but I didn't close it so the interior light would remain on. It didn't take more than a few seconds to catch a glimpse of his cell phone that was tucked between his thighs. I wasn't certain at first, but it appeared to be a fourth-generation iPhone. This was late 2011, and that iPhone had just been released a few months prior, so I knew that it was worth a pretty penny. I could sell it for up to a couple hundred bucks on Sixth and Los Angeles Street come morning. Satisfied with just stealing the phone, I saw no need to investigate further, when two men opened both rear doors and joined us in the vehicle.

"Whatchyou doin' in this kid's car, bruh?" The man behind the driver's seat inquired. At this point, the kid was coming to life—and was even showing signs of distress over the three strangers that now sat around him—but he was still too fucked up to verbalize anything that made sense.

"Hey, it's cool, man, I just noticed this kid passed out at the wheel, and I'm like, just tryin' to help him out. There's cops parked up the block, I don't want him to get in trouble."

"Aight, blud, you cool on that, cuz he don't need yo *help* no more. *We* finna help him now." The other man responded.

"Ayyyy wayyyyat…whoooo…gehh outttt!" The driver was slowly remembering how to speak English.

"Listen, I was here first, so I think I should help him, I mean…this is too many people, right? He doesn't need that much help." I said as the tension dredged on. We all knew that there was a limited amount of time before this kid was fully back to reality, at which point violence might become unavoidable.

"You best just get the fuck out the car right now, cuz you probably just tryin' to rob this kid, man. We finna actually *help* him." He said with a half-believable tone.

"Aight, I got an idea.... How 'bout I *help* him with his phone, and then you guys can *help* him with his car and anything else he might have. That work?" I proposed.

A moment went by as the two other assailants looked at each other, nodded, then looked back at me, and the one behind me said, "That'll work."

I swiped the driver's iPhone and hustled out the door. To my surprise, the kid was able to process what had happened, and attempted to chase after me for about half a block north up Crocker. I looked back and watched him stumble in my direction, until his lack of coordination caused him to come crashing down into the pavement. Seconds after the plummet, his car came screeching down Crocker, speeding past his flattened body moments before crossing my path. I gave the car thieves a polite wave, which they did not reciprocate.

I felt nothing but jubilation after my first quasi-robbery. I, of course, detest this behavior now, but at the time I experienced a feeling of self-worth that had previously been unrivaled. I felt like a man. An adult criminal, as opposed to a delinquent kid. I had done something reprehensible against someone who hadn't harmed me in any way, but acknowledgment of this would not come to fruition for years. In the moment I was a force to be reckoned with, or so I thought for the first time in my life. In my mind, I had graduated from a measly street addict to a legit crook. A bit far-fetched given the rather tame event, but still, I had crossed a line that I was savagely proud of.

I, a homeless drug addict, was doing what I needed to survive—I thought—and I was damn proud of myself. My ability at attaining the means to get high was self-evident; it would no longer *ever* be a question for me of whether I would be able to get my next hit. From that point on, hustling up funds to get high became a high in itself. The psychotropic effects of hardcore narcotics—no matter how celestially dynamic they truly are—become monotonous after months of daily intake, in which case an addict becomes equally dependent on the adventure that comes with *remaining* under their influence. For me it would become a dual addiction.

Three in the morning on Skid Row is different from three in the afternoon, but not as much as you might think. Heroin and crack are readily available around the clock—and nowadays meth as well—but back in 2011, the gangs did what they could to keep meth out of the area in order to keep it from impeding on cocaine sales. You could only get meth from a select few people on Sixth and Wall back then, but now it's sold on every square foot of Skid Row.

I wanted heroin *and* meth, but I didn't have cash—only the iPhone. I could have waited until the morning and sold it for a decent price to the Paisas, but I was willing to take a loss if I could find someone willing to trade me dope for it immediately.

I knew a defunct gangbanger named Li'l Boy from Eighteenth Street, who sold good heroin from midnight until the sun came up. He had a house, a wife, and kids, but every night he set up a tent on Skid Row and sold dope in order to pay his bills. He got high too. I knew he was open to certain trades, so I made my way over to Seventh and San Pedro to show him the phone.

"Ayyy, my boy, whatchyou need?" Li'l Boy peered through the opening of his tent.

"Hey, man, check this out," I looked around before pulling the phone out of my pocket. "I got a iPhone Four, and this thing is like brand new, newest model. And the Paisas are payin' like one-fifty, two hundred for 'em."

"Ah, shit, my boy! My wife been talkin' 'bout that new iPhone! Damn, wood…I can't give you cash, though, I need to re-up soon. You down to trade for some black?"

"Yeah, I'm down. How 'bout a bundle? Or maybe like twelve balloons and a couple shards? And ten bucks if you can so I can buy some cigarettes and shit," I proposed.

"Damn, wood, twelve balloons and some chris? *And* ten dollas? My boy…I'll give you ten balloons, ten bucks, naw, fuck that—I'll give you my tent instead of the cash, you can sell that shit if you want but I need all my money right now." Li'l Boy spoke as he removed his glasses and cleaned them with his Raiders sweatshirt. "And a fat-ass shard for that shit, but that's the best I can do, my boy."

"Aight, but Li'l Boy, you know you robbin' me right now. You gettin' the bargain of a lifetime on this shit…but fuck it, let's do it."

Li'l Boy waved me into the tent and doled me out my payment. After I handed him the phone, Li'l Boy removed his items from the tent with haste, then took off in his car to go re-up his stash.

I had a good chunk of dope on my hands, enough to keep me pretty damn high for a whole day—maybe a day and a half. This was a blessing in my eyes, but once I'd run out, I would be in for the rude awakening of no longer having transportation.

Having a bike was a *necessity* for me to hustle. Relying on my feet alone to get around wouldn't get me more than a few blocks, because the soles of my feet were now in a constant state of homeless decay. Having run a few blocks earlier from the owner of the iPhone only exacerbated this issue tenfold. I would have my fun and get high for the rest of the night, but come morning time, my feet would be bloodied and squealing with pain.

I sat alone in my tent with an empty bag of crystal meth as the rats scurried back into the sewers to escape the rising sun. Other than a now-vacant meth pipe, all I had were a few balloons of heroin and two feet that were out of commission. I exited the tent and hobbled myself to the corner in anguish to find a smoke.

I traded one of the balloons I had left for two packs of Sheriff brand cigarettes and a warm Steel Reserve, my first beer in months. I didn't have a drop of desire for alcohol at the moment—nor did I ever when heroin was available—but when bartering, you always try to get as much as you can or you look weak.

I gulped down three-quarters of the beer, tossed the can to the curb, and lit up one of the cheap cigarettes. I was done for. Who would have thought that something as simple as losing my bike would be the crux of my downfall on Skid Row? My train station hustle and petty thievery had now come to a grinding halt.

It was getting close to Christmas, and I figured there was no better time to throw in the towel. Maybe I'd get in contact with one of my high school friends up north, and in the Christmas spirit, they would buy me a bus ticket "home" and let me crash at their place until I figured out a viable plan. However, I was strung out to the gills and knew I'd have to kick heroin before I could put any energy towards a full-scale relocation. I lugged myself down to the end of the block, where I found a rolled-up carpet leaning against a chain link fence.

My mind was teetering between sleep-deprived hallucinations and complete unconsciousness; I'd be willing to bet that I hadn't slept in over a hundred hours, and flipping the autopilot switch was becoming less and less of a choice by the second. Moments later I found myself sitting cross-legged on the still-rolled-up carpet and smoking my last two balloons of heroin. I knew they would be my last for quite some time—maybe forever, maybe not, probably not—but I still treated the act in a ceremonious fashion. I was done *for now*.

After taking my last hit, I balled up the sooty piece of foil and tossed it through the fence. After unrolling the carpet, I laid myself across one side, grabbed the edge, and rolled myself up in the middle of the cylinder. Despite the mild dampness and stench of urine, my provisional carpet womb was optimal for hibernation. I then fell asleep for maybe twenty hours. When I awoke for the first time, the sun was just starting to creep through the opening of my cocoon as I shifted my body so I could vomit out the hole. Already very dopesick, I was fortunately so sleep-deprived that I managed to snooze on and off over the next twenty-four hours.

When I stopped vomiting and began to only dry heave from dehydration, I found the will to unravel myself and go in search of water. The temperature was maybe in the mid-seventies, which was above average for Christmastime in LA, but I was in no state to enjoy the weather. When you're in the throes of heroin withdrawal, there's no ideal climate. Everything is freezingly hot and leaves you drowning in a cold sweat.

Lucky for me, my kick has always been more prone to violent bouts of vomiting and dry heaving over diarrhea. Some people have the opposite reaction. Not having this predisposition was especially ideal in my circumstance, given that my kick was occurring within the confines of a semi-permeable rug. Puking out of the rolled-up carpet was much easier than shitting, I presumed. Either way, it was far from detoxing in a hospital bed with a slew of medications and a flatscreen TV, but this was my only option. I was too weak to even figure out a way to get arrested, where I'd at least have access to a toilet and running water.

I wrapped myself up once again and spent another day and night excreting the illness from my pores. Upon unraveling the carpet when the sun rose again, there was a group of middle-aged women shooting heroin adjacent to where I had been laying. They glanced down at me and immediately discerned that I was kicking hard. A junkie can practically smell it on their own vile kind and feel it reverberate between their two souls.

"Awwwwchhh! Poor baby, you look terrible!" one coughed at me.

"Yeah…I'm 'bout…forty-eight hours without dope. Was tryin' to kick, but now I actually think I'm gonna die. You think I could…can I get a little bit of your shot? Or maybe just suck on the cotton? I'll take anything." The words creaked out of my vomit-coated lips.

"Oh, baby, naw, baby, no…you should stay strong, you don't want none o' this shit, you've gone too far, baby, forty-eight hours! You're practically done!" said another, offering a bit of closed-fist sympathy.

I begged. "Listen…I don't care if you have hep C…. I don't care if you have HIV…. I will lick the blood that drips outta your arm if there's a chance that a bit of dope seeps out."

"Damn boy, you fucked up in the head for sayin' some shit like that, tellin' me you think I might have HIV! Bitch, I don't got no fuckin' AIDS!" she squawked.

"But you *do* got hep C, bitch!" her friend jumped in and started laughing.

She laughed too. I wasn't in the mood for jokes but managed to crack a little smile before retreating back into the carpet.

Unable to sleep and at my wits end, I managed to erect myself out of the carpet and push my weight up the block towards the Fred Jordan Mission later that day. They gave out bottles of cheap cola, and I was desperately craving anything sweet. My muscles felt like cuts of meat that had been stapled together, being simultaneously animated and electrocuted by a wet car battery. The last thing I wanted to do was walk in such a condition, but I needed to try and shake it out. This is the dopesick shuffle: when it's simply too painful to lay still.

After receiving my free soda and several bottles of water, I collapsed about ten feet from the entrance of the Mission and crawled towards its cinder-block wall. I perched myself up against it, pacing my water and soda consumption so I wouldn't vomit. If anything ever symbolized the opposite of dignity, this was it.

A passing Chevy Silverado pulled over past where I was sitting, and a small redheaded man hopped out from the driver's seat. Blinded by pain, I squinted as his cloudy figure made its way over and stared down at my corpse.

"Hey there, bud. You don't look so hot right now. You kickin'?" the blurry Irish-looking man asked me.

"Yes…about two days in." I struggled to spit out a complete sentence. "Not feelin' good…came over here to get some water."

"Gosh, well, I've been there, myself. I know what it feels like. My name's Michael McCutcheon, by the way. What's your name?"

"Me? I'm…Jared."

"Jared? That's a great name," Michael proclaimed. "Hell, it's biblical! Son, you got a name that shows up in one of the first few pages of the Bible. It's a good Christian name."

"Yeah, you're right, I guess, I mean, shit…it beats…Braydon," I said, followed by a sharp snort. My nose was leaking bad.

"Braydon? That ain't a proper Christian name, I'll tell you that. Abraham didn't have any sons named *Braydon*, and he sure as hell didn't have any sons named *Tanner* neither."

I couldn't tell if Michael was joking or not, but either way, I liked it. He was genuinely funny in a simple kind of way, almost like he belonged in an old-time Western film. By the way he spoke, dressed, and even the way he walked—holding a tight posture with his hands resting on his short hips—he was a breath of fresh air compared to the surrounding cretins. Don't get me wrong—I was a cretin of the highest caliber myself, but I truly appreciated the civilized company in that moment. He was an agent of normality and made me feel welcomed.

"Agreed, Michael. So you've kicked heroin yourself before?"

"I been clean damn near eleven months now, and shit, it's a complete miracle. Been on and off dope since I was a young buck; it ain't nothin' new to me…. Hey, I was thinkin', you could probably use a bite to eat, right? You wanna tag along with me and get some, I dunno…how 'bout some Shakey's pizza?" Michael said as he reached out his hand to help me up.

I grabbed on to Michael and let out a painful grunt as I made my way up onto my nimble frame. I wasn't sure what Michael's true intentions were. After all, he was a stranger inviting a weakened junkie into his car. Maybe he just wanted to help a guy that was down on his luck, or maybe he was going to take me to his home, tie me up, and keep me in his basement. Anything was possible. Worse things have happened to vagrant junkies, but this was a chance I was willing to take. Anything seemed better than spending the rest of my days throwing up out of the peephole of a rolled-up carpet. Regardless, I felt warmth from Michael. Warmth that I hadn't felt in months since living on the streets. Connection existed between Chinola, Shadow, Boxer, and I, but any of us would have double crossed each other if it meant we could make a few bucks. On the contrary, Michael seemed to be offering help with no expectations of financial gain. He made me feel worthy of another human's care, and therefore, I agreed to go with him.

Michael and I drove a few blocks up to one of the Christian missions that had just had a church service of some kind. I remained lying down across the backseat of his truck while he went out to talk to some of the attendees. Moments later, Michael returned with about half a dozen homeless church goers and opened both back passenger doors of his truck.

"Hey, Jared, I brought you some folks that would really love to say a prayer over you, if that would be OK?" Michael asked as he patted my shoulder.

This was something I would have normally scoffed at, but for some reason it felt like it was exactly what I needed. "Sure…that's fine by me."

Despite having limited room, everyone managed to put at least one hand somewhere on my body, while one of them led the group in an animated prayer. It was electrifying. Maybe not in a biblical sense, but a group of strangers converged on me and showered me with the energy of love for the first time in…forever. It was unconditional. Furthermore, I was open-minded to it, which was more electrifying than the act itself. By being receptive to such a foreign concept such as group prayer, I showed the first sign ever in my life of raising a white flag. I'm not saying that religion would end up saving me. It didn't. In fact, I never even gave it a try. But opening my mind to the idea that maybe all of my preconceived opinions weren't fact was the first step in a psychic change being possible. This was a critical moment in humility.

It's easy for any drug addict to have sympathy for another drug addict, but there's something particularly unique between fellow heroin addicts. The scourge of heroin withdrawal is transcendent. After your first time, its magnitude of suffering permanently changes you—both physically and mentally—to a degree that rivals most modern hardships. It's not the level of pain associated with dopesickness that's excruciating; it's the constant and perpetual momentum of agony that seems to never take a break for days on end—a seemingly permanent fiasco. One will literally not sleep a wink for six or seven days during this period of terror, followed by at least a month of only an hour or two each night of second-rate shut-eye. If you're lucky enough to go through this hellish experience in a bed, be assured that it will be soaked through with cold and musty sweat at every moment. The smell is like nothing you've ever encountered: soggy crotch mixed with rotting earth matter and chemicals excreting from every pore. Your joints *itch* (for lack of a better term) so badly that sometimes the only solution you can think of is trying to break your own elbows and knees. Fortunately, the sickness makes you so weak that you can't muster up the strength to ever pull it off. Those who have gone through the ordeal, like Michael and I, forever share a bond on a reptilian level. We have a relationship with the oldest parts of our own brains that few humans in modernity can relate to.

Once at Shakey's, I drank a lot of Mountain Dew and had less than a dozen small nibbles of fried chicken before I made my way to the bathroom and threw most of it back up. Some people can't eat anything for a whole week when they begin withdrawals. I can successfully hold down certain things when I'm dopesick—candy, pastries, peanut butter and jelly sandwiches, anything sweet—but food that's complex, meat-based, heavily spiced, loaded with fat, or over a certain temperature won't agree with my stomach for at least five days. Just a whiff of deli meat will send me running to a toilet to puke.

Upon my return to the table, Michael said, "Listen, Jared, we got some food in your stomach, which is good—you definitely needed it—but I don't feel right if I were to just drive you back to Skid Row and drop you where I found you. You seem like a good kid, but the dope's got you by the balls, and this could be the biggest mistake of my life…." Michael took his time after appearing to give some thought to what came out of his mouth next. "I think I'm gonna offer you to come to my home…stay a few nights until you get through the sickness. Would you wanna do that?"

Before answering, I contemplated my options of whether I truly wanted to clean up. This sounds like an easy decision for anyone sane to make, but for people like me, those that are *literally* insane when it comes to drugs, it just isn't. I wanted the nightmare to end, but I didn't know if I was ready to feel feelings again. The kick was one thing, but having to figure my life out after detoxing was what terrified me to my core.

"Well, that's a big offer.... Are you sure? I don't wanna take advantage or make you feel uncomfortable, but yeah…I don't see myself havin' much of a chance gettin' clean if I went back downtown right now."

"There'd be some rules," Michael said abruptly, "and I want you to know I've never done *anything* like this. I just get a feelin' about you…. I dunno how to explain it, but I wanna help you. I see potential. I see… something. Just know that if you try to rip me off or steal any of my shit, God will be watchin'. He's always watchin', over me, over you, over all our decisions. Shit, he's watchin' over the one I just made, and he'll be watchin' over what you do with this opportunity if you take it."

"I understand. I promise, well…I know my promise ain't worth much right now…but I'll take you up on the offer. Thank you, Michael."

On the ride home, I got to scratch beyond the surface of Michael McCutcheon. He could be back on dope and serving a life sentence in prison now for all I know, but in that moment, he was honorable to the point of confusion. Selflessness was not a term I was familiar with back then, and much like trying to explain calculus to a Jack Russell terrier, I had no ability to understand the idea of thinking about anyone besides myself. Michael planted that seed for me.

He was a family man, an active church member, and a lifelong blue-collar worker who had been running his own construction company for decades. Nothing about that seems odd, except when you throw in the fact that he'd been on and off heroin since he was practically a child. His and my dad's stories weren't exceptionally different on paper—barring the church stuff—but it wasn't so much his story as it was his aura that made him enchanting to me. He just had an energy about him that made him come off as an idyllic member of society. Sure, he wasn't well educated, and he didn't have a pristine record with the law, but that would have only worked against his unruffled energy. He was the guy that you'd want to pull over if you were stranded on the freeway with a flat tire.

Sitting just above my adoration for him was a glimpse of fear for his power; would he somehow be able to convert me into a man of religion? The answer would be no, but he'd have a lasting effect on my relative perception. I once despised religious people. I looked down on them as closed-minded bigots who wouldn't piss on you if you were on fire unless you declared Jesus your savior. Michael changed that perception. Whether God was "real" or not, he inspired Michael to possibly save my life, and therefore the question of God's tangible existence would no longer matter to me.

We arrived at his empty townhouse less than an hour after finishing lunch. In that time, I gave Michael the abbreviated version of my life story, as did he. His wife and stepchildren were up north with her parents for the holidays, being that it was only a few days before Christmas, but Michael implied that his three other children from a previous marriage would be joining us at some point. Still in disbelief that I was going to be detoxing at a stranger's house, I was even more perplexed at the idea of spending Christmas with him and his family. Shit, just the fact that Christmas was a few days away was completely novel. Homelessness and staying current with the upcoming holiday schedule don't exactly go hand in hand.

I was shown upstairs to his youngest son's room, where Michael gave me fresh linens to line the bed with, along with a youth-sized sleeping bag.

"You'll be sleeping in the youngster's room. I know the bed's a bit small, but the other kids are teenagers, and you know how teenagers are about no one goin' in their rooms! I gave you two sets of sheets on account of all the cold sweatin' you'll be doin'. And if the sleeping bag doesn't do you justice, there's a few blankets folded up in the closet. Now try to get a few hours of rest because later tonight we have church group."

"Church group?" This caught me off guard. "Michael…I've never been to church. Plus, I'm really sick, you know, maybe I should just stay in for a few—"

"We'll discuss it on the way to church group in a few hours," he interrupted before closing the door.

The next few days aren't the easiest to remember. This is the "top of the curve" segment of heroin withdrawal. What amounts to something best described as a waking nightmare unfolds, complete with minor hallucinations and a healthy fear of drowning in your own sweat. Sprinkle in bouts of running between a child's bed and a stranger's bathroom to vomit out of every orifice if you want a clearer picture. Nothing out of the ordinary for a real winner like me. It wasn't my first time, it sure as hell wouldn't be my last, yet somehow, I seem to forget just how bad it is every time I get a hankering for the poison.

Utter madness. Rinse and repeat.

Once a night, Michael would take me to his church groups for alcoholics and drug addicts, which, although similar to a standard twelve-step meeting, were completely Christ-based. I don't remember much about the meetings, other than that the people were very welcoming and often embraced me as if this would somehow transmit Jesus into my nervous system and rid me of the junk.

Oh, how I wished it worked—I really did. For a lifelong religion despiser up until that point, these people and their prayers not only helped in the moment but were welcomed. I figured that it wouldn't hurt to attempt embracing whatever this was—Christianity, spirituality, non-denominational worship, a bunch of fuckups eating stale cookies in a church basement—I wasn't sure, but being a spiteful atheist hadn't worked in life thus far, and I was at least willing to give anything a try temporarily.

Throughout the stay, Michael gave me chunks of his leftover Subutex pills from when he kicked to ease the withdrawal symptoms. Unbeknownst to Michael, I would only pretend to place these under my tongue (which is the way they're intended to be ingested). Subutex is a prescription narcotic, and despite it being illegal to hand out to a homeless kid you found on Skid Row, it can be quite helpful to someone withdrawing from opiates. Subutex doesn't eradicate all withdrawal symptoms—especially when taking the doses that Michael was giving me—but it does make them a lot more bearable. I chose to hoard the doses Michael gave me, so I could snort them in the bathroom once I had enough stashed away to attain some sort of buzz. Remember: I was still a shitbag, and being shitty doesn't just go away, even when you're trying to get clean and do the right thing. It's a slow and mechanized *daily* process, which I haven't even come close to perfecting at the time of writing this. The degeneracy will always lay dormant and can be awoken at any time if I don't keep myself in tune.

Michael's kids came to the house on Christmas Eve, and following their awkward introduction to the homeless guy hanging out with their father, we all ate honey ham, macaroni and cheese, and green bean casserole. It was all anyone could ever want out of a Christmas meal. Simple, comforting, and paired with hot cocoa.

At that point I was able to clean up nice and stave off the vomiting bouts for long enough to hold a civilized conversation. They didn't need to know the whole truth, or even most of it—just that their dad used to do drugs, he no longer did, and I was simply a fellow church group member who had fallen on hard times. It may have seemed strange, and yes, had I come to Christmas dinner to find my dad accompanied by a street bum, I would have felt uncomfortable too, but I tried my damnedest to present myself as a fellow normal human being. They were good kids, all of them either in college or working and starting their own families, and although they were kind and accepting, I couldn't help but feel alone at the table.

I envied them—even resented them, like I did to all relatively stable people in my age range. I've always had a knack for turning others' success into self-hatred. How morbidly selfish.

For years I suffered from believing that I *deserved* happiness and stability just as much as anyone. What I've come to realize is that stability is not something you *deserve* per se, it's something that you *create*. No one can hand it to you; they can hand you an opportunity, but it's you that must *maintain* the structural integrity of that contingency. That's really all that stability is: maintaining a situation, whether it be a minimum-wage job or running a Fortune 500 company. I couldn't maintain anything—and I mean *anything*—besides a drug addiction, which happened to bring about nothing but instability in my case. The nonexistent loophole in my warped thinking was that, unlike most others, I *deserved* to have both.

I may have been competent enough to possess substantial value in the job market—or I may not have been—but it didn't matter. I had never been able to maintain anything because of my penchant for self-sabotage. When broken down and measured, my self-induced liabilities annulled any value that I appeared to have as an employee, boyfriend, son, student, you name it—I would ultimately disappoint anyone and everyone who put any amount of faith in me. This remained a constant until I focused on the stability of not getting high, above the stability of everything else. Lo and behold, here we are. On that particular Christmas in Michael's home, however, I was still light-years away from such a notion.

A day or two after Christmas, both Michael and I could tell that the meat and potatoes of my withdrawals were coming to an end. I was entering what some call the "post-acute withdrawal" phase, which can last months and is mostly defined by general insomnia, anxiety, fatigue, and intense cravings for heroin. Michael urged me to start contemplating a safe exit plan from his house, because his wife and stepchildren were going to be home by New Year's Eve.

He drove me by the local Salvation Army and introduced me to some of the employees/graduates of their rehabilitation program, who seemed to come from a similar situation as myself. Entering the Salvation Army program seemed logical, considering I was homeless, penniless, and needed some kind of structured environment to reacquaint myself with society. A no-brainer. It was one of those moments when I knew it was the right thing to do, and therefore I was immediately turned off by it. Besides, I was fed up with Los Angeles.

I figured as long as I got far enough away, I'd be able to get my life together. Clouded with naïveté, I zeroed in on my problem: Skid Row. No way I'd go back to anything that even resembled the horror of the past few months as long as I got away from the streets that staged it. To me at the time, this was sound logic.

Little did I know, I would apply this logic many times to every corner of the United States, until I would come full circle and find myself right back on Sixth and San Pedro Street years later. Only then would I consider that maybe my logic, regarding *everything*, was flawed. Many years of my best thinking would get me right back to the place I started, and it would make the first round seem like child's play. Like I've said, addiction typically only moves one direction, and by the time I made it back to Skid Row for a second rendezvous, it would have me on nothing less than a death march.

CHAPTER 5

A MOST TENDER YEAR

After some discussion and crafty manipulation, Michael and I came to the agreement that if I could reach a friend by the end of the day who could help me in Oakland, then he would take me to the Greyhound station. If not, I agreed that I'd give the Salvation Army a shot. Michael knew that the Salvation Army would have been the wiser decision, and deep down I knew it too—but I also knew that I wasn't done trying to do things my way.

Not getting high wasn't an option—and it never would be as far as I was concerned back then—but being smart about the way I got high seemed feasible. If I could get to Oakland, I'd have a fresh start, giving me the opportunity to get high in a responsible way. No more heroin. Well, no more doing heroin *daily*—I didn't wanna get too ahead of myself.

Meth use was going to be tricky, but it would be necessary if I were to get back on my (now partially healed) feet in a timely manner. So, no meth once I was grounded with a steady job and a place to live, I told myself. Once again, "solid logic."

I phoned a few people to no avail, until I tried calling my good friend Alex. I left a message with Michael's callback number, which Alex called a few minutes later. Alex knew me well, having been one of my very first friends after I came to live with my aunt in Piedmont, and we remained buddies when we both attended UC Santa Cruz. As mentioned earlier, in high school we played together in several bands, partied hard on the weekends, and may have put more value in our social lives than our studies, but Alex always managed to stay diligent and make responsible life decisions. He was—and still is—a person who knows how to live vibrantly while retaining a stern sense of foresight. Alex is most certainly *not* an alcoholic or a drug addict, and although he's an upstanding man of high character, these two qualities aren't mutually inclusive. I may not be alive today if it wasn't for him.

Alex and my other friend, Ethan, put some money together to get a me a Greyhound ticket up to Oakland, but assured me that they'd only remain willing to help as long as I remained putting in effort to better myself. Put plainly, they weren't going to buy me a ticket so I could come home and fuck off. Alex told me that depending on my mental state, he could maybe let me stay with him for a few weeks until I found a job, and then we could discuss further options.

To me, it sounded perfect, and it was: perfect for someone capable of making constructive life choices. For an actively using drug addict, however, it would be a train wreck, but only someone with experience like Michael could see between the lines. Loving someone who isn't ready to get clean isn't a bad thing, and trying to "help" them is only natural. It can, however, be extremely counterproductive to all parties involved. The problem is that most people don't know this until it's too late, and the damage an addict can inflict when given free rein is often unforgivable. My buddy Alex, God bless his soul, would come to learn this in the coming months.

This bus ride, unlike my last one, was drug-free—at least on my end—but I can't account for any of the other passengers. Because I wasn't high, not to mention still relatively dopesick, my ride was not as enjoyable as rides prior. In fact, I was consumed with anxiety about the fact that I still didn't have a stable place I could call home. In addition, I was returning to a place in which I already had a history of feeling othered. Now with a crippling drug addiction and a homeless stint under my belt, how would I not feel even more out of place? I was grateful to still have a few friends that cared deeply for me, but this didn't help much in the way of making me not feel like a hometown pariah. I had been the one kid from Piedmont with hardcore drug-addict parents. Now I was returning as the one kid from Piedmont who became one, himself.

I had left most of my belongings behind on Skid Row, excluding what I could fit in a small backpack, but fortunately Michael packed me a small bag with some clean underwear and other essentials. He also gave me twenty dollars and his business card, which I still keep in my wallet to this day. I usually send him a text or an email around Christmas time every year, thanking him for what he did for me. He's never responded, and I'm not even sure if he would remember me. Shit, I'm not even sure that he's still sober. I can only hope that he is, but even the best of us can fall.

As the bus encroached its way up to the Bay Area, I became less and less enthusiastic about my "plan." Reality began to sink in; I had just spent months successfully adapting to homelessness on Skid Row and was now traveling three hundred miles away with no long-term guaranteed shelter. Sure, if things didn't go smoothly up in Oakland, I could probably figure out how to be homeless up there, but what if it was different? Downtown LA was set up for homelessness; it was like an amusement park for drug addicts and undesirables. San Francisco came to mind, given that it was world-renowned for its homeless, so this made me feel slightly more at ease. If Oakland didn't pan out, then maybe the toxic paradise I was destined for was just one bridge away. Regardless, I was leaving behind a place where I had perfected a routine and feared having to figure it out all over again.

I rolled into the Oakland Greyhound station a few minutes earlier than our expected 8:00 AM arrival. Some Greyhound stations in the middle of nowhere are quaint and welcoming. The station in West Oakland is not one of these. It's claustrophobic, unkempt, overtly dangerous, and you only have to go so far as the bathroom to be offered narcotics. One thing that remains a constant across this great country is that if you need drugs and you don't know where to get them, go to the closest bus station. It's almost guaranteed that you'll find something to purchase that will get you high. You may get robbed in the process, and the dope most likely won't be of the highest quality, but it's the best place to start if you don't know where else to go. Methadone clinics usually work as well, but they're typically only open very early in the morning.

Ethan, who remains one of my closest friends to this day, picked me up and took me for a cup of coffee. Happy to see me, he was more than willing to help me out, but after catching up over breakfast, he addressed the fact that he had no suggestions on how to go about this. There were no valid suggestions because the situation made little sense to someone with no experience with addiction. He figured that since I'd been clean for a week or two, my best bet was to try and stay with Alex. Get a job, save some money, get my own place, and put this all behind me. Those with some experience would know that this plan wasn't likely to work, and that the best decision would have been to go to long-term treatment. But I had no health insurance, and there weren't many resources for free rehabs that I knew of. I'm sure there were shelters and waiting lists for permanent housing, which I'd eventually sign up for, but that's not what I really needed. What I needed was a long-term program like the Salvation Army Michael had tried to get me into. I'd come to learn over the next year that he had been absolutely right.

My aunt wasn't speaking to me; I had no other family; I was disheveled, unemployable, and broke. All of this in addition to the fact that I essentially needed to be babysat in order to not use drugs was a major handicap. Arriving relatively sober-minded, I knew how to present well, but Ethan and I both knew that this could change at the flip of a switch. One minute I'm talking about changing my life, and the next I have a pipe in my mouth. We've all seen the movies, read the books, or have that one uncle that ruins Thanksgiving every year. I was no different. I was a liability.

We drove to the cemetery, where I chugged the remainder of a bottle of Smirnoff that I had found in Ethan's trunk (not a good start) in order to calm the nerves before I "picked myself up by my bootstraps." However, it was New Year's Eve weekend, and I hadn't seen some of my high school friends in years, so I wasn't going to tie up my boots just yet.

I floated around for weeks, crashing on couches in a rotation that was far from stable. Drinking heavily to ward off the fleeting withdrawals, booze veiled me from the reality of disequilibrium. Ritalin entered the picture at some point—which, when snorted, was like meth on training wheels—but I was able to refrain from seeking out the real stuff. This, in combination with the booze, satiated my thirst for heavier thrills. It didn't help in the way of getting my footing or finding a job, but it might have kept me from jumping off the Golden Gate Bridge during that first month of being home.

Alex got in contact with me sometime in January, telling me that he had spoken with his father about my predicament. They shared a small home on Grand Avenue with a spare bedroom that wasn't being used. Not without qualms, they offered to temporarily move me in, as long as I stayed off drugs and went out to look for work every day. If things went smoothly, I could live there for a couple of months and eventually start paying rent, at which point I could start saving to eventually get my own apartment.

Yet another perfect opportunity lay at my feet to get on track.

With the utmost grace, these men took a chance on me like no one ever had besides my family. Unfortunately, like I had with my family prior, I would make a waste of their sacrifice and end up doing everything just the same—selfish death-wish behavior with no regard for those who were trying to help me.

I did make some half-hearted attempts at improving myself while living with Alex, but ultimately my blind adherence to my own self-destruction always took hold. I got several jobs within the first few months but couldn't keep one for more than a few days. Some would consider these small attempts at getting myself back on my feet, but these actions occurred from time to time just to keep up appearances. No one's going to let you latch on to their wagon unless you make occasional displays of supposed self-advancement. Any successful drug addict knows this (or at least carries it out subconsciously).

A seemingly endless free fall at terminal velocity towards a juncture between an early death and chronic homelessness just about summed me up. Loved ones tried to reach out and catch me every so often, but no matter how hard they tried, all they did was briefly slow the fall. This isn't to say that their actions didn't potentially save my life, but the unfortunate fact is that no one has the power to *thoroughly* help a drug addict who isn't ready to meet them halfway. And a drug addict who's afforded every leniency in the world will *never* make that trip.

From the get-go with Alex and my team of childhood friends, everything was expected to go off without a single issue—as long as I refrained from getting high. Due to the horrors of what I'd told them about my Skid Row experience, my friends believed that I'd surely never turn to hard drugs again. Anyone who had gone through such hell would be disgusted by the thought of jumping back into drug use, right? Maybe a select few, but more than anything, my time in Los Angeles provided an exceptional exercise in keeping junkiedom afloat.

I had had enough of heroin addiction—this much was true. I had just gone through quite the detox down south at Michael's house and was still feeling slight symptoms weeks later. I was prepared to not get strung out on heroin ever again, even if it meant going full force with the uppers. Being dead tired from all the uncertainty and lingering dopesickness, I figured it would be nearly impossible to go out and find employment without a little bit of a pick-me-up.

Alex gave me twenty dollars to aid in my job search—for practical things like bus fare and maybe a nice shirt from Goodwill—but I thought the twenty dollars would be best spent on meth; my logic was that energy and pep were more important in a job interview than a clean shirt. The problem was, I had never bought crystal in the Bay Area and didn't know where to start. I knew that the Tenderloin neighborhood of San Francisco was flooded with all kinds of depravity, but I questioned whether they would have quality speed.

I was going to head into the city by myself, but I figured I'd give my good friend Kevin a call and see if he wanted to make the trip with me. Kevin, my former college roommate and junkie buddy, had gotten onto a Suboxone program since leaving Santa Cruz and done exceptionally well for himself. After staying away from heroin for a few years and transferring to NYU, he was back from school on winter break, staying with his parents. I knew he didn't mess with opiates anymore, but since he still had a hankering for stimulants, I thought he would make a good companion on my journey.

Kevin picked me up in his parents' beige Corolla sometime in the early evening, and we made our way over the Bay Bridge into the city. I'd probably only been to San Francisco a handful of times in my life, despite living thirty minutes away from it for nearly ten years. I didn't know how to navigate the place at all, but I knew that Kevin had copped morphine there in the past. He knew exactly where to get all kinds of pills and crack—but we were both skeptical about our chances of finding crystal.

We drove west on Market until we hit Van Ness, then pulled over. We were in what seemed to be "normie" territory. There was a Starbucks, a bookstore, and an upper-middle-class couple walking with a stroller; it just didn't feel "methy" enough. Nowadays that same neighborhood is rife with all kinds of meth-induced antics, but remember, this was 2012.

"Kevin, where the fuck are we? We're not looking for a Bed Bath & Beyond. We're looking for crystal meth."

"Dude, trust me—it's SF," said Kevin. "It's fuckin' weird. One street looks normal then all of a sudden you hit The Tenderloin and it's mayhem." We drove north on Van Ness, took a quick right, then another right on Leavenworth, which Kevin insisted was a practical starting point for us to get out and start walking.

The atmosphere was getting odder by the step, suddenly feeling reminiscent of Skid Row. Certain smells, primal screeches from the mentally ill, and the all-too-familiar sidewalk blood drippings that seemed to be a staple of Downtown Los Angeles were making me feel at home.

Kevin was right: we were on the right path. I could feel it—I could sense the dope—and then before I knew it, someone offered to sell us Oxycontin. This was a good sign.

I had entered the open-air drug market of downtown San Francisco for my first time, and unbeknownst to me, it would become my daily stomping ground. This was my introduction to the Tenderloin—which although smaller and less violent than LA's Skid Row, was somehow more frightening. Its eccentricity induced a flavor of paranoia in the vein of getting kidnapped and sold into sex slavery rather than just plain old murder. Compared to the harsher parts of LA, the Tenderloin was more like a steampunk version of a typical drug-slum. There were tweakers riding around on triple-decker bicycles, top hat–wearing fiends openly puffing on crack pipes, and various androgynous characters dressed up like they were walking off the set of a post-apocalyptic film. Fading bright colors littered the signs of closed storefronts at the base of daunting turn-of-the-century architecture, as billows of crack smoke wafted every which way in the style of a third-world street market. It was bizarre, nightmarish, and crawling with negative ambiance. It was the creepiest place I'd ever seen. On one hand, Skid Row was strictly just addiction, violence, and poverty, whereas the Tenderloin was all of that in the middle of a bad acid trip that had gone on for half a century too long.

The avant-garde, "do as thou wilt" doctrine of the city is what's made it a national treasure, but from a brief stroll through the Tenderloin (or a number of the city's neighborhoods nowadays), it's clear that this conduct may have finally gone too far. It's bled into the politics, which has resulted in a current fentanyl crisis unrivaled to any other American city. I admire San Francisco for considering novel approaches to these issues, but unfortunately, they've chosen the wrong ones. The result has been catastrophic in terms of overdose deaths, crime, and general reduction in the standard of living for many of its residents. I would end up wreaking havoc in the city for many months, not once getting arrested or even pointed in the direction of treatment. And this was *years* before the current epidemic, where leniency has increased tenfold and the open-air fentanyl markets are *completely* condoned. For being one of the most "leftist" cities in the country, it certainly felt like an anarcho-libertarian's wet dream (minus the right to self-defense). It was lawless, decrepit, and fully enabling of every one of my favorite worst behaviors. And although I'd just arrived and didn't know it yet, my addiction would come to flourish in its disorder.

The urchins were now coming out of the woodwork, and we were being offered all kinds of pills—just pills—and no sign of crystal. Kevin told me that pills were the foundation of the Tenderloin drug market, and that the majority of the heroin being sold was little more than dime bags of instant coffee and shoe polish. If you wanted an opiate, you'd be much more satisfied trying to score morphine or oxys than anything that wasn't FDA approved. This all changed by 2019 with fentanyl, but back in the old days, it was still a prescription-pill-based economy. Crack was also widely available, and so was meth, as I would shortly find out.

As we passed the Fairfax Hotel on Eddy Street, a handsome yet brutish man with a 49ers wave cap around his head gave out a whistle. Our heads swiveled as the man stated that whatever we were looking for, he had it.

Before I could tell him what we wanted, he said, "Y'all lookin' for some crystal, ain't you?"

"Well, Goddamn, we've been offered everything *but*." I grinned back.

"Well, y'all betta not be no police.... I ain't never seen you around," he replied.

"No, not police, we're just from Oakland, but we need a new connect."

"Aight, well, my name's T-Bone, and I got the best chris out here. Always do, and I got that good *heron* too, if you fuck with that. How much y'all want?"

"Uh, just give us a twenty. You got a pipe for sale?" I asked.

"Naw, y'all gotta handle that part on your own. I'm just the dope man." T-Bone joked. He looked like a former linebacker, mid-forties, and most importantly to me, not a drug addict. It's always good to find a drug dealer that isn't an addict themself. This guy seemed genuine for some reason, and I took his number just in case I decided to keep this relapse going. Who's kidding who? This train was now off and running—and I would definitely need a guy like T-Bone in my corner if his dope turned out to be as good as he said it was.

After exchanging the cash for the crystal, we scampered back to Kevin's car like the rats we were. Having no pipe, we were still in luck given that I always kept a piece of foil folded up in my wallet for times of emergency. That's a good test to see how much of a piece of shit someone is: search their wallet, and if you locate a secret stash of aluminum foil—chances are you're not in the presence of a winner.

I showed Kevin the ropes of free-basing meth off foil, which he unsurprisingly got the hang of almost immediately. The dope was good. It was *really* good, which meant that T-Bone's number would be utilized in the near future.

We lurked around the downtown area with galloping jawbones, enjoying a few hours of intense euphoria. Having a life to get back to, however, Kevin didn't do any more crystal because he wanted to be in bed before midnight. He was in for a rude awakening; there's no such thing as a quick meth high. Given my fiendish nature, not doing any more crystal wasn't an option, but that didn't even matter. Just the amount I initially did with Kevin had me in a predicament that I've encountered all too often: I was very high with nowhere to go and nothing to do. This is a problem strictly associated with crystal meth, because a meth high can't be slept off like other drugs. A few hits of meth is a multi-day commitment to rabid activity—yet most people on meth are the furthest thing from productive. For some reason there's always a disconnect between the massive amount of energy and applying it towards anything that *isn't* self-destructive. They say the slowest thing in the world is a tweaker in a hurry.

Usually once I get a single dose in me, I come up with a quick scheme to make some cash, and before I know it, a few months have passed, and I have a raving staph infection somewhere on my torso. These marathons of sleep deprivation are what got me into most of my trouble for the foreseeable future: job loss, mental deterioration, physical fatigue, visits to psych wards, you name it. If I could have just tweaked for a few hours, fallen asleep, and woken up the next day like nothing had ever happened, life might have played out a bit differently. Thank God it didn't.

Alex routinely kept tabs on my well-being over the following months, and I somehow managed to hide the extent of my drug abuse. This was mostly due to his inexperience with drug addicts as opposed to any cleverness on my part. Maybe deep down he knew the entire time, but his brotherly love guarded him from seeing the horrid truth. He certainly knew I wasn't keeping my nose clean, but he didn't know that it was a constant.

Either way, my shameful behavior had peaked. I would leave during the day to go look for employment—according to my lies—but I would always end up getting my hands on some easy cash and taking the train to San Francisco.

I would sneak in and out of the house on midnight adventures, which if I wasn't knocked out in a speed coma, I participated in every night. Running around all night and returning home with a garbage bag full of dumpster treasure doesn't exactly scream sobriety, so I stashed most of my goods behind a shed in the backyard. My nighttime activity had to remain top secret if I was going to convince anyone I wasn't a full-fledged tweaker.

I got a few jobs here and there, but I couldn't hold them. I couldn't even show up to my first day of work half the time, because I didn't plan on holding the job in the first place. As long as I could come home with a business card and show Alex that I was going to interviews, I figured it would extend this period of freeloading. When immersed in drugs, my little pea-brain could only handle instantaneous survival: "How can I maintain my safety net for just one more night?" was the extent of brain power I was willing to dedicate to anything besides supporting my habit.

Alex went out on a limb, sacrificed time and money, and even was letting me live in his house free of charge in order to help me get on my feet. But I was convinced sobriety wasn't possible for me, so no amount of help could lift me up for good. I had lost all contact with any family—who had seemingly achieved erasing me from their lives—and the only conclusion I could draw from that fact was that I didn't deserve another chance.

I was ready to live out the short remainder of my life as a doped-up lingerer.

This was when my love affair with trash began to blossom. Although sounding like a joke, this was the furthest thing from a laughing matter during this period of my decline. I was obsessed. Most people don't get excited about half-working electronics soaked in garbage water, but to this day it gets my blood pumping.

The way I saw it was that every garbage can and dumpster might as well have had a rainbow swelling out from its grizzled lid. Every night a different neighborhood was lined with pots of gold, just waiting for a maniacal trash goblin like myself to plunder my way towards another twenty-dollar bag of poison. The drugs gave me the energy for the nightly hunt, the findings gave me the funds to buy the drugs, and the cycle went on and on.

I bled for trash. I contracted infections and climbed over fences and squeezed my way through gaps that didn't even make physical sense, all for the sweet, ever-providing trash. It's free, it's everywhere, and if you're on enough meth, you can turn a broken vacuum cleaner into seven dollars. The trash gave me purpose, provided sustenance, and made me feel like I was worthy, not unlike the way I felt after I robbed that kid on Skid Row. Give me a wrench, a broken printer covered in raccoon urine, and most importantly a few hits of speed, and I'll show you a twenty-dollar bill by lunch time. Not anyone can do that, but I could, and I probably still can. God forbid I ever go back to that life, but hypothetically, I'd be glad I knew how to turn a dumpster into an ATM machine with a little bit of elbow grease. I'm not proud of this particular skill, but I have to say, it doesn't lack a certain type of glory. Many people develop far more sinister passions in the world of meth.

I started mapping out territory around Oakland, San Francisco, and any other town that was close enough with a trash can worth diving into.

Free piles of clothes, donation bins, and dumpsters behind outlet stores were a mainstay, given that I could always sell something to the trendy used-clothing shops in Berkeley, but often I'd find certain items that just needed basic fixing and cleaning up, which I would place for sale on Craigslist and play the long game. Pretty soon I had enough items listed that I was making multiple sales a day and maintaining a steady cash flow. More often than not, the majority of my findings were worthless, but that didn't stop me from lugging them all over town in a frenzy.

When I would eventually pass out and wake up in a sober mind frame, my mountain of dumpster gold appeared in its true form for what it was: mostly worthless garbage. Something like a set of broken windshield wipers seems nice in the moment when you're hopped up on tweak, but when the head clears and reality sets in, you realize that you may've been too liberal in your pickings.

As I got to know T-Bone better, I came to find that he was very willing to trade me drugs for certain items that he fancied. His girlfriend, Shawntal, took a strong liking to me upon realizing my expertise at pilfering. I started getting invited up to their hotel room when I'd drop by to make a purchase, as opposed to having to wait on the corner for T-Bone to make his way to the street.

Despite their nourished appearances, I learned that Shawntal and T-Bone were avid meth users as well. T-Bone was not only impressively muscular, but his fingernails were always shimmering and perfectly trimmed. He must have been six foot three and 240 pounds, which is far from the typical build of someone on meth, but upon spending more time with him, I came to learn that he was a constant user. He even liked to snort heroin every few days to combat the comedown, so I followed in his footsteps and developed a similar regimen. I would get high out of my gourd on speed for three days, using alcohol and marijuana sparingly to calm the nerves when I was around Alex, then buy a half gram of mid-grade heroin from T-Bone, smoke it, and drift into a forty-hour coma to recharge. This actually worked quite well, and even more surprisingly, I was able to maintain the rhythm. Heroin remained my drug of choice (although I only used it twice a week), but meth was keeping the clock synchronized.

When Alex questioned my erratic schedule—not to mention my failure at retaining employment—I would pull out the two magic words that temporarily work for any drug addict: manic depression. The saving grace and golden scapegoat for all our problems. Alex—like most well-adjusted individuals—didn't suffer from mental illness, and therefore didn't completely understand it. I had a better grasp on mental illness, but more importantly, I understood that it could be used as a weapon.

Manic depression (also known as bipolar disorder) is not something that I have in the slightest. However, when I'm using copious amounts of drugs, my behavior resembles that of someone who does. When Alex questioned whether I might be bipolar, I ran with it in hopes that it would help veil the truth. Not only this, but it also instilled a fear in Alex that he mustn't kick me out, despite my inability to maintain a job. I was "mentally ill" after all, and Alex wasn't someone that would throw a sick person on the streets.

This was the level of cutthroat manipulation beset upon the innocent bystanders within my reach. Zero consideration for the sanctity of human compassion. Alex was far from a fool, but no amount of intelligence can get past the astigmatism of love. That's where he fucked up: he had love for me, and I was truly in no position to deserve such a thing yet.

Maybe I'm being rough on myself. Does every person deserve love, no matter how little they regard the welfare of others? The thought of my impact on Alex's well-being *literally* never crossed my mind. In fact, I resented him for his lack of cooperation with my instability. A mere request that I clean my dishes—the dishes that I filled with the food that Alex would buy for me—was met with contempt from my end. Self-pity is not always a victimless crime. The disdain I had for myself was so heavy that it worked its way into every human interaction I had, often leaving Alex a casualty of my own self-obsession. "I hate myself" turns into "don't they know how much pain I'm in" turns into "well, they can go fuck themselves" turns into "how dare they!?"

Alex knew I had no one else to turn to, and that I was disillusioned over Aunt Ina disowning me. Every conversation we had turned into me blaming her for everything that I had become, thus making the burden I was creating for him and his father *her* responsibility. *She* had been my legal guardian, and therefore it was *her* job to clean up the mess (in my juvenile, distorted opinion).

This was the level of insanity that I crushed him with for the better part of a year, and I genuinely believed it as well. Not to sound campy, but the old saying, "Resentment is drinking poison and expecting the other person to die," could not ring truer when examining my downfall from beginning to end. The world owed me nothing.

On my nightly excursions, I started breaking into garages and climbing over fences to get better loot, which I would be able to sell much more readily by advertising on Craigslist. A stolen bike that I might be able to get ten dollars for in the Tenderloin I could now post online with ease and get a hundred dollars. There was also a bartering section on Craigslist, which I took advantage of to start with a small item and trade my way towards a more valuable one. I could start out with a stolen cordless drill, trade it for a decent bike, trade that bike for a bricked iPhone, fix the iPhone, and sell it for $250. It didn't always work out like that, but it worked out enough for me to continue the charade and show Alex that I was making an income.

Through dedicating many hours a day to perusing Craigslist, I started coming across cryptic postings in the "Wanted" section for painkillers. To my astonishment, there was a flourishing local market (back then) on message boards and classified listings. I couldn't believe there were people soliciting drugs online, but upon searching for "oxy" in the "for sale" section, I was blown away at the volume of digital dealers. These posts would attempt to be coded in some way, but for the most part, they were little less than online billboards for black-market prescription opioids.

The heroin that T-Bone sold had become very hit or miss, so I decided to take a chance and hook up with one of these Craigslist pill dealers. We arranged a meet up down the street on Pleasant Valley and Piedmont Avenue—eighty dollars for five Roxys—and when I walked over to the spot at the agreed meeting time, I saw a middle-aged woman sitting in a newer-model sedan.

Gesturing towards the passenger door to enter the vehicle, I was met by a small aggressive dog that began barking uncontrollably. After lowering the window a few inches, the woman insisted that I wasn't allowed to enter the car on account of the dog. Although I didn't trust her, I had no other choice—I wanted the pills bad—so I followed her instructions and slipped the money through the window.

She grabbed the cash and then her dog before instructing me to walk around to the driver's side. Now with her window cracked, she threw a bag with five green pills at my chest and drove off. Everything seemed legit. I inspected the pills, which were not marked with a familiar numerical inscription but looked enough like generic Roxys to me, so I cast away my doubts. Once home I figured it wouldn't hurt to double-check, so I googled the inscription and nearly ripped my hair out in rage: they were over-the-counter heartburn pills.

After thirty seconds of mental convulsions, a wave of relief came over me: at least I wasn't dopesick. Could you imagine? Spending your last eighty bucks on some fake pills at the height of opiate withdrawals? That's practically a recipe for homicide.

Now don't get me wrong—I wanted to torture this bitch, but her phone was turned off, and I knew the faster I could accept that I had been ripped off, the quicker I could consolidate my energy towards hustling up more cash.

More than anything I was intrigued by the event, and quite impressed at the ease in which this hellion had made eighty dollars out of thin air. Was it lower than low? Yes, because it was cowardly. An armed robber at least has the fortitude of keeping their victim in the loop.

Notwithstanding, I was the dunce that didn't verify the pills before handing over my money. Was I the victim? Yes, but I learned a valuable lesson. I was also doing something illegal, and in the drug game, there really are no rules. A dollar is a dollar at the end of the day, and it must be procured to satisfy the beast. No one's off limits when it comes to opiates, including a fellow user.

Regardless of my post-initial cooperation with getting played, the pain of losing eighty bucks was not easily quelled. I knew I wouldn't be able to locate her anytime soon—so payback was out of the question—but somehow I'd have to rectify this situation. Getting robbed had come and gone; it was now about the issue at hand: I was broke again. How on earth could I amend the financial loss as fast as it had been taken from me?

Well, I figured I could learn from this experience and replicate the hustle. Fuck over others as they've fucked over you: the ancient junkie proverb that every good drug addict lives by.

I started selling fake pills on Craigslist, and—in my honest opinion—it was the most loathsome thing I'd ever done. When you look a dopesick junkie in their watering eyes, take their last hundred bucks, and hand them a bag of worthless generic sleeping pills you stole from a CVS, you've engaged in one of the most heinous acts that a junkie can pull on one of their own. Most of us (junkies) have been there too, and if you haven't yet, don't be surprised if you find yourself in such a predicament. For some of us, it happens early, perhaps back in middle school when we sold a sixth grader a bag of oregano, and for some of us it carries on well into adulthood. I've taken $500 from a soccer mom strung out on Percocet and handed her a bag of off-brand Acetaminophen. The threatening texts that followed regarding my imminent murder were one thing, but knowing that I ripped someone off that was going through the same pain that I was will be something I'll never come to terms with. Whether it's your children, your grandmother, your job, your future, or the sanctity of your sex organs, if it stands between you and the dope, the dope will always win. It has all the time in the world and nothing to lose, especially another worthless junkie. There'll always be a young up-and-comer waiting around the corner to fill your bloodstained shoes.

I did my research and was able to find certain over-the-counter pills that resembled various opioids. It was easier than I thought. You'd be surprised at how much a generic Tylenol looks like a generic ten-milligram Norco. However, the key component to my success in selling fake pills was my customer base. Real addicts aren't scared to step into the hood and find their drug of choice, so if you're looking for pain pills on Craigslist, chances are you're not exceptionally streetwise. You know the type: an accountant who got hooked on oxycodone after a back surgery, or a college kid that just started to develop a taste for ruining his life. We all know someone like this, whether we're aware of it or not. Most of the people I found online that were willing to buy pills from a complete stranger were deathly naïve: suburban housewives, white-collar dads in New Balance running shoes, rich teenagers, and anyone else that was too scared to step foot in a poor neighborhood. This made selling fake pills easy for multiple reasons: one, I wasn't usually intimidated by these types of customers; two, the fact that they often appeared well-to-do eased my sense of guilt; and three, I was always able to contort myself into the "real victim."

A few times T-Bone fronted me a handful of real oxy, which was used to sell to new customers, only to secure their trust and rip them off on a larger deal in the future. T-Bone was happy to do this for me because it only meant that more cash would eventually make it into his pocket. What became clear was that this new hustle was not only disgusting, but also eerily personable. In comparison to breaking into a car or stealing a bicycle, I actually had to see my victims face to face. Conversate, smile, pitch a loaded backstory, hope they didn't have their wits about them, and pray they didn't bring a gun. There aren't many gigs out there that are more sadistic. It was twisted, gut-wrenchingly shameful, exciting, harrowing, and disturbingly easy for someone with an inborn death wish.

Unpleasant news came one day when I found out that T-Bone had been arrested. After trying to reach him all afternoon, I was out of the loop until I ran into Shawntal on Market Street. Flustered, she told me he had been involved in a fight, and when the police arrived and searched him, they found bagged out meth and heroin. This was back when they'd still occasionally arrest people in San Francisco for drug dealing, unlike now where selling fentanyl is all but state-sanctioned.

Although we were quite different in many ways and had absolutely nothing in common besides our shared appreciation for drugs, T-Bone and I had become very personable. Unlike Shawntal, T-Bone was present when you spoke to him, almost as if the drugs hadn't completely ripped out his innards from the shell. This was not the case with Shawntal, who was moderately friendly on the surface, but it was obvious that the drugs were always in control of her thoughts and actions. I probably fell somewhere in the middle of this spectrum, but I couldn't tell you with confidence that I was ever truly present. I lacked the sadism that lay behind the eyes of most of my cohorts, and so did T-Bone. We could talk about politics or old-school Bay Area hip-hop while we passed the pipe to one another, whereas

Shawntal was usually only concerned with what she could get out of you. I wasn't excited to have to deal strictly with her without T-Bone around.

Despite continuing to make good money selling fake pills, dumpster diving never left my daily agenda. It no longer served as my main source of income, but an artist can't just stop making art. No matter how much money I made during the day, I couldn't keep my dirty little hands out of trash receptacles come night. It was my bona fide "tweak"—the only thing I enjoyed doing to pass the long stretches of being incredibly high on meth. It was as much fun as it was unsafe. Drugs deteriorate the immune system, and a healthy immune system comes in handy when your favorite pastime is burrowing into garbage cans. I eventually learned this lesson the hard way by way of half a dozen MRSA infections that all landed me in the hospital.

They were clearly all drug-induced injuries, at which point a social worker should have stepped in and directed me towards treatment, but I was always sent "home" with just a prescription for antibiotics and pain-killers. I know it wasn't really any of their business to recommend I clean up from my drug problem, but the fact that I had no insurance and was getting tens of thousands of dollars in medical care should highlight the needed change in our approach. Yes, long-term public treatment is expensive, but by the end of my run I'd rack up close to half a million dollars in surgeries and medical bills on the taxpayer's dime. Combine that with my time incarcerated and general damage to society, and my rampage certainly passed the seven-figure mark. Perhaps if I had been incentivized to go to a public treatment program, much of this cost could have been avoided, but more importantly, I may have gotten clean far earlier and gotten a head start on this new life.

These MRSA infections were mild in comparison to some of the health issues I'd suffer later in my using, but they were a good introduction to the concept that drugs do have a very real negative impact on the body. It's common for an addict in the middle of an act of self-destruction to think, "Well, if I could just figure out how to have enough money to never run out of drugs, I'd be totally fine." As the severity of my health consequences began to increase, however, it became easier to accept that it wasn't that simple.

Nevertheless, it was the close calls with death that began to take a major toll on my humanity. As I sunk deeper into the drug world and started to bump shoulders with true evil, the psychological pain was turning me into something I was afraid I could never come back from. My level of criminality would increase, my capacity for empathy would wane, and the drive to stay intoxicated would take on a demonic tone. The remaining time I spent in the Tenderloin would be grim, and although not nearly as grim as the bottom I would eventually hit during my second run on Skid Row, one of the most terrifying things that's ever happened to me was about to occur. The following event perfectly encapsulates addiction's potentiality for evil. And although not guaranteed, those that become engrained in the dark underworld of hardcore drugs—especially methamphetamine—will usually stumble upon a situation close in caliber.

CHAPTER 6

THE SUITCASE STORY

I remember the day Whitney Houston died quite vividly because I was the one to break the news to Shawntal personally. She cried for what seemed like an entire hour as we sat together in her hotel room and passed the pipe back and forth. A few days later, with the singer's death still fresh on my mind, I called Shawntal with the expectation of my still-grieving drug dealer to pick up her own phone.

To my surprise, it was a man who answered. He told me that Shawntal was out of town for a few days, and that he was "taking over business" for her while she was gone.

It seemed odd, but I couldn't really care less at the time; I just wanted to purchase drugs and really didn't care who or where they came from. The unknown man told me to meet him at Seventh and Howard, which wasn't anywhere near where Shawntal normally operated but was easy enough to get to from the Civic Center on my stolen bicycle.

I called him when I got to the meeting spot, and within a few minutes, I saw a large heavyset Black man approach me from the east side of Howard. I recognized him as Shawntal's uncle, who I had met one time prior when we both helped her move to a new hotel after T-Bone had been arrested.

The man came up to me and said, "Ay, you remember me? Shawntal gonna be gone for a while, but you can just call me from now on." He handed me a piece of folded-up paper that presumably had his number on it.

"OK, sounds good, is she alright, though? Everything OK?" I asked as I slipped the piece of paper in my pocket.

"Yeah, she all good, just had to handle somethin' outta town, you know? Just call me when you need somethin' until she come back," he said dismissively.

"Aight, well if you talk to her say whatsup for me. You got the shit?" I asked, which was shortly followed by a hand-to-hand exchange.

"Listen, man, I put a li'l extra in there for you." He shot me a fiendish smirk and then continued, "I know you used to that shit Shawntal be slangin', but trust me—my shit better. You'll see what I'm talkin' about. Hit me up anytime."

Everything seemed legit, and yes, his heroin was a bit stronger than what I was getting from Shawntal, so I had no qualms for the time being. Shawntal had been struggling in her attempt to handle T-Bone's business while he was in jail, so it wasn't surprising to hear that she may have taken a break and left town for a bit.

I continued to buy dope from her uncle for about a week straight, before I got an unexpected call from Shawntal on her original cell line. She told me to meet her at a hotel on Van Ness and Bush Street, and that she needed to discuss something with me in person. I needed to buy some heroin anyway, and her uncle wasn't picking up the phone at the moment, so I made the trip out to SF and hiked my way up Van Ness.

It was your typical Tenderloin hotel: desk person behind bulletproof glass, drug addicts and hookers meandering up and down the hallways, shared bathrooms in remarkably disgusting condition, and an overall morbid vibe that you could taste in your nostrils.

I went upstairs to room nineteen where Shawntal said she'd be waiting and knocked on the door. She welcomed me into the surprisingly kempt room, which was currently being occupied by her and her younger sister. I had seen Shawntal's sister a few times, but having never been formally introduced, our communication rarely went beyond a head nod. Nevertheless, I knew her name was Shanice, and I could almost guarantee that she didn't know mine.

Aside from her trademark sinister glare, Shanice intimidated me for a number of reasons. First off, she was very attractive. Not in a standard sense—due to the years of street prostitution, transient living, and drug abuse—but underneath the layers of untreated trauma, anyone could see that this was a very beautiful woman. She had short, straightened hair that was partially dyed purple, and her body was quite voluptuous despite her skinny frame, which was impressive given her extensive history of using meth. Sure, she was tattered from drugs, but you could tell that if she cleaned herself up, she would be stunning.

On the contrary, Shawntal was not exceptionally beautiful. She wasn't ugly, but her many years of meth use was more pronounced on the skin of her weathered face. Some might have called her a "handsome gal"; she definitely had some overtly masculine features. Regardless, she was still attractive in her own way, albeit with her more stalwart qualities. Although curvy, Shawntal was equally muscular without an ounce of extra fat.

She may have been a few inches shorter than her sister, but she was still about the same height as me. My fighting weight is about a 165 pounds— meaning my meth weight was no higher than 130—but in either circumstance, Shawntal would put higher numbers on a scale. This isn't saying much, but for a lady who shot up crystal meth daily, you'd expect her to be just skin and bones. Far from it, Shawntal was ripped; she had a strapping frame to begin with, accompanied by an almost nonsensical amount of muscle for a female drug addict. Throw in an assortment of psychopathic tendencies, and you wound up with someone you wouldn't want to fuck with while you were strung out. Fortunately, I was passive even in my own lunacy, on top of the fact that we had grown to get along relatively well.

Keep in mind that I had been awake at this point for about seventy-two hours on a meth bender, and I was trying to buy some heroin from Shawntal so I could bring about a smooth comedown. Despite being in a state of complete physical and mental fatigue, when Shawntal's sister offered me a hit of the meth pipe, I didn't hesitate for a moment. I took a large hit, blew out a sweet chemical plume, and passed the pipe over to Shawntal.

She shook her head suggesting that she didn't want to take a hit.

"So, Girard,"—Shawntal never could remember my actual name— "why you haven't called? Don't look like you stopped gettin' high."

"I called your number like a week ago, your uncle picked up, said that you went out of town or some shit…. Why? What's goin' on?" I already knew something was up when Shawntal said she needed to talk, but I figured the issue would be between her and her uncle.

"Well, shit, Girard…you didn't know that someone stole my phone? You didn't know nothin' 'bout that? Somehow my uncle wound up with it, and that nigga been stealin' all my clients." Shawntal spoke with a faint hint of sarcasm. When she paused, I stayed silent and was worried that I knew where this was heading. "So I got a new phone from the Metro store, but you ain't call me since I did that. Then I heard from my cousin that you been buyin' dope from my uncle."

"Well, shit, I didn't know about any of that. Your uncle told me you left town, gave me his number…said he was takin' over until you got back," I said.

"Yeah, well fuck that nigga," Shanice chimed in.

I was confused at where any guilt on my part could be found and saw the whole issue solely between Shawntal and her uncle. Despite this, Shawntal seemed marginally suspicious that I may have played a role in it. Due to my contact with her uncle soon after the phone incident—and more importantly, my lack of contact with *her*—she had gotten to thinking I was in on the uncle's scheme. These suspicions weren't entirely ludicrous but seemed to be dismissed after our short conversation.

She looked me up and down for a few moments, then put her arms on my shoulders as she said, "Alright, Girard, you good, homie. But I had to feel it out, you feel me?" and then sat back down on the bed.

I knew I was innocent, and now Shawntal appeared to think so as well, but I remained hesitant to believe that she was fully convinced. I was sitting on a chair opposite the bed where the two girls sat, now hunched over to unzip my backpack and retrieve a pair of shoes I'd found. They were women's Air Jordans, and I figured Shawntal might want to trade me some dope for them, but as I reached into the open bag and pointed my head down, I got hit with a sucker punch directly to my left ear.

It dazed me good, and after tipping over in the fetal position, the ringing in my ear pierced through to the other side of my skull. After getting beat on for another thirty seconds or so, the kicks and punches subsided as it became clear I wasn't going to fight back. I was strung out, underweight, and too malnourished to stand a chance against two toddlers, let alone two full-figured women.

Aside from a few kicks, Shanice refrained from striking me. However, at some point during the commotion, I caught a glimpse of the large knife she was wielding, which was the main reason I didn't even attempt to retaliate. Shawntal backed away from me, allowed me to get a few of my bearings straight, and ordered me to strip naked.

I was baffled at this request, yet slightly intrigued about this new direction. "Are they going to kill me, or fuck me?" I thought to myself, not ruling anything out of the realm of possibility. Stranger things have happened on meth. This wasn't the typical kind of foreplay that I was accustomed to, but it was working in some capacity. I'll be honest—there was something sort of erotic about getting the shit kicked out of me by two sexy, demonically high, well-built ladies. Meth is good at crossing wires in the brain and inspiring anything to become sexual. However, when Shanice then punched me in the mouth and told me to lay my cracker ass on the floor, I ruled out the possibility of this taking a romantic direction.

From under the bed, Shawntal pulled two large suitcases into the center of the floor, while a knife-wielding Shanice kept me confined to the corner.

"Listen, bitch! I dunno if you gonna fit in one of these suitcases, but you gonna shove yo ass in one of 'em and try." Shawntal threw the seemingly larger bag towards me, implying for me to try that one out first.

"Listen…Shawntal, what the fuck is going on here? What did—"

"Shut the fuck up! You only allowed to speak if you answerin' a question, otherwise, you gettin' smacked," Shawntal interrupted.

"But just before we get into this can we just—" I didn't get to finish the sentence before I got a slap across my face.

"Nigga, what did I just say! Get yo skinny little ass in the suitcase!"

I took a moment to breathe deep and gauge the weight of what was happening. I knew there was nothing I could do for now other than provide my cooperation and buy time. With only minor squirming and adjustment, I actually fit surprisingly snug, and despite being frightened by the confinement, I felt apathetic about the crisis in general. Immobilized by the dimensions of the suitcase, I sat in complete darkness and tuned out the voices of my captors. For some reason, I had a cosmic hunch that I would maybe be alright as long as I remained calm.

In fact, I was halfway disappointed by my favorable suspicion; my desire to improve my life had crumbled away over the prior months, and an early death not only seemed inevitable, but it was nearly preferable to the alternative. What better way to die than get murdered by two attractive women in the depths of meth psychosis? It wasn't honorable, but it certainly wasn't a boring way to go out.

No more than three minutes passed before my being naked trapped in the suitcase had become unbearable. It also made no sense; why did I have to *stay* in the suitcase? I had been totally compliant thus far and saw no reason why I couldn't be tied up in the corner instead of sealed up like a bag of laundry. Respiratory panic ensued, so I decided to make an attempt at negotiations. I was going to *negotiate* myself out of this suitcase.

"Yo, Shawntal! You *gotta* please let me outta this thing.... I promise I'll do whatever you want; we can discuss anything that you wanna talk about.... Just please let me the fuck outta here." I tried to beg calmly, taking pauses between my statements. It was incredibly difficult to breathe in the suitcase when I was silent, let alone pleading for mercy, but it was the only way I figured I could get out before suffocating.

"Oh, you best not be talkin', Girard!" Shawntal gave the suitcase a light kick. "Or yo ass gonna be in a worse place than that suitcase."

"Yo! You know I'm not gonna try and pull anything, Shawntal.... I'm gonna stay cooperative...but you can't leave me hyperventilatin' in here, or you're gonna have a pre-packaged dead body on your hands," I said, then continued after I got no response, "I'm gonna die without a chance to talk about this? You know I'm a good dude...."

"We gonna have to take him out anyway once Cousin Meth get here. He ain't gonna do nothin' girl, you know that. With his shriveled-up ass!" Shanice threw in her two cents.

Part of my concern now shifted towards this "Cousin Meth" fellow. Who was Cousin Meth, and why was he joining this already crowded affair? More importantly, "Cousin Meth" isn't the kind of moniker that paints a picture of a tender soul. My release from the suitcase was encouraging— however, I was *not* thrilled about meeting anyone named Cousin Meth. When being held captive in an article of luggage, I'd imagine it's much more comforting when your potential killer has a conventional name. Give me a Kevin, a Tyler, or even a Chuck—anything or anyone other than a Cousin Meth. It's just not a name that you'd associate with leniency, and trust me—he would live up to this appraisal.

Shawntal gave in, "Alright, let's get this bitch out the bag and put him in the closet."

Knives in hand, they unzipped my nylon coffin and dumped me out on the floor. After taking a few deep breaths and recalibrating my upgrade in freedom, I thought carefully about my first words in a post-suitcase world.

"Thank you...so much...for letting me out." I struggled for air as Stockholm Syndrome took hold. "Maybe I can sit in the closet with the door open, you know...that way I'm still confined, but we can still discuss this?"

"We ain't talkin' 'bout shit 'til Cousin Meth get here, but yeah, we gotta keep an eye on you. Just get in the closet and we'll leave the door open. Can't trust yo shiesty ass behind closed doors," Shawntal said with the slightest hint of a smile. This combined with her abrasive tone was as confusing as it was appalling.

Her contrasting expressions of borderline glee and rage implied that she was incapable of compromise, all the while influencing me to see my captor in a more playful light. Maybe this was a defense mechanism—or maybe it was due to my high level of intoxication—but something about gestating the insanity within the room was consolatory. However it would end, it was going to be "one for the books" so to speak, and whether I would be murdered or released, either way I would be free in a certain sense. A part of me recognized the excitement of it all, or at least its potentiality for a good story. Years later in jail I'd tell it over and over again, at the request of the Mexican shotcaller, but back in that room upon my release from the suitcase, I wasn't sure if I'd be able to live to tell the tale. Everything relied upon my ability to convince Shawntal I wasn't guilty.

When someone beats you, makes you strip naked, and forces you to cram yourself into a suitcase, it's hard to maintain faith in your own innocence, especially when you also happen to be a total piece of shit. I would betray anyone for the right-sized bag of dope, so what I was being accused of wasn't exactly unfathomable. Nevertheless, I no longer contested whether there had been any wrongdoing on my part and accepted that I had simply ended up on the wrong side of someone else's hallucination. From a certain angle, it was acceptable behavior—if not relatable. I had never gone to this extent in my revenge but had certainly concocted similar stories of false impropriety. This was a bit over the top, but perhaps not completely unexpected. Violence, kidnapping, rape, and murder were all normal components of the perverted culture of methamphetamine. They all fell under the umbrella of Business As Usual for this particular drug, which I was already fully aware of.

Still naked, I was moved to the closet and sat down inside a hamper of folded clothes—from one receptacle to another. I understood why they stripped me in the first place—to make sure I had no concealed weapons, valuables, or cell phone to call the police—but we were already an hour into the affair, so there was no need to remain cautious on this front. If I had been hiding a Blackberry in my rectum, it almost certainly would have been propelled out during the suitcase segment of the evening. They had taken my cell phone already—a jailbroken iPhone 3GS that could only make calls over Wi-Fi (the tweaker special)—along with the few dollars I had on me and my passport. I had lost my driver's license during my time on Skid Row, so Aunt Ina had dropped my passport off with Alex for me to use to get a job.

Breaking the silence rule, I tried to clear the air, "So can we maybe talk about what's goin' on…and what exactly you think I did?"

"Girard, you stole my mothafuckin' cell phone!" Shawntal's eyes were glowing. "You stole that shit, sold it to my uncle—he told me all about your bullshit."

Shanice jumped in. "We know you been workin' with our uncle and shit, like he been hookin' you up with free dope."

"I mean I was buyin' dope from your uncle, yeah…but I sure as hell didn't steal your fuckin' phone, Shawntal! I really don't know what the fuck you guys are talking about." I started to get upset. "I sold your uncle *your* phone? He said I did that shit!? He doesn't even know my name!"

"He said the white boy that always ride a bike that's too small, and always wears a hat…he said that's who sold him the phone. And who the fuck does that sound like? Who else he be talkin' 'bout?" Shawntal paced as she spoke with a tad bit more clarity. "I mean, shit, I can't believe you went and did me like that after me and T-Bone been trustin' you, hookin' you up and shit."

"White boy on a little bike with a hat? What does that even mean? This city is full of white people riding bikes and…wearing fucking hats! What kind of fucked up description is that!?"

Once again, Shanice butted in. "Yeah, but the nigga said a white boy on a *small* bike, and you know you always be ridin' a small-ass li'l BMX, and wearin' fuckin' hats and shit. Mothafucka, that's you!"

The finality in their version of the truth was almost comforting. I didn't have a single calorie left to burn on forming a logical argument, so there was relief in knowing that it wouldn't be necessary. I made myself comfortable on the pile of laundry, leaned my head back, silently prayed— to something—and accepted that this might be my last rodeo.

Bay Area rap played in the room as the girls talked and passed the pipe back and forth. They even let me hit it a few times, as long as I kept my hands behind my back while they lit it for me. I was no longer being pun- ished for speaking, but at the same time I wasn't exactly *encouraged* to join in the conversation. I would jump in now and then, trying to make a joke about what the girls were saying, and either get a laugh or an empty threat. In the midst of our semi-peaceful interlude, Shawntal's phone rang, and when she saw who was calling, her eyes widened in congruence with a gro- tesque smirk. The light from the phone reflected off her pockmarked face as she glanced towards her sister, who shared an equally serpentine stare.

"Well, shit! It look like Cousin Meth finally here!" she exclaimed, before answering his call and promptly telling him to come upstairs to the room.

A drawn-out minute passed before there was a heavy knock on the door.

In came two men: both Black, one tall and skinny, and the other aver- age height but built like a linebacker. The skinny man greeted the room with an animated, sinister presence suggesting that *he* was most likely Cousin Meth. The other man, who was infinitely more reserved, quickly took a seat in the opposite corner of the closet I was poking out of.

"Shit, this the little nigga right here?" Cousin Meth pointed towards me.

"Damn right that's him." Shanice shook her head.

Cousin Meth approached me, looked me up and down, smiled, extended his hand for me to shake, and politely introduced himself, "How you doin', bro? They call me Cousin Meth from Fillmo'."

"Hey, Cousin Meth. nice to meet you…I mean, I hope it's nice to meet you—no disrespect. But my name's Jared, and ah, these girls—"

"Nigga, these ain't no girls! These grown-ass women! You best not be showin' them any disrespect right now, and don't even *think* about pullin' any funny shit, cuz I'll put a mothafuckin' hole in you, real quick." Cousin Meth turned his tone on a dime, as he lifted up his jacket and revealed a pistol tucked in his belt.

"I'm sorry, Cousin Meth, I meant no disrespect, really, and I don't intend on showing you anything *but* respect, but I just need to let you know…this all right here, this is a mistake—"

Before I could finish my thought, Shanice interrupted with something loud and incoherent, but Cousin Meth gestured for her to stop and let me finish my statement.

"What they think I did I actually didn't do…like, for real. I wouldn't do Shawntal like that, ever. I mean it…I mean, do I look like the kind of guy that would do something that stupid?"

"Listen… What you say your name was? Girard? Well listen here, Girard, you done got your ass beat, stripped naked, and you bein' held hostage in this here room, so whether you really did it or not is sorta not relevant anymore…. What I mean is this is already a pretty committed situation. We too far now to just back up and re-examine the case, you feel me?" Cousin Meth, although I wasn't too fond of what he was telling me, was at least speaking with some diplomacy. "Shawntal my girl, and she call me down here to handle this, and that's what I'ma do. I got plenty more reason to believe her than you, cuz the bottom line is, well, I never seen you in my life, and Shawntal been my homegirl since elementary."

He certainly was a puzzling character, and it would be safe to say that he had several psychological disorders, but in comparison to Shawntal and Shanice, Cousin Meth's magnetic persona was nothing less than a breath of fresh air.

Despite my admiration for the man's idiosyncrasies, I quickly grew unsure of whether Cousin Meth's lightheartedness would endure. He was oddly conversational at one moment, and then would suddenly snap into an ephemeral rage and threaten to squeeze my dick off. His threats became increasingly sexualized, which although hilarious, didn't make for a positive outlook on the way in which I would be murdered. Even his voice would change during these inversions of his personality—and not just in volume and tone. He would literally sound like a different person with a separate identity. The man was clearly plagued with some form of mental illness, so I had to be careful with every word and every mannerism that I displayed. This became increasingly difficult when he started freestyle rapping.

Why, you ask? Because he was utterly spectacular at it.

I was so blown away with how talented he was that I couldn't help but voice my praise from time to time. In fact, he was so phenomenal that it momentarily distracted me from my own impending rape/murder. He was flattered but eventually grew paranoid that I was merely brown-nosing, and this is when the other—much more terrifying—side of Cousin Meth would spring up, and the threats of gutting my bowels with a screwdriver would replace his poetry.

What felt like many hours had passed, which slowly brought about an extreme awkwardness that radiated throughout the hotel room. What exactly was going on here, and what was the holdup? What started as a potential murder scene had devolved into an apathetic kidnapping. I began to question my captors' intentions.

Cousin Meth's cell phone eventually rang, and he requested silence from everyone in the room. Within the first few exchanges of words, it became apparent that whoever had called Cousin Meth was calling in regard to me. This was an interesting addition to the plot, and although I was excited by a sense of progress, I wasn't sure how this new variable was going to impact my chance of survival.

"Yo, Girard, how tall are you?" Cousin Meth asked.

"What? Why? Um…like five foot eight?"

"Come on, Girard, I'm not askin' for an estimate; I need to know exact height. I can't fudge the numbers on the size of the product, you feel me?" Cousin Meth had the phone tucked between his ear and his shoulder now, gesturing with one hand, and holding a Newport 100 cigarette in the other.

"What!? No, I don't *feel you*, Cousin Meth, fuck. I'm five foot eight…but what did you say about the size of the product or something, what do you—"

Cousin Meth interrupted, "Yeah man, he five foot eight. Now how much you weigh, bruh?"

"What? Cousin Meth, you gotta let me know what—"

"Nigga, it's a simple question. How much do you weigh?" he asked before taking another drag from his cigarette.

"Jesus," I paused momentarily, "I dunno man, probably one-thirty right now. I'm pretty sucked up."

"Aight, aight…you got brown hair, brown eyes, right? Also, you in pretty good health? You got HIV or anything I need to know about?" Cousin Meth stared at me with his mouth open while he waited for an affirmation.

"What? No, I mean…I dunno, I hope not, probably not, but what the fuck, man, this line of questioning is not fuckin' good!" I paused and waited for an answer from anybody. "Like you're tryin' to trade me to some Jeffrey Dahmer–type motherfucker, I mean, what the fuck is happening? This is how I'm goin' down, Shawntal!? Like a fucking episode of *Law and Order SVU*?" I didn't want to come off as hostile, yet I couldn't help but raise my voice. We had entered a broader dimension of savagery—one that really came out of left field—and I could no longer lay back and just hope for a quick death.

Cousin Meth ignored me and diverted his attention back to the phone. "Yeah, man, he a decent lookin' white boy, a li'l sucked up from the speed and all, but he still got meat left on him. Talk to your peoples, and give me a call back when you can, and let's work something out."

The conversation finished, and Cousin Meth hung up the phone.

This had now gone from a very shitty situation to a complete lack of adherence for human decency. Things weren't exactly smooth sailing prior to Cousin Meth's disturbing phone call, but at least the worst-case scenario I had imagined for myself was just plain old-fashioned murder. Now I was on the market for God knows what, reduced to a group of measurements like a piece of meat on a butcher's scale. *Is there a deeper layer of hell that you could find yourself on the brink of?* I can't personally think of one off the top of my head, and in that moment my imagination was equally limited. I was only thinking about how the fuck I was going to wiggle my way out from sexual enslavement. I figured I'd stay calm, because nothing was set in stone—I wasn't being carried off to the sex dungeon just yet—and it wasn't guaranteed that the customer in question would like "the product" upon viewing me in person. I'd have to present myself in the most vile, unattractive manner during the "test-drive," and I could only hope that the kind of people that like to test-drive strangers' assholes were a picky bunch. Seemed unlikely, but these are the times that you need to keep faith.

"Turn your body towards me. I want him to get a square look at you." Cousin Meth had his camera phone aimed towards me. "Say cheese, playah."

Cousin Meth smirked as he snapped a few pictures, then took a moment to examine how they turned out. My demeanor was far from enthusiastic, which Cousin Meth took notice of, and ordered me to sit up straight and put a more friendly smile on display.

This is the sort of predicament that they don't teach you about in D.A.R.E. class. Sure, they tell you that drugs will make you lose your teeth and put you in jail, but they never tell you that you might end up naked in a closet, getting photographed by a man named after an actual narcotic who is attempting to sell you to a human trafficker. I'm not saying that this is a normal issue that most drug addicts face at one time or another, but I *am* saying that methamphetamine tends to lead its users out of the realm of what you thought was even possible—both in your own mind, as well as in the physical world—and with time it will most certainly drag you to the outer limits of unencumbered evil. Rick James once famously said that coke was "one hell of a drug," and you know what? It is. But let me tell you something about meth: "one hell of a drug" doesn't come close to describing its utter disregard for any moral code. It sucks you bone-dry, eating its way through every ounce of muscle and strand of sanity; the toxic levels of euphoria leave you frothing at the mouth for a chance to burn yet another hole in your brain. You're left with a train of thought whose boxcars have come undone from the engine, wheels shattered and derailed, without a single passenger left alive by the time your inertia comes grinding to a halt. Meth had not only physically gotten me caught up in all of this, but it was also the source of paranoia that fueled my captor's actions. It was one small hotel room filled to the brim with dementia. Maybe meth had dissolved my mind to a point where I hallucinated the whole thing—some would eventually accuse me of this, causing me to temporarily question it myself—but either way, does it matter? In fact, if it was all a product of my imagination run amok, doesn't it only make the drug that much more petrifying?

I had been on quite the tirade for several days prior to my squabble with the sisters—and subsequent imprisonment—so naturally, I was dehydrated even before the endeavor started. I had been asking for water for hours, but my requests were ignored. There was no sink in the room, and although there was a communal bathroom down the hall, they obviously weren't going to let me out. They could have gone and filled an empty bottle with water for me, but I had already peed in the only empty bottle in the room.

Eventually, everyone developed a thirst to quench, so Cousin Meth sent his quiet partner to the corner store for some food and drinks. Before he left, Cousin Meth took him outside the room to discuss something in private. It seemed odd, and upon their return to the room, the girls joined them in a whispered huddle. Maybe they were talking about letting me go, or maybe they were talking about putting a bullet in my brain; all I knew was that they didn't seem to want me to hear what they were saying. It didn't seem reassuring, but given that this kidnapping had been going on for almost half a day with no movement, I thought maybe they were getting ready to throw in the towel.

Upon his return, Cousin Meth's partner offered me no snacks—nor did I want any—but I was handed a bottle of red Gatorade. The bottle was full, yet the cap was not factory sealed—which would normally be a red flag—but given the state of desperation my throat was in, I took a chance. After taking a single large gulp, I was almost certain that it wasn't Gatorade, but it did have a peculiar familiarity.

"Thank you for the drink." I took a small sip then continued, "Hey, maybe I'm trippin' but it tastes kinda funny?" The unsealed cap couldn't be refuted, but I was hoping that the strange flavor was just a side effect of my unrested mind.

Shawntal shot back, "Man, that's Kool-Aid. We mixed it up special for you, Girard. Why, you ain't never been in the hood somewhere and been offered some Kool-Aid? Since you fucked up my whole business, I ain't exactly have the budget to get yo ass name-brand shit right now."

"What? Yes, I've had Kool-Aid before, but this shit tastes different. It tastes, like, sweaty or something, I dunno, it's hard to describe."

"Nigga never drank Kool-Aid in his life," Shanice piped up. "Fancy-pants-ass Gatorade-drinkin' bitch. Probably racist too."

"Hey! I'm not like that, OK? I like Black people, I ain't fuckin' racist. I mean, shit, I liked you guys, didn't I?" I tried to defend myself. The *last* thing I needed in that moment was a false accusation of racism.

"Girard, you buy drugs from us! That shit's different; we don't go to the movies and play video games with each other 'n' shit, like you probably do with all y'all li'l white friends. You call us when you need dope, and that's it." Shawntal seemed genuinely offended.

"Well, damn, I still thought we were sort of friends, I mean, until all this kidnappin' shit happened I thought so. But what about that time we went shopping at Ross? Remember that? Or the time I helped you move? Shit, remember when we got Chinese food and you took pictures of me and T-Bone together? I mean, damn, we got pictures together, Shawntal. I considered...and would still be willing to consider you guys friends. You're actually like, the only friends I have at this point."

Disgruntled, Cousin Meth jumped in the conversation and got it back on topic. "Hey! Y'all gotta shut the fuck up right now, about the friend shit, the race shit, the Chinese food...just drink the damn Kool-Aid, bruh!"

My thirst had become overbearing, so I sipped slowly. Cousin Meth and Shawntal seemed to quiet down, and I noticed that their eyes kept trailing towards the bottle every time I raised it to my lips. I had already consumed about three-fourths of it when Shanice asked me to finish it off so she could throw it in the bin for me.

That irked me—she didn't strike me as an avid recycler—but maybe the natural paranoia of being kidnapped had me cracking at the seams. I didn't want to expose any of my suspicion, so I nonchalantly said that I was done with it and handed it to her. An array of cock-eyed exchanges fluttered about the room momentarily before the bottle was snatched out of my hand and placed by the sink.

"Well, excuse us for bein' nice and makin' yo ass some Kool-Aid. I'll hold onto it over here in case you change your mind." Shanice couldn't play it off. It was clearly bullshit.

This didn't sit well with me; in fact, I was now convinced that I had most likely been drugged—probably not with a fun drug either. It was more likely that it would be one of those drugs that you take unknowingly, and then wake up a few hours later in a tub full of ice with a missing organ.

Whatever it was that was in that Kool-Aid, it was already settling in my stomach like a chunk of lead. Within minutes my system felt saturated, although the substance's caustic nature was matched by a deeply seeded warmth. On one hand, it was enjoyable—in the same manner I imagine freezing to death might feel—and on the other hand, I was haunted by the repercussions that would come from falling under its spell. With nerves that were sapped to their last drops of moxie, I knew that I would soon have to fight—possibly for my life—to stay awake. I figured that they must have put a thimble's worth of GHB in the drink, but to this day I still don't know what the cocktail was comprised of.

Twice prior I had used GHB, and it seemed to mimic those experiences to a certain extent, but in that moment I couldn't trust my own scrutiny. The horrifying conditions that encompassed my high had tainted any potential analysis, so delving into the logistics would have proven worthless. Still, I figured that it wouldn't hurt to proceed with caution, navigating forward under the assumption that I had been drugged. After all, they had a motive, the cap wasn't sealed, the Kool-Aid tasted like horse piss, and I was on the brink of passing out. All signs pointed the same direction.

Reality churned slow like cold butter, but my lingering meth high was keeping the lights on for the time being. Shawntal's cell phone rang out "Don't Give Me No Bammer Weed" by RBL Posse as its ringtone, and upon checking the caller ID, she shot up to her feet and exclaimed "T!"

This of course was short for T-Bone, who was calling Shawntal from a smuggled cell phone in jail. It took me a moment to realize the significance of this phone call. Shawntal would most likely inform T-Bone of the "hostage crisis" she had on her hands, which I hoped T-Bone might react to strongly in my favor.

It could go either way; he might believe her nonsense claim that I had done her wrong—although at this point I think we all forgot exactly what her theory was in the first place—or there was a chance he could take a rational stance. He *was* in jail, and therefore probably sober—at least more sober than any of us in the hotel room—so I was counting on him to take a judicious approach. Furthermore, T-Bone had outlined his trust for me in the past, and although he tried to suppress it at times, he was fully aware of his girlfriend's erratic mind frame. Everyone was, so whether my capture was justified or not was irrelevant.

The underlying issue was the long-term implications of a shoddy plan. My cell phone was pinging to our location, there was video surveillance in the hallway—even my identifiable bike was locked to a pole outside the hotel. There was even a chance that my passport could wind up in some evidence room and get a fingerprint lifted off it. These were not ideal set-backs if you wanted to make someone disappear and get away with it. It wasn't unlikely that T-Bone was well versed in the art of getting away with such a crime, so I was confident he would recognize the long list of flaws.

Everyone knows that if you shoot a complete stranger with no wit-nesses, you have a decent chance of getting away with murder. If you kill someone in a hotel room—or even just drug them—you have a body on your hands that you have to deal with. Eventually you must do something with it, whether you sell it to a human trafficker or toss it over a bridge, but either way, you're taking a big chance when you have to carry it through a hotel lobby (even if it's in a suitcase).

Shawntal was ecstatic upon hearing T-Bone's voice, and after a few seconds of flirty banter, she broke the news that she had kidnapped me. Hoping for his approval, she explained that she was merely "protecting the nest" while he was locked up. Incoherently, she quickly cataloged my sup-posed crimes, but her underlying point was that regardless of the specifics, she had zero tolerance for my betrayal.

I could tell that T-Bone was more interested in the specifics than Shawntal was willing to explain, and furthermore, he seemed to be con-cerned with her plan from here on out. Although I couldn't make out the exact words, I could hear T-Bone yelling at her from the earpiece of her phone.

Her disorganized attempt at an explanation was proof that she no longer grasped the reasoning behind what was happening anymore. The only thing she was able to prove to T-Bone was that she was in dire need of sleep. My decaying strand of hope suddenly calcified when Shawntal removed the phone from her ear, took a deep breath, and said to me, "Girard...T wanna talk to you."

Shawntal reluctantly handed the phone over to me, and I began to speak softly, "...T-Bone...how are you? How's jail?"

"Girard, man, what the fuck is goin' on? This bitch tellin' me you stole her phone and sold it to Gilbert...which I don't understand, I mean, what the fuck she talkin' about?" To my relief, T-Bone didn't sound angry *at me*.

"T...listen...I didn't do anything wrong, and I didn't steal anything. I don't really know what's goin' on, but whatever really did happen, it wasn't me, man. Shawntal might have gotten her phone stolen, but I had absolutely nothin' to do with that. You know I wouldn't do you guys like that, I mean, so little to gain and so much to lose, T." I stayed calm and spoke quietly, trying to keep Shawntal from hearing exactly what I was saying.

"Listen, bruh, we both know this bitch can get crazy, and shit, she sound fucked up right now...I just dunno bro, I just don't see it. I don't see Girard the li'l white boy stealin' from some niggas like that; I know you ain't that stupid. But I'm not there, man, so I really don't know nothin' for sure. But either way, they can't be holdin' you up in that hotel room like that. How long they got you up in there for?" T-Bone asked.

"I dunno, T...I'm pretty fucked up myself, I'd guess twelve hours maybe, but, T..."—I began to whisper—"I think they drugged me, man, I think they gave me Kool-Aid with GHB in it, I'm not totally sure, but I feel like I'm underwater...I just gotta get outta here, T, you gotta talk to Shawntal and get her to let me go—"

"This crazy bitch think she can just kidnap muthafuckas 'n' shit! What other crazy shit this bitch been up to since I left?" T-Bone grew livid. "You can't just kidnap a white boy on some dumb shit, cuz you the niggas police actually gonna look for! Shit, you probably already on the ten o' clock news, Girard. How this bitch not already in jail!?"

I tried to quell T-Bone. "No, T, this can all come to an end, and we can pretend it never happened, because she'll listen to you.... If you tell

her to just let me go, everything will be fine. No one's looking for me…
yet, T-Bone…*not yet*…so let's just put an end to this right now, you got the
power to make that happen."

"Alright, I'll see what I can do…but I might not be able to control this
bitch anymore, you know what I mean?" T-Bone paused. "You might have
to start workin' on an escape plan yourself, you feel me?"

"Yeah, well…hopefully that won't be necessary, cuz Cousin Meth is
runnin' a pretty tight ship over here. I'm gonna hand the phone back now,
but thank you, T. Please just try and get me the fuck outta here."

I lifted the phone from my ear and then waved it to get Shawntal's
attention, before she lurked over to the closet where I was still sitting and
snatched it. She looked tired—too tired to keep this charade going. This
ordeal seemed like it was finding its way towards a conclusion, if only
T-Bone could somehow tame its orchestrator. Shawntal practically wor-
shipped T-Bone, so it wasn't her loyalty to his orders that I was worried
about; I was concerned about her—and possibly T-Bone's—paranoia about
whether I'd go to the police. They might think that it had already gone too
far, and I would have to be eliminated to ensure no criminal repercussions.
I can guarantee that the thought ran through all our minds, but T-Bone
was surely smart enough to know that in the drug world, a strung-out
tweaker is the last person a cop is going to believe. At any rate, I could only
hope that he knew I wasn't the kind of guy that would go to the police in
the first place. In the case of people like T-Bone and Shawntal, I was well
aware of how they dealt with snitching, and fortunately, it turned out that
T-Bone had confidence that I would keep quiet.

He told Shawntal that she had to let me go.

"Aight, Girard, listen: we gonna give you back your clothes 'n' shit.
T-Bone must really like yo ass, cuz he trustin' you right now over his own
people." Shawntal lit a cigarette then continued, "This don't mean it's over,
though, cuz we gonna have to get to the bottom of this shit eventually, but
for now, we gonna let yo skinny ass go home."

"Thank you guys, thank you so much. I know you had your reasons
for what you did, and don't worry, it is what it is. No hard feelings…I just
want you to believe me," I paused to stand up and put my underwear back
on. "I really would never do you guys like that."

"Yeah, I wanna believe that, but I think we gonna have to keep some of yo shit as collateral. Like the passport, so in case you do feel like snitchin', we got some info on you," Shawntal explained as she held up my passport before tucking it into her nightstand drawer. "That way, if you try to pull some shit, we got yo address where yo family live, and you know T ain't afraid to fuck yo shit up."

"And I ain't afraid to fuck yo life up neither, so just believe that. You fuck with my girl Shawntal, you gonna find yourself in a landfill, my nigga." Cousin Meth, who had been quiet since T-Bone called, got his empty threats in too.

I knew that my passport was useless to them—it didn't have much information in it at all, let alone a home address—and by letting them keep it, it was nothing more than an inconvenience to me. Regardless, I didn't have much of a family or a real address anyway. It was my only form of photo ID at the moment, and I had no intention of seeing it ever again. I played along though and pretended I would return for the item, but I never wanted to take the chance of being alone in a room with any of these people ever again. If there ever was a line that a drug dealer could cross to lose your business, this was fucking it.

With a depthless sense of hope after yet another escape from death, I truly believed it when I told myself that I was done. I should be more specific: it wasn't literal death that I was afraid of, but rather the drawn-out panic of dancing with it on a twenty-four-hour loop.

What was more disturbing was that the cycle of ceaseless horror had become all too familiar, to the point that it was now the foundation of my identity. Pride in reverse. Overdose didn't scare me, and dying quickly in any other fashion was welcomed. It was the constant shimmy down to Hell and then getting thrown another undeserved chance at life that I could no longer bear.

I was done. Done with meth. No further departure from sanity was necessary. The consequences of getting high were now in a different league than the benefits, leaving me on a scale so askew that I couldn't help but slide off.

This is actually a pivotal point in generalized addiction: when you discover the disproportionate amount of suffering that drugs cause in relation to the pleasures that they grant. The real tragedy of this juncture, however, is that you believe for a short period of time that this newfound knowledge might actually put an end to the nightmare. When you finally accept that it absolutely won't, the breadth of demoralization knows no bounds. No matter how awful of a place drugs knowingly take you, that immediate high—the numbing relief of releasing the pressure—always seems to be worth it when a real addict is convulsing for a hit.

Some adults used to tell me that the reason why my parents couldn't stop getting high was because they loved drugs more than they loved me. That's not quite it. I believe they loved me more than drugs, as I have loved many people in my life more than drugs, but getting high becomes a sub-conscious necessity—like eating food and drinking water. For some, like my parents and I, love doesn't trump the physiological nature of our rewritten hard drives. Most of us hate the drugs that bridle us. Unfortunately, our chemical allegiance knows no bounds. With tears bursting from our faces as we picture the life we're about to torch once again, nothing can stop the mechanism of destruction that now pulls our strings.

Like malware, it's deep-seated in parts of the mind misunderstood by the greatest doctors the world has ever known. It will hide, regenerate, and like the devil himself, convince you that it doesn't exist. Then, before you even adjust to your newfound confidence, it will prevail in overriding self-preservation at all costs. Calling it an affliction is demeaning. It's super-natural. At the very least, it's otherworldly.

The exact time I was set free was unknown to me, but it definitely fell within the terrifying window of not quite nighttime, but not quite morning either. This meant that I didn't have a chance of catching the subway anytime soon. I could barely walk, given my lack of sleep and the potential date-rape drug running through my system, but I managed to zig-zag my way down Van Ness without falling into oncoming traffic—or to be more accurate, where oncoming traffic would be had it been rush hour. After a few moments of stumbling, the last remaining pixels of comprehension drifted out of my consciousness.

I awoke on the side of the road in the early morning and managed to get back to Alex's house. For the first week I was absolutely traumatized and feared stepping outside of my room, let alone venturing out to the street. This level of fear was discomforting, but it was helping me not get high. By the second week, this feeling had faded a bit, but the reptilian gaze of Shawntal was still unshakeable. Regardless, the mental obsession to smoke meth began to quietly ring through my thoughts. I lasted another week, and then like all good junkies, I cracked.

It was unavoidable in a situation absolved of hope. Willpower always folds to obsession, and like a domesticated rat, I squirmed back into my cage once again. It took two weeks to gather enough evidence that I had no more reason to live. This sounds like a brief chunk of time, but for me it had been my longest stretch without drugs since I'd started using. What was I *supposed* to do? Get a job, stay out of trouble, and move in the direction of financial independence? Yes. But a junkie never tries to swim upstream before putting on a weighted vest. We always put more effort into setting ourselves up for failure than actually trying to win the game. Making such a decision is a cakewalk when you have no ambition, self-esteem, a sense of identity, community, or family, and not a single soul to love—when you're outside the realm of humanity. The very essence of the human condition is made obsolete under chemical dominion. I, like millions of others, had found a shortcut: a self-inflicted chokehold of counterfeit gratification.

Mom and Dad, Boston 1970s.

Mom, Boston late-1970s.

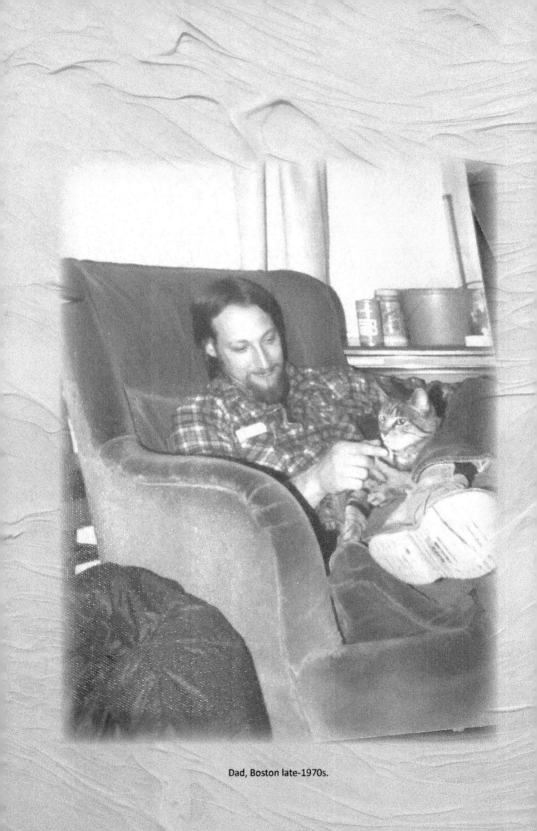

Dad, Boston late-1970s.

Me and Mom, Boston 1994.

Mom and Dad during a brief stint on methadone, 1999.

Dad's mugshot, Florida 2010.

Me in a friend's SRO on Skid Row, Los Angeles 2015.

Getting high in an SRO, Los Angeles 2015.

Me and Richie on Skid Row, Los Angeles 2015.

Me and Jay high on Skid Row, Los Angeles 2015.

Me a few days after getting out of jail, Los Angeles 2016.

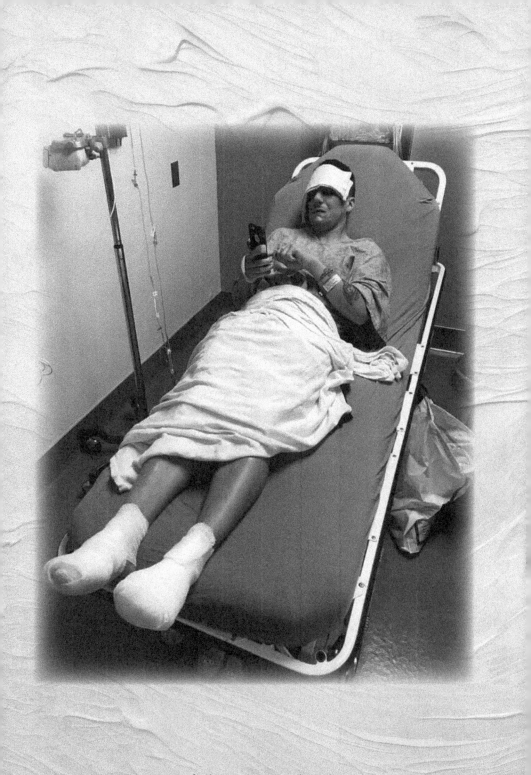

Me after losing a toe, Los Angeles 2018.

Me and Pierceon two years sober, Los Angeles 2020.

Dad, retirement home in Florida, 2023.

Five years sober, Texas 2023.

CHAPTER 7

BARRY'S REVIVAL

Heroin withdrawals are in a league of their own, but withdrawing from meth is no picnic either. There's virtually no physical pain, but the emotional throes and suicidal emptiness can be more disturbing and less methodical than that of ceasing heroin use. You actually fight to not kill yourself, whereas with heroin, the amount of pain is simply too distracting. You still want to die sometimes—trust me—but you know that you're just too brittle to pull it off.

I had just turned twenty-three, had no contact with family, had no foreseeable future, was a college dropout, was a full-blown drug addict, and possessed no will to try to get my life in order. Things weren't good by any measure, but they were so bad that depression would have been a luxury. Depression takes hold when you have something to live for, but the confines of your own mental instability prevent you from moving forward.

This wasn't that. I was waiting out the days until Alex kicked me out of his house, and I would go back to living on the streets until I wound up in jail or dead—either from an outside source or self-inflicted. I accepted all of this, and it left me to only dwell on the present. With no concern for the near future—or even the next hour—I was at peace with the gradient of my downfall; I knew that I had already been dredging myself along the bottom of my storyline for quite some time. This is freedom in reverse. Of course, I was wrong about this notion, but a drug addict usually is. You can—and will—always sink deeper, and you'll most certainly find death before you dig your way to sovereignty.

Had it been available, this would have been the perfect time to commit to long-term treatment. I had hit an emotional bottom, was scared shitless from the repercussions of my drug use, and would have been willing to go into any program. But upon going to the social services office, all they offered me was information on a methadone clinic. Fortunately, I didn't take them up on this suggestion, and returned to Alex's house to wait out my eventual relapse.

Meth, it turned out, was not easy to quit. Although it lacks the physical addiction of heroin, the obsession is monolithic. The noise between my ears grew louder with each day, until a fortnight had passed, and I sold one of my spare bikes on Craigslist. Now with cash in my pocket, the noise grew deafening, vibrating down into my torso and steering me back to San Francisco.

The street heroin in SF was garbage in those days—it would be more accurate to call it shoe polish cut with heroin than heroin cut with shoe polish—so I wasn't going to buy any tar until I could find a reliable connect. However, crystal was relatively decent across the board in the city and could be purchased on the street without much concern of getting ripped off. Downtown San Francisco was filled to the brim with cheap, mid-quality meth, so there wasn't much need for anyone to sell fake shit.

Being a heroin addict at heart, I can deal with sub-par meth, but when it comes to my drug of choice, I either want something of superior quality or nothing at all. This was mostly due to the fact that I was still smoking it; when I eventually started to shoot heroin, I became more open-minded towards inferior product—at first. In a needle, even low-quality heroin can provide some amount of a head change. Eventually this levels out and you go back to being a snob.

The relapse commenced, and so did the same old loathsome behavior. After traversing back alleys in hopes of finding a decent pile of trash, I lurked across the intersection of Eighth and Market around dawn. Just as I took a seat at the bus stop to gather the chaos, I heard a genial voice hollering to get my attention. Darting my eyes across the four-lane road, I made eye contact with a very small human. A person of unknown gender waved at me, I responded with a nod, and then they motioned with the same hand for me to cross the street and approach. Normally I'd be cautious, but this tiny person posed no foreseeable threat.

He was no more than five foot four, had long, gleaming black hair, and was dressed in a style that could most easily be described as sexually ambiguous. I assumed he was going to offer me money to have sex with him. This assumption wasn't made with prejudice; I was offered money and/or drugs for sex on a near daily basis whenever I was in San Francisco. Believe me, I'm not trying to brag; I was far from a stud. Realistically I was nothing more than a scraggy young kid who looked desperate—which is apparently all you need to get laid in that city. Of course, a woman never made this offer to me, and although flattered in a way, I never accepted any of the hundred or so proposals I received from men while roaming the SF streets. Fortunately, I was able to sustain my drug habit by other means, but sometimes I think about how much easier it could have been if I were willing to cross that boundary. I know a lot of people that did, and I have nothing but respect for them. I was just never man enough.

The mystery person introduced himself to me as Jme—pronounced Jamie, but I would later find out that he spelled it with just three letters—and asked me if I had any crystal for sale. I didn't want to sell the amount that I had, but one thing led to another, and he invited me to his apartment to get high. It turned out he had quite a bit of crystal himself, and he eventually admitted that he was merely lonely and looking to make a friend. Shit, so was I. He was clearly gay, and I told him that I was straight and had no desire to even discuss sex. This wasn't out of bigotry, but rather out of paranoia due to my recent run-in with the world of human trafficking.

After the trauma of the suitcase situation, I was overly cautious in the realm of mixing meth with strangers. In the drug world, discrimination is an ugly yet necessary safety precaution—especially if you're in San Francisco and dealing with meth. Going into the wrong hotel room or following a person down the wrong alley could mean the sacrifice of your manhood. Trust me, I've had to jump out of a window once or twice to keep mine intact. When you enter some unknown tweaker's apartment, you never know how many depraved fiends might be lurking. You always keep one hand in your jacket pocket, clutching a knife that's ready to slice a jugular just in case a first introduction goes south. Jme's apartment, however, turned out to be quite orderly, absent of any additional people, and devoid of potential threats.

Jme and I developed an oddly close relationship rather quickly. Having nothing in common besides a shared appreciation for smoking speed, we somehow enjoyed each other's company enough to form a daily friendship. The simple answer was neither one of us was afraid of the other, which is an absolute rarity in relationships based around meth.

Jme's already natural boyish figure contributed to his androgyny, but he also carried himself and dressed in such a manner that suggested he was transgender. However, I'd come to learn that he now identified as a gay man. A self-described "ex-tranny," Jme spent about twenty years dressing like a woman and working the streets as a prostitute. Despite having a previous life as a "transsexual" (again, these were *his* words), he insisted that he only presented as female in the past for more lucrative opportunities as a prostitute, and not because it was something that he naturally identified with. I assured Jme that there was absolutely no judgment from my end, but from my estimation he may have struggled with shame around his former lifestyle. After all, he was part of the pioneering generation of LGBTQ rights, and I couldn't imagine the amount of trauma and hate he had endured in his youth. He was a good man and the only tweaker I ever met that genuinely cared about me.

I saw Alex and my other high school friends from time to time, but when I was in the depths of heavy meth use, I was practically in a different dimension that ran against the grain of the sober world. Jme and I shared paranoia, thoughts of grandiosity, spiritual emptiness, and most of all, heart-rending pain. I wasn't alone when I was with Jme. I can't say the same for when I was around others. I despised myself in the company of normal people, whereas I felt oddly whole when I was in Jme's apartment.

After a long absence since Melissa left me, having an emotional connection to someone bolstered my opinion of life's potentiality. Most of my lived experience was nothing more than forcing myself underwater as I imagined the rest of humanity stayed afloat with ease. When I finally found Melissa—someone who I was able to pull underwater beside me—I wasn't alone for the first time in my life. I told these things to Jme, and not only did he listen, but in a drug-induced stupor he always managed to contribute a meaningful response. I told him I needed to get Melissa back, and he told me that our relationship sounded unhealthy and codependent. I'd say I needed to call her, and he'd tell me I needed to call my dad instead. He gave me a first glimpse at my misguided, false sense of abandonment—which I always used to justify my destructive behavior but never considered that it could be utilized just the same for something positive. Jme, despite being high all the time, was often gently profound. He planted the seed in my mind to reconnect with my father.

Dad was never unwilling to answer a phone call, but I was too self-obsessed to ever find a reason to reach out. After all, there wasn't much to discuss. What could we have possibly provided each other, other than our traumatic linkage—the ugly familial reminder of what we had both lost with my mother's death: the event that had left the both of us in a seemingly permanent state of disillusion.

Jme still insisted that I give him a call. Besides, what amount of spirit did I have left to lose? I was in an aimless nosedive, waiting for the first mountaintop to slap the life out of me, and maybe what I needed was a father to tell me to pull up on the throttle. Although this sentiment sounds nice, it wasn't the product of a sound, fully matured mind, but rather that of a selfish child. Ultimately, no one else is going to be able to sort through your emotional baggage and organize the mess that drives your own self-destruction. I may have figured this out by now, but back then sitting in Jme's apartment, I thought that maybe my dad could do it for me. Maybe having a father, something I hadn't had in many years, could fix my broken brain.

There are more than several interpretations of the "American Dream," and if you huffed enough ether to sleep for a week, you'd eventually stumble upon the version that plagued my father. The man did "America" right. Like the proper countryman that he was, he escaped his own life at the last second and ran away to Florida as the house of cards came crumbling down. It didn't hurt that he was born at exactly the right moment, although it certainly didn't help when he dined-and-ditched on the "free lunch" of the American century before he could order dessert.

I was his burden. We—Millennials—are their punishment. An era defined by inflation—not of currency, but rather quality of life—has imploded at the hands of its own opulence. They birthed us, raised us, and prepared us for a world that simply doesn't exist. However, we are not victims as much as they are not culprits. Both parties represent separate stages within a system of cyclical balance. We—the "failed" generation—are nothing more than the diminishing returns of short-lived prosperity. They—the "successful" generation—are timely prize-winners of the most artificial era in human history. A cabinetmaker nowadays makes no more than what my dad made thirty years ago, whereas the price of a house has gone up 600 percent in my childhood neighborhood. Hopefully, after we eat the rebound and pick up the check, our kids will live on the cusp of equilibrium. May God have mercy on the next generation that's forcibly drowned in as much fraudulent hope as we were.

Tucked away in an email from long ago, I found Dad's cell phone number using Jme's computer. Not sure if it was still valid, I took Jme's portable house phone into the spare bedroom and gave it a shot. It had been a couple years since we'd last spoken, and many more since we'd had a coherent conversation. I had been emotionally checked out for nearly a decade, and Dad had been equally stale from a vicious regiment of self-medicating. Once addicted to heroin, I had a hard time picking up the phone for anyone unless I could weasel a few bucks out of them. Talking to my dad, however, was too painful. Overwhelmed with shame that I had been unable to avoid the very mistakes that had destroyed his life, I found it too unnerving to confront our flawed relationship over the phone. I wouldn't say that I didn't love him, nor would I say he didn't love me, but we were both too damaged from our shared past to actively give a shit about anything. We were both addicts—therefore, selfish to the bone—which makes it hard to rekindle a bond when both parties put self-indulgence before everything else. I had a grip on my own problems, but Dad was truly broken, seemingly destroyed with no hope of redemption for having lost his nuclear family. It saddened me to such an extent when I acknowledged his existence, that rather than processing my feelings, I simply compressed every thought I had about him into the predecessor of an ulcer. I could only imagine the decrepit state of his own gut; the man was entirely unable to forgive himself.

PHONE CALL BETWEEN ME AND DAD IN JME'S APARTMENT, SOMETIME IN JUNE 2012

"Hello?"

"Hey, Dad...how's it going?"

"Jared? Jesus, it's been months...or years...how ah you?"

"Me, uh...I'm alright, Dad, I'm alive.... I'm in San Francisco right now."

"Yeah? Well, ah yah doin' OK? You still gettin' high?"

"Yeah, well...I'm gettin' high.... I'm still usin' heroin here and there. But it's really the meth this time, I mean, it's bad.... It's fuckin' making me go insane, and I don't think I can quit in this place. It's fuckin' everywhere, and I just got nothin' to live for, and Aunt Ina won't speak to me; it's all fucked. Dad, I gotta get outta here."

"Yeah, well, I haven't seen any of that meth stuff here in Florida, it's all crack and oxy; everyone's on that shit, but listen, Jared...I'm actually sobah right now. Been sobah a few months now."

"Really? Wow, that's...that's crazy, Dad, like completely sober? Not even drinking?"

"Yeah, I been completely sobah fah almost four months now. I was in jail last year; have we spoke since I got out? Probably not.... I just had nowhere to go, but I found a pretty nice halfway house in Fort Laudahdale.... I'm actually doin' real good, kid, really...like the best I've done in years. I'm with a sponsah, doin' my twelve steps; it's goin' real good."

"Damn, that's great, Dad, I'm happy for you.... That sounds really good. Sounds like something I need. Why haven't you called me, though?"

"Whatta yah mean? You been homeless and fahkin' around for what, a year now? How was I supposed to call you? I didn't know yah numbah, if you even had a phone...fuck, Jared, I didn't even know if you were still alive.... Ina wouldn't really tell me anything, just said you were, ah... fahkin' up."

"Yeah, I'm sorry. I have been fuckin' up...fuckin' up pretty bad. I should have called, I've just...not been doin' great, you know? I figured you weren't doin' much better, but it sounds like I was wrong. I just got to a place, like a rock-bottom kind of place, you know? And got the idea to give you a call."

"Yeah, well I was in real bad shape. The fahkin' cops lost my sneakahs so all I had was my socks on when they let me outta jail…figured I wasn't gonna staht runnin' around, gettin' high with no shoes on, you know? Kinda hit a bottom myself. So I called a friend, got the numbah to this halfway house, and called 'em up, moved right in."

"Well I'm proud of you, Dad. Honestly, it sounds like what I need to do too. Like even when I do stop gettin' high for a few days here, I just have no will to do anything right, like it's just a fuckin' toxic environment for me, you know? Maybe I should come to Florida?"

"Yeah, you could, it could help, but Jared, just movin' somewhere new isn't gonna fix you…. You gotta put a lot of work in besides just movin'. Why don't yah think about it for a day or two…and if yah really ready to stop, I'll getchya out here somehow. Getchya a bus ticket or somethin'."

"OK, Dad. I'll think about it. I'll call you back soon…OK? I love yah."

"Love yah too, honey."

What an odd state of reality this was: Dad was not only sober but sounded coherent and…maybe even happy. He sounded like a dad, which as simple as that may seem, wasn't the way he had sounded since the prior century.

I, on the other hand, was damaged on every front and was nothing less than the spitting image of Mom at her rock bottom. Rotting from the inside by various chemicals found at your local hardware store, my mind was plagued with constant bouts of paranoia and thoughts of self-divinity. Meth was literally seeping from my skin in the form of boils on every appendage, which only aided in my delusion that I was the reincarnation of Job. From my pores I leaked a pungent scent of gasoline and other less-than-appetizing smells that were potentially flammable. Wandering the streets of San Francisco after losing everything I once possessed, homeless, no family left, and plagued with sores all over my body, it was only natural for the delusions to float in a biblical direction. It was close enough to Job's story that I was eerily convinced that God not only existed but was perpetually yanking my chain.

Having been obnoxiously atheist my entire meager life, this was a surprising change of heart since my encounter with Michael McCutcheon. It's not often that someone in the span of a year goes from believing in nothing to cursing God at the top of his lungs in the middle of a Wendy's dining area. This was it: I had joined the club. I was one of the thousands of homeless men that violently scream in public across this great nation. Every town has at least one. In San Francisco, they seem to outnumber the regular folk nowadays, but back then, they were just a sizable minority.

I found myself bouncing around the SoMa district of San Francisco for a few days after the phone call, eventually parking my corpse on a soggy couch cushion that was lying unoccupied in an alley. I was not only out of dope but was also drained of any willingness to conjure up a few dollars to buy another bag. My hustle had been worn thin.

However, I did have an HTC Google Nexus One Android cell phone. Where had it come from? Not entirely sure, but all that mattered was that it was in my back pocket at that moment. Remember, this was 2012—when that phone was worth a pretty penny. I'd had the phone for quite some time and was able to use it to strike up deals to sell fake pills on Craigslist. It wasn't connected to a plan, but with a little bit of finesse and public Wi-Fi, I used it to conduct my business. This *job*—if you can call it that—required what would be considered strenuous effort for someone that hadn't had a wink of sleep for days on end. Not being in the condition to properly work, I needed a way to make a quick buck in order to knock myself out medicinally with a half gram of heroin. My career depended on it.

A man who appeared to be in his late fifties came meandering through the alley and walked past me before stopping and doubling back to start a conversation. Given his nervous gait and sunken facial structure, I determined that he was on a similar amount of drugs as me.

Although biologically old enough to be my grandfather, nothing about him was age-appropriate. Everything he wore was baggy—even his hat somehow—and the patches of Looney Tunes characters on his jeans didn't exactly scream "Baby Boomer." This sort of fashion had been out of style for nearly two decades, but even if it had been a currently acceptable trend, this man—who may have been born as early as the Eisenhower administration—should not have been dressed this way. Anyone who qualifies for an AARP subscription should never have decals of cartoon characters on their denim. That's a general rule of thumb that I still stand by to this day.

The man introduced himself with a bit of small talk, maybe about the weather and such, followed by a handshake and a formal introduction. His name was Richard. He asked me what my plans were for the holiday, and when I asked him what he meant exactly, he informed me that it was the Fourth of July. This was news to me. Normally this holiday was one I looked forward to, given the drinking, fireworks, and other summer she-nanigans, but this Fourth of July I was in no mood for festivities. I was crashing hard—practically in an early state of decomposition.

"Well, bud," Richard took a seat on the curb, "you don't look so hot. Maybe you could use a hit?"

A glimmer of hope for my dopamine receptors was all it took for me to muster up a quick answer: "Well...I'm sorta comin' down right now, been awake for close to a week...pretty much tapped out. But I wouldn't say no if you were offerin'."

"Shit, how could you tap out on the Fourth of July? It's America's fuckin' birthday, brother. I'll tell you what: I was about to go get some— and it's real good shit too.... I'm willin' to share, but you gotta kick in a few dollars cuz I'm a li'l short right now." Richard said.

I paused a moment to think about my options, quickly realizing that the smartest thing to do was to bid Richard farewell and knock out for a day or two. I had no cash, and the cell phone was way too big of an item to trade for dope in my current state. It would serve me much more efficiently if I held onto it until after I gave the brain a few days to recuperate.

Meth, like all stimulants, loses its pizazz on a user that's been up for days and running on an empty tank. After a good night's rest, a few hits of meth will have you charged up for a whole weekend, as opposed to only a few minutes by the end of a binge. However, it's very difficult for an addicted mind to take this into account.

"Well, I appreciate the offer." I lit a half-smoked cigarette butt that I had already removed from my Altoids can, then continued, "But to be hon-est, I think if I got a good hit of crystal in me right now, I'd use the energy to jump off the Golden Gate bridge."

"Shit, they got nets all around that thing to catch whack-jobs like you." Richard gestured towards my half-smoked cigarette, silently requesting a puff before continuing, "I dunno what a young kid like you could be sad about, especially on the greatest holiday of the whole Goddamn year. It's the fuckin' Fourth of July! Ain't no day to jump off a damn bridge."

"Well, I was kiddin'…sorta, you know how it is when you been up for too many fuckin' days. Either way, I don't got no money. I mean I got this cell phone, but—"

Richard interrupted, "Cell phone? What kind of cell phone? I'm actually in the market for one right now, but I want one a them smart phones that you can play poker games on. What kind you got?"

"Well, it is a smart phone…but I'm not really tryin' to sell it. I use it a lot and…it's worth at least a hundred bucks. I'd need a decent chunk of dope for that." I tried to hold back my temptation.

"Well, you were just talkin' about jumping off a bridge, so what's a phone gonna be worth to you then? You seem like a smart kid, and if you're high, I'm sure you could get your hands on another one before dark." Richard made a compelling point.

"If I did end up tradin' the phone, I'd need a li'l bit of cash—like twenty bucks so I could buy some H to help me knock out…so if you could do that with say, a gram of crystal, I could maybe make that work." I laid my offer out to see if he'd bite.

Richard contemplated, scratched his head with his sweat-stained base-ball cap, and said, "Well, I'll tell you what: if I can manage to get a front, we can split a gram of speed. Then I got some H on me, I could give you a solid twenty of that…and fuck it, you can come with me down to the Chinese market, and I'll buy us some chicken wings on my food stamps. That sound fair?"

Out of options and lacking any sense of foresight, I agreed. "Yeah, I'm down with that."

Several hours passed—or maybe it was twenty minutes. I lost track of several dimensions as I sunk deeper into an already-tapped reserve of neural chemistry. Richard and I had a crackheads' version of a playdate, where I got the chance to meet some of his "neighborhood friends." I was the youngest of the bunch, whereas the rest of the crew looked like senior citizens that had recently escaped from a Yugoslavian labor camp. Some were armed with canes and walkers, each slumping around and guarding their individual shopping carts and piles of debris. One gentleman was even wearing Styrofoam floaties not unlike what you would find on a geri-atric swimmer. I can only assume that he was in a permanent hallucinatory state of being underwater, despite looking like he hadn't bathed since Josip Tito was president. These men and women—probably in their late forties—had spent half of their lives shooting speed and sleeping on concrete, making their shells of flesh appear to be twice the years in age. Drugs had erased their identities and left them to rot forever in the back alley of an industrial San Francisco neighborhood. Some might have once been talented hookers, and others might have been prosperous two-bit thieves, but they were all now withering away in early retirement, living off thrills from permanent psychosis and measly Social Security checks.

This was my destiny. These were my trailblazers. A generation on the brink of burning out, preparing to hand off the torch.

I sat next to the youngest-looking person in the alley besides myself—a girl that appeared close to my age. Despite being covered in open sores and dirt, her natural beauty remained intact beneath a layer of poor life choices. She was transfixed on a single crack in the sidewalk and appeared to be trying to crush invisible insects emerging from the crevasse.

I tried to make conversation, but the severity of her mental illness made this a harrowing task. I do remember that she told me she was a student at UC Davis once upon a time, and that over a short period of being introduced to drugs, she wound up strung out on the city streets. A lovely young woman once pursuing a university degree now sat rotting and forgotten with a permanently broken mind. This haunts me to this day.

She not only knew Richard, but she had also given birth to one of his children a few years back, who was immediately confiscated by the state. I couldn't believe it. There was a kid out there somewhere that was the product of a young schizophrenic girl and a much older homeless man that most certainly took advantage of her. I nearly started tearing up when Richard came over and entered the conversation. He only spoke briefly before pulling the girl away to a makeshift cardboard shelter about ten yards down the block. As she dragged her feet in the direction Richard pulled, I heard him say, "It's time for us to have a little date."

A few minutes passed, and although most of their two bodies were concealed by cardboard, it was clear that Richard had begun having sex with her. I could see her head rocking as it poked out from behind the cardboard, and she didn't appear to be fighting him off in any way. Yet her head eventually turned towards mine, and we locked eyes as Richard grinded away at her docile frame. I became certain that I was witnessing a crime. Zero emotion emitted from her gaze as Richard continued with the deed, nor did her eyes shift away from my petrified stare. After what felt like an entire minute of solid eye contact, I turned my head away and dry heaved until the crumbs from the fried chicken wings scattered across my taste buds. These were my people now.

What looked to be a disheveled prostitute in her mid-thirties stood a few yards deeper within the alley, who upon hearing the echo of my gagging came over to offer some solace. She sidled up beside me on the curb and rubbed my back with a strong grip. This, along with now being in close visual proximity, allowed me to surmise the fact that she was not a biological female.

"What's wrong with you? You eat somethin' bad, baby?"

I kept my head pointed towards the cement and muttered, "No...I dunno...I just don't feel good. I think I gotta get out of here."

"Well, damn, baby, I got a place we could go, ain't too far... You like to get your dick sucked?" she asked as she squeezed my emaciated thigh. "Oooh you got nice skinny legs, don't you, baby?"

"What? No! I mean—" I removed her hand from my leg and continued, "It's not a good time for me." I didn't want to hurt her feelings.

"Ha! You funny, baby. Let me guess, you 'straight'?" She said as she smiled and made air quotes with her fingers.

"What? Yes...why? You don't believe that?" I asked.

"You runnin' round, smokin' dope in San Francisco. No such thing as gay or straight anymore. Everybody havin' fun, baby." Despite her bubbly attitude, I couldn't shake the image of the sexual assault that was occurring close by.

"Yeah, well, I ain't havin' much fun anymore. I think I gotta leave... not because of people like you, I don't mean it like that...I mean, I love San Francisco, but I'm stuck in a fuckin' spiral here. Like the drugs, the sleepin' outside, the fuckin' hospitals and staph infections..." My gaze lifted from the concrete and caught one last glimpse of the rape. "Yeah, I think I gotta leave right fucking now."

CHAPTER 8

THE BIG ORANGE

I asked for help. Real help. Not help with a Western Union wire but help to escape. Was it sincere? Yes, but as I've said before, sincerity isn't enough in the long run. In the short term it can be enough to get what you want, and that's what I got: a Greyhound ticket to Fort Lauderdale.

It took me about an hour to get from my outing with Richard to Alex's doorstep, where he let me use his phone to contact my dad. Although Alex wasn't thrilled about my unannounced arrival, he was relieved once I explained that my dad would be buying me a Greyhound ticket out of the state. In fact, I would be leaving for Florida that very evening. Alex, despite loving me, knew that my lack of drive to better myself had made me the worst kind of burden. He had done all he could, and if anything, he kept me alive for the better part of a year. But moving across the country to reunite with my father was much more promising than continuing to waste away rent-free at the cost of Alex's peace of mind.

Alex dropped me off at the Oakland Greyhound station with a bag full of snacks, ten dollars cash, and a pack of Camel cigarettes. He waited with me until my bus left out of fear that I wouldn't get on it. Had he not, I probably would have left with those ten dollars and tried to get high one last time.

The trip would be four days in total, with over twenty-five stops and seven bus changes. Despite the major inconveniences of bus travel, it isn't much cheaper than flying, but can be the preferable form of transportation in several specific circumstances. For example, if you need to leave town ASAP, you can drive to a bus station and most likely be gone within the hour. Air travel usually requires more time and planning. Another key benefit of bus travel is that you don't need an ID or a passport. This is convenient for transient folk like me that aren't responsible enough to hold onto a form of identification. It also comes in handy if you've just committed a major crime and need to skip town without leaving a paper trail. These three types of people make up a significant portion of bus travelers, including myself. We may not be from the top tiers of society, but we certainly have some grit. Let's just say that people who've taken a cross-country bus ride usually aren't the ones who would complain about a crying baby on a three-hour flight. When a baby cries on a Greyhound bus, everyone takes turns holding it and tries to calm it down. There's more of a *Grapes of Wrath* feel to bus folk, unlike the sniveling nature of those that stick to commercial flight.

I brought some weed with me (Alex gave me about a joint's worth), even though I didn't much care for marijuana anymore. Before the bus departed from a pit stop in Arizona, I smoked it with a random kid on his way to Texas. I charged him five bucks because I would need as much cash as I could get to help feed me along the way.

Unbeknownst to me at the time, this would be the last time I ingested drugs for several months—the longest period I'd stay abstinent since I was twelve years old. I would have much preferred some heroin at a time like this—and I most likely could have found some on my bus—but with the little amount of money I had, my chances were too slim to put much of an effort towards it. If a conversation was struck up between me and a fellow degenerate passenger, I'd pry to see if they had any drugs available to share. Either they didn't have enough to give away, or I didn't have enough money to buy a hit. After a few failures, I decided to utilize my time on the bus to get some much-needed rest.

My nerves spiked as we rolled past the Georgia/Florida border a few hours after a layover at the Atlanta Greyhound station. There I was offered heroin outside of the bus terminal, but by then I hadn't a dollar to spend. This wasn't the source of my anxiety, though, for I was nervous about seeing my father for the first time in many years. It had been many more years since we'd had anything close to a normal parent-child relationship—long enough that I was wary of even the possibility of rebuilding an untarnished connection.

The father that I had grown up with was an imposter of sorts, having kept his double life of addiction and criminality hidden beneath a veil of the all-American working-class fantasy. Exhausted of all identity, Dad had been heavily medicated throughout the entirety of our relationship, and now I was a couple hundred miles out from seeing the man truly sober for the first time.

I arrived in Fort Lauderdale after midnight, where to my surprise it was still nearly ninety degrees despite the sun being nowhere in sight. This soiled my first impression of the city, but with the way my life had been going back in California, I was in no position to be judgmental. However, I was still emotionally erratic from the meth comedown, so the obnoxious amount of humidity wasn't helping convince me that I'd made the right decision. My first thought was that if it was this hot in the middle of the night, what sort of hell awaited once the sun rose in the morning?

I borrowed a fellow passenger's cell phone to call Dad and requested to be picked up. He arrived shortly after in his 2006 Toyota Tacoma, which although just a few years old, looked like it had survived several accidents. Silver-haired with a vagrantly long goatee, he exited the truck, and we approached one another. He was old. Wide-shouldered and stout, he appeared to have shrunk a couple of inches in height, which he made up for with the extra inches of hair that sat shoulder-length behind his skull. He was now a mulleted Jew, wearing a thrift-store-purchased Tommy Bahama shirt and a pair of jean shorts with oversized cargo pockets. Florida had conquered every fiber of his being.

Before we went in to hug, I noticed the silver hoop earring dangling from his right ear, which only further confirmed this notion. This was far from the dad I remembered—a blue-collar Bostonian with the smell of liquor on his breath at most moments—but it was the dad that I'd be more than willing to accept. The guy was clearly sober, with a twinkle in his eye and timidness about him that was so far removed from his inebriated former self. I was more than happy to meet this man.

We embraced for a long hug and then shared a moment of simply observing each other in the damp Florida moonlight. The feelings were as pleasant as they were awkward. We hopped in the truck and did our best to conversate during the drive back to the halfway house where he—and now I—lived.

Catching up is rarely easy, and this encounter was no exception. I had nothing much to talk about other than how bad I'd fucked my life up. Dad's topic of conversation was about the same. He had been living in a very structured halfway house for nearly half a year after doing a long enough stint in jail to detox, and in all honesty, he probably wouldn't have been able to get sober if he had wound up anywhere else. He credited the place's militancy for his success, claiming that no program that he had attended prior was half as organized as the one that I was now a part of.

This frightened me, but at the same time stimulated my trifling impulse to actually change my life. Fortunately, there was an open bed at the time I contacted Dad, and they were more than happy to reserve it for the suffering son of a fellow resident.

It was not a literal house; it was more of a large portion within an apartment complex. There were many rows of apartments on the street, and three of these rows closest to the intersection made up the sober living establishment. Each row had four apartments, each apartment had two bedrooms, and two men lived in each bedroom. Although several beds were empty, no fewer than forty men were ever living on the premises. I didn't move into the same apartment as Dad, but rather an apartment that was catty-corner to his. Having arrived after midnight, I slept on the couch in Dad's apartment that first night and was shown my actual room the following morning.

Not many men can say they got to live in the same halfway house as their dad, nor should anyone desire such a thing, but most of the other guys on the compound thought me and my dad getting sober together was pretty uplifting. It really was an inspirational concept, although at the same time emotionally complex. Our fragile reunification lacked any sense of privacy.

I was back with my father after not being in his life for nearly a decade, which was fantastic, but a halfway house may not have been the greatest place for us to naturally redevelop a bond. Alongside forty or so other men, many of whom were close to my age, my dad had already taken form as the halfway-house father figure to a dozen or so of these young delinquents.

Contrary to my experience in high school, I was now in a social setting where I was the *only* person with a dad. Although some would consider this advantageous, it made me feel similarly unique to how I felt being the only "orphan" in my high school. The combination of feeling different than everyone else, alongside the fact that most of the residents felt more comfortable with my own father than I did, made for a rugged social terrain that I simply wasn't mature enough to handle.

I barely knew the man anymore, so I had issues right away with the fact that most of the other residents knew him better than me. They had inside jokes and recent, shared experiences, while I just had ominous memories from decades prior. I was an emotionally stunted twenty-three-year-old, who had found himself in a pit of resentment and jealousy almost immediately. Were these feelings justified? Maybe. Did I handle them maturely? No, but what twenty-three-year-old with a brain temporarily fried from meth would?

I did, however, reestablish some sort of relationship with my father—whether it was a promotive atmosphere or not—and formed some sense of familial structure that I had been lacking for many years. He *was* the man who created me, and therefore we couldn't help but notice our inherited similarities. From our lopsided gait to our self-deprecating humor, we were of the same blood, and despite the cumbersome environment of a felon-filled sober living, a connection remained intact. A second chance at family was granted to both of us.

In a sense, Florida is the worst of America in its purest form: a graveyard of broken dreams, refinanced delusions of grandeur, and an aura of grift so strong that you'd feel left out if you weren't getting ripped off. People rarely move to the state for a *good* reason; most of its inhabitants seem to be running from their past. Whether they be senile retirees, fugitives on the run, or newly divorced fathers with a penchant for abandoning their children, Florida is a place to live out your second act with complete disregard for reality.

I was no different, having moved to Florida to flee from myself, and like many of my fellow Floridians at the time, the state would ultimately prove to be of no use against our own lunacy. Moving to a new geographic location can't cure the problems we carry within our own minds, and it usually takes a few of these maneuvers before a drug addict comes to this conclusion. During this trip, however, I really believed I could start fresh and catapult myself into a new tropical mindset. Having cut my own hair for nearly a year, my accidental mullet was appropriately crass, and I figured that with a good pair of sandals and a couple of tank tops, I could melt right into the culture.

This fantasy dissipated within about forty-eight hours. I soon began to despise every detail about the place, and although I'm still not in love with the Sunshine State, I've come to question whether the source of my resentment for Florida was purely internal.

What if I hated Florida because I subconsciously felt it took my dad away from me? He didn't care for the place all that much, but it had clearly become his permanent home. Getting on probation shortly after his arrival had kept him trapped there for years, and by the time he was legally allowed to leave the state, his roots were already set. If I wanted Dad in my life, I now had the opportunity, but Florida was the compromise. Selfishly, I expected that my father would cater to my wants, and eventually move back to California with me. This was the least he owed me, I believed.

But he had the wisdom to know that location meant little in the battle of maintaining abstinence from heroin. No variable mattered if sobriety wasn't the number one priority—which sounds corny, but it's the harsh, boring truth. Florida was where he happened to be when this concept finally stuck, and therefore he was in no rush to leave. Hastily moving across the country to satisfy his mentally unwell son was not in the best interest of his sobriety and, therefore, his survival. His chances of long-term success were rooted in him staying right where he was. Florida was where his people were: a vast, sober community of unconditional love and support. For me, it was there for the taking as well. But I wouldn't let it happen.

My greased-up mind was too slick to catch a rational thought, and, therefore, I was more concerned with changing everything around me over fixing what was inside. This was normal for a child—which I still was—and only additional hardship would invoke a craving for sanity.

Dad paid my first two weeks' rent—three hundred dollars—to provide a buffer while I went out to find a job. We were in the middle of a bad recession, so jobs weren't easy to come by for someone with a nearly blank resume, even if they had four years of college under their belt. Remember, this was back in the before-times when the fantasy of a liberal arts degree being a job-qualifier still existed. Turns out that when shit hits the fan and people are fighting over minimum-wage jobs, employers don't care much about your knowledge of European history.

My first gig was working as a sign holder for a pawn shop. It paid eight bucks an hour and consisted of holding a sign that said "We Pawn Guns" on a street median. This was a devastatingly boring task, and after standing in the hot August sun for about forty-five minutes, I shoved the sign in a bush and took the bus home. Although an act of cowardice, it wasn't that I was afraid to work. I feared a job so mundane that it couldn't mute my own thoughts. Because of this, I sought intense manual labor as a form of mental distraction.

A graduate from the halfway house came by one afternoon looking for guys in need of work, and I volunteered to join his crew. The gig was hard labor, and regardless of not having any experience or skills, he figured I could be worth something. This gig paid nine dollars an hour cash and was nothing less than backbreaking. I loved it.

We did various jobs for a few days here and there in all facets of construction. Although the most arduous, our roofing gig was my favorite because I had gained enough trust at that point to use power tools. At first, my only responsibility was to constantly climb up the ladder with roofing material across my shoulder, but as the week progressed, I was taking measurements and cutting plywood. The insufferable heat, along with the body wreckage of labor, kept my mind blank until my head hit my pillow each day. Heroin and meth temporarily became a distant memory.

The taste of sobriety was on my tongue, and although I enjoyed having a steady income and not waking up dopesick every morning, I wasn't happy. My unreasonable expectations of life weren't panning out exactly the way I wanted. They never do, nor should they. I've found that once I accepted this years later, life started to grow beyond what I imagined was even possible. But back then I was still far too impatient and domineering of what I thought reality should be.

Fantasy plagued my distorted sense of justice with what life owed me after several months of good behavior. I wanted to be the director of the show, with the ability to pick the shooting location and have the actors take my cues. The location was California, the actors were me and Dad, and the set was an apartment that we would both rent. This was as selfish as it was disjointed of a plan, which only my father was mature enough to understand. After many years of an irregular family life, I wanted to feel normal. I wanted to play *house* with Dad.

Unable to accept life aside from my unripe desires, my tracks were set towards inevitable failure. I absolutely abhorred my life in Florida, for which I blamed Florida and not my own warped thinking. This set in motion the countdown to making a poor decision to run away once again. It could have taken days, or it could have taken years, but regardless of the time frame, my fate was set. I was simply too young, dumb, and closed-minded to see the immensity of my troubles within.

Remaining sober permanently was still out of the question, although I desired to stay away from heroin. Many people had been able to still drink and not use heroin ever again, so why couldn't I? It's a legitimate question for any heroin addict to ponder. Some figure out the answer quickly, some slowly, and some die along the way. I was convinced I could still drink alcohol and use drugs responsibly—aside from heroin. With this notion, any intention of remaining in Florida long term was null, and my escape was imminent.

Ramen replaced steak, and Pall Malls replaced Marlboros in order to feed the nest egg.

Several months of misery passed, and my savings grew to a whopping $1,600—more money than I'd ever had in my life. This wasn't even half of the bare minimum someone should save before moving across the country, but it was enough for me to start looking for any excuse to leave. That moment came when my roommate woke me up with the vacuum cleaner on my day off.

I packed my bags (as I'd done in a fit of rage several times before), but this time I knew I'd be leaving for real. My dad wasn't thrilled, but he was perceptive enough to know that I wasn't ready to fix my life. After pretending to think about my decision for several hours, I walked back to his apartment and laid out my plan.

California was out of the question, for I had burned every bridge once available to me, but a bridge still ripe like a tinderbox stood between me and New York City. My old college roommate, Kevin (the friend that had been with me when I first met T-Bone), had gotten off heroin and turned his life around in the Big Apple, where he had been attending NYU since escaping from Santa Cruz.

I'd previously floated the idea past him of someday joining him in New York, and he was hesitantly receptive. Maybe he thought it would never materialize, but the nightmare was now coming to fruition.

I called him, told him my intention of moving to New York, and like my dad, he was far from thrilled. Kevin wasn't opposed to the idea of me moving to New York per se, but my request to temporarily stay with him was not welcomed with enthusiasm. I assured him that I'd quickly get a job and find my own place, only needing a couch to sleep on for a few weeks at most. In my head I knew that this timeframe was unrealistic, but bending the truth was necessary for the greater (selfish) good.

I needed more pain. New York would surely deliver some amount of it, but no city alone was capable of giving me my fill. A compiled list of bad decisions would one day bring me to my knees, and leaving Florida for the first (of several) times was only one notch in my belt. My father knew this, but there was nothing within his power to convince me otherwise, so we went out for one last meal and told lies about the next chapter of my life. Before nightfall he dropped me off at the Greyhound station, where we shared a hug and some soon-to-be broken promises.

And just like that, I was gone. I grinned with reckless excitement as the bus pulled away from the Fort Lauderdale terminal and thought to myself, "Never...will I ever...step foot in Florida again." I imagined New York would be the perfect place to find equilibrium as a post-heroin addict. With one of my best friends by my side, I'd relearn how to drink and drug, establish a successful white-collar career, and rendezvous with Dad in California once I could prove to him that I wasn't a liability. I was the director, and this was how my movie would play out. This was how I'd finally achieve normalcy.

Several years prior, Kevin had seemingly escaped from drugs—and in a way, it may have been because he escaped from me. He'd been attending New York University, acquiring a bachelor's degree in psychology and working towards his goal of one day becoming a therapist. He had been off heroin for years and was building a respectable life for himself, when like a cold sore on prom night, I re-emerged at the worst time possible.

With a subversive attitude and a half-packed suitcase, I once again trampled my way into Kevin's life and practically forged his signature on the suicide pact that was our friendship.

Kevin loved me, and like anyone else who did, he became a victim. We still love each other to this day, however that love is free of self-indulgence. My younger self saw love as an opportunity, and I was practically trained to prey upon it when it came to my parents' guilt. Our home was broken on account of my parents' behavior, and therefore the love they had for me was easily weaponized and manipulated. I was a seasoned pro, and when I showed up at Kevin's Lower East Side apartment, I came bursting out of retirement.

Kevin was in class until the early evening, so I went to a bar up the street from his place and drank four pints of beer. I had been completely sober for nearly six months, but drinking was never much of a problem for me—or so I thought at the time—and although I never became homeless as a result of alcohol, who could say I had the ability to drink without eventually seeking out hard drugs? I wasn't convinced it would lead anywhere besides a colorful social life in a new city.

This experiment of attempting to drink responsibly after years of abhorrent drug abuse was something I'd never tried before, and therefore I honestly didn't know if it would work like so many had told me it probably wouldn't. Many sober people I'd met in Florida had advised me against this experiment, on account of their own failed attempts, but after expressing my stubbornness, they explained that there was only one way to find out. Some people truly can drink like a normal person after having a history of drug abuse. More importantly, some people can even drink like a normal person and refrain from going back to their drug of choice. Although confident, I really didn't know for sure if I was one of these people, but it was necessary that I find out.

At the onset of the experiment, I drank those four beers, and thus threw away my sobriety. Everything seemed fine. I had zero desire to seek out heroin and had total control of ceasing my alcohol consumption before I got completely wasted. I did ponder, however, that since I had thrown away my sobriety with positive results, what was the big deal if I snorted some Adderall or took some Subutex? By the end of my first night in New York, I would end up doing both of these things without resorting back to heroin, so as far as I was concerned, my experiment was a success.

Kevin had quit heroin years earlier and was on a prescription drug called Subutex. This drug has been mentioned a few times in earlier chapters, but now I'll provide a more thorough description. Both Subutex and Suboxone's main ingredient is buprenorphine, a synthetic opiate derivative that serves a similar purpose to methadone in the world of addiction rehabilitation. It is prescribed to people to replace their addiction to heroin with something that is legal, much cheaper (if covered by insurance), and non-lethal. In addition to buprenorphine, Suboxone contains naloxone, which blocks your opiate receptors and prevents all other opiates from working for about twenty-four hours after consumption. This makes heroin abuse while on Suboxone virtually impossible. On the other hand, *Subutex* doesn't contain naloxone, but will still deplete the effects of other opiates for about twelve hours after consumption. Both these drugs induce a head-change, but don't provide an overtly euphoric high, and therefore are much less prone to abuse than other opiates. If you snort Subutex, however, a decent buzz can be attained. The effects of Suboxone, even if snorted, are slightly less desirable.

Still a little drunk later that evening when I reunited with Kevin, I pressured him to give me a Subutex pill and promptly snorted it off one of his textbooks. Regardless of how reckless a move it was to introduce an opioid into my freshly relapsed system, I hadn't an ounce of anxiety about the downward spiral this could lead to. In fact, abusing Subutex only added to my confidence in my ability to avoid heroin. Afterall, even if I did get my hands on some, the Subutex would negate heroin's effects on my brain.

Therefore, snorting Subutex was actually the *most* responsible thing I could do during this vulnerable time, I concluded. A drug addict is always a master of justifying the worst possible decision.

My first few days in New York were quite a thrill. Having found temporary housing with Kevin, I spent my days bustling around the nooks and crannies of the megalopolis, inhaling Adderall and pretending to look for a job. Fortunately, Kevin had introduced me to an NYU student that sold various pills, which I self-prescribed to make for a smooth transition into New York life.

After grabbing coffee every morning, I would peruse Craigslist for employment with no real direction, and spend more of my time riding the subway to random corners of the city to take in the culture and stare up at the skyscrapers in awe. Not once during this first week of exploration did I consider hunting for heroin. This secured my confidence that the experiment was a success.

"It's all good" is often the repeated mantra of a junkie on the brink of disaster.

Before the end of my second week, I found myself drunk in a stranger's bathroom, snorting China-white heroin. I had met some jazz students while out drinking, and the direction of our conversation had landed my nose straight into a bag of dope within the hour. As it turns out, alcohol lowers your inhibitions, especially when it comes to snorting various powders.

By month's end I was out of money and strung out. This was the first time in my life that I had been sober for a considerable amount of time and got to experience a clean-slate relapse. I watched in slow motion as the progression from "fun night out" to "I'm throwing up by noon if I don't get my fix" played out in a predictable fashion, just like everyone in Florida had accurately predicted.

This solidified the notion in my mind that I was indeed an addict.

If I touch any substance, it's only a matter of time until I seek out heroin and wind up physically dependent, without fail.

What an epiphany.

That must have been the ultimate wake-up call, right? One would think, but this was simply the transition from "doing the same thing over and over, expecting different results" to "doing the same thing over and over, knowing exactly how it will play out, and still having zero ability from within to not repeat it." This is where we enter the deep psychological abyss. The true mystery of addiction—a black hole that defies logic and leaves someone like me penniless, crying in the gutter on a cyclical basis. This is what baffles us.

With no cell phone service during the long subway rides, I needed to occupy my mind while traveling around the city. Just buying heroin required nearly ninety minutes of subway travel back and forth. Like most cringe-worthy dissidents in their early twenties, I wanted to read a book about drugs, and given that my drug of choice was heroin, I asked a hip bookstore employee for a recommendation.

He recommended *Junky* by William S. Burroughs. Over the next several months, I read it many times, front to back. Half the time I was reading it, I was on my way to buy heroin, and the other half of the time, I was on my way home. During these return trips I was always very high, barely able to keep my eyes open, and often unable to remember anything I'd read. This led to complications in following the plot, thus explaining the need to read the book many more times than once.

Junky is a major novel in the canon of beatnik literature. It's a thorough history lesson in the pre-counterculture era of drug addiction in a major American city. I was obviously drawn to the book because of its subject matter, but more importantly, this book inspired me to think about the possibility of my own writing. The book isn't a masterpiece of character development and prose; it's easily approachable. It's gripping, hilarious, and simple. Upon reading it, for the first time since my delusions of becoming a professional wrestler, I found something I might want to do with my life if I was ever able to get my shit together.

I was a heroin addict, and with heroin addiction comes good stories. However, one must be skilled in storytelling to have anyone give a damn about what they're telling a story about. My addiction provided me many years of misery above all else, but I'd be lying if I said it didn't furnish me with many hours of compelling material. The concept of being able to turn my suffering into something entertaining and emotionally moving onto paper was formed by *Junky*, and upon discovering my ability at storytelling years later in jail, I would finally find the courage to write, myself. I had something inside me all along, but sometimes it takes an outside view of someone else's creation to discover your own potential for creation within.

For the next six months, I kicked around NYC while working a shit job, occasionally selling fake Oxycontin to stockbrokers on Craigslist, and weaseling a few bucks out of my dad here and there to maintain my habit. I'd work forty, sometimes fifty, hours a week washing dishes, and even though I was living rent-free sleeping on Kevin's carpet, I'd still spend my week's paycheck on heroin before the week was half over. I could snort up to fifteen bags a day, and at ten dollars a pop, a budgeting crisis ensued.

I eventually found a job apprenticing as a carpenter in the Bronx, which paid me a bit more and allowed some breathing room with my expenses. I'm using the term "apprenticeship" loosely. I was merely a laborer that unloaded the trucks, sanded wood, and prepped cabinets for the finisher to paint. Besides a Puerto Rican fellow who worked there as an installer, I was the only employee that was fluent in English. I had no issue with this and got along great with my mostly Ecuadorian co-workers, but the language barrier made training difficult. However, this didn't concern me much since I'd only taken the job because it was a pay-bump from washing dishes. Regardless of my lack of enthusiasm, my coworkers taught me a few things over time, and I took a remote interest in the trade. I came in at fifteen dollars an hour—an astronomical wage for me at the time—but the back-breaking labor of carrying millwork up countless flights of stairs made for a paycheck well earned.

Our shop was off 146th Street and the Grand Concourse, which was by far the worst neighborhood I'd laid eyes on throughout New York City's five boroughs. There were always various types of fiends lingering outside of the shop, so one day on my lunch break, I figured I'd snoop around and scope the scene.

It turned out that there was a methadone clinic around the corner from where I worked, which wasn't very exciting in itself, but what did intrigue me was the needle exchange next to it. I had never shot heroin so I'd never been to a needle exchange, but now that I knew that I worked within a block of one, I couldn't help but begin a slow obsession.

I was snorting more and more heroin and getting less and less high from my acquired tolerance, and anyone with a D.A.R.E. graduation certificate knows that shooting heroin is far more powerful (a.k.a. economically sound). Still, I had pretty much sworn to myself that I'd never stick a needle in my arm. My mother died this way, which although troubling, didn't contribute to my concern. I wasn't scared of death; I feared the consummation of my addiction. Intravenous drug use was the final frontier, and I knew that there was never any turning back from such an escalation. I wasn't "that kind of junkie," as us highfalutin snorters and smokers loved to say, defensively ignoring reality and patting each other on the back.

One late spring afternoon, an interesting thought floated into my head about an hour before I got off work. What if I went and got a few needles, and just did a muscle shot? This is when you inject heroin directly into a muscle instead of a vein. Injecting into a vein is called "mainlining" and creates a far more intensive rush from the drug than shooting it into a muscle. Muscling heroin was more economical than smoking it, but less euphorically intense than mainlining, so I concluded that it was a logical middle ground to take. To save a few dollars, I'd muscle from time to time instead of smoking or snorting every bag I got. This sounded manageable.

According to some people's opinion, any form of consumption involving a needle makes the high more addictive, however I find this sort of argument hard to prove. Opiates are the most addictive drugs on the planet, regardless of how you ingest them. I was already fully addicted just from *smoking* heroin, so the idea of becoming *more* addicted was nonsensical. What is true, however, is that your route of consumption usually only moves in one direction. Once you smoke an oxy, you'll never swallow one again, and once you mainline heroin, you'll never again freebase unless a needle isn't available. The fear was that mainlining was an escalation in debauchery: increased health risks, visible track marks that would need to be hidden, and a daily routine made more visceral by the constant sight of your own blood.

Mainlining is also more difficult to pull off. Entering a muscle requires much less dexterity than entering a vein, meaning that without practice, mistakes can be frequent. Even once you get the hang of it and mistakes become rare, a single vein can only handle so much poking, and therefore the crooks of your arms become unusable and more deplorable spots of the body are utilized. This is the point you wind up with track marks scattered across your appendages (from head to literal toes), essentially unlocking the final character of junkiedom.

To my surprise, the bag of needles I got from the exchange included a pamphlet on how to properly mainline. Not only this, but the pamphlet advised *against* muscling because it was much more likely to cause an abscess. Who knew? Not being one to turn down government-sanctioned advice, I now questioned my original plan of avoiding my veins. What the pamphlet didn't have was any information about accessing drug treatment or detox. I'm all for trying to prevent the spread of diseases with clean needles, but at the same time, it's probably best to discourage further drug addiction by promoting avenues of recovery. There are services out there for getting off drugs, and you'd think while in the process of handing a twenty-three-year-old kid with no track marks a bag of needles, there would have been at least a comment about local detox programs. I'm not blaming the needle exchange for exacerbating my habit; eventually I would have gotten my hands on a spike. But it does seem counterproductive to completely cater to addicts' worst behavior without an ounce of encouragement to clean up their act.

Nowadays there's a lot of talk about destigmatizing drug abuse across the board. Advocates say we should let addicts quit on their own timeline without shame, which sounds compassionate, but a junkie on his own timeline with nothing in his way is a recipe for an entire life wasted. Shame is powerful. It's actually one of the most influential tools within society to shape behavior. Before I'd end up quitting drugs for good, I would be shamed into non-existence. Because my actions hurt people, especially those that loved me, I believe the shame I experienced was not only deserved, but necessary for a successful redemptive journey. And I wholeheartedly believe that I'm lucky this narrative wasn't very popular yet when I finally got clean. Had I kept using during this new era of unbridled state and social apathy, I can't imagine how I'd not end up being one of the hundred thousand or so people in this country that die from opiates every year.

A little before my time, needle exchanges used to be run by ex-junkies, and often encouraged a path towards recovery. The ultimate goal was to help people get off drugs. But now that the harm reduction industry pulls in *billions* of public dollars a year, it's grown vastly bigger than the initial small network of needle exchanges. The motive to continually justify more funding doesn't merge smoothly with *solving* the problem. It encourages those that stand to make a great deal of money to "ethically" *maintain* the problem. And so, with state approval in places like California, the ideology of recovery-first has been thrown out the window. Those involved are often politically motivated, careerists, and aren't recovered drug addicts themselves. And if they haven't been addicted to these drugs and successfully recovered from addiction, there is only so much they can understand about the epidemic. I'm not saying they aren't good people with their hearts in the right places most of the time, but what I am saying is that a lot of them don't understand the mechanisms of what truly helps or hinders a drug addict. Without the active encouragement and provision of *recovery* resources above all else, we are doing very little other than enabling suicide in slow motion.

After arriving back to the flophouse I'd recently moved into with my hypodermic goodie bag, I pulled several glassine packets of heroin out from the coin pocket of my jeans. With the pamphlet spread out on my bare mattress, I set up the metal cooker and tapped a few pinheads' worth of heroin into the container. Shooting up for the first time was about as safe as a game of Russian roulette, so I started with a dose that didn't surpass one-third of a dime bag. I measured out about forty milliliters of water by plunging it out of a bottle with a syringe, then squirted that into the metal cooker where it became slightly tinted by the greyish powder. The heroin seemed to dissolve quickly after a bit of stirring, but the pamphlet said to run a flame under the cooker regardless. After that step was done, I placed a tiny, balled-up piece of cotton into the cooker—which was used as a filter—then sucked up the mixture with the needle pressed gently into it. I wound up with about thirty milliliters of a light brown liquid in the chamber of my syringe, which was intended to be injected directly into my bloodstream.

With the needle cradled in my left hand, I surveilled the crook of my right arm. Never having shot up before, my circulatory system was untarnished; my veins were plump with chastity. So much so that they radiated in their final moments of innocence. Time crunched by slowly as tunnel vision formed towards my vein of choice—followed by my quivering left hand, as if it was gripping a loaded gun to my own temple. I pressed the needle gently into the vein and watched the thin barrier of skin give.

With the needle seemingly inside my vein—but not deep enough to exit through the other side—I carefully pulled back the plunger with my index finger, making sure that the rest of the apparatus remained as stationary as possible. I saw a plume of red manifest within the brown tinted liquid, appearing not unlike the aftermath of a nuclear bomb detonation. A tiny mushroom cloud of my DNA had joined hands with the most lethal substance humans voluntarily consume.

I paused with caution for several seconds, realizing the actuality of what could be the most important decision of my life, and then—eyes closed—firmly pressed down on the plunger.

First second, I felt nothing. Three seconds went by: nothing.

And then, like she had never left my side, I felt what negated a decade's absence of motherly love.

Pure detachment from the painful truth. Unadulterated composure with oneself. Finally, something so reminiscent of the final moments before death that it was actually worth living for.

This was yet another line I said I would never cross, and another slice of dignity lost in an attempt to fill the hole she left me with. And shortly after I was off and running with the needle, I found myself once again unsatisfied. Every escalation in habit only works for a brief moment before you feel the emptiness again. So naturally I added to the pile and began my love affair with crack.

Kevin, who several years prior had had a brief crack cocaine habit, was flirting with the idea of starting it up again as a plan to get off heroin—a bad move, but like all drug addicts, Kevin had a funny way with logic. We're all timeless philosophers when it comes to justifying the absolute worst decisions you could ever imagine.

Like I detailed previously, I had tried crack a couple of times, but never really got a kick out of it. I'd smoke it for a night here and there during my first run on Skid Row, like the night I saw my first stabbing, but it never hooked me the way heroin and meth did. Until New York.

I had resorted to a mostly unreliable heroin connect in Chelsea, a high-end mostly gay neighborhood in the lower west side of Manhattan. It had great restaurants, culture, and atmosphere for those whose social life consisted of much more than nodding off in a subway station. Although not a place known for substantial drug activity, it happened to have a housing project in between Eighth and Ninth Avenue where heroin could be found sporadically. Crack, on the other hand, was readily available.

During my initial investigation of the area, I discovered several teenage crack dealers who were more than happy to take my business. The problem was that I was looking for heroin—which none of them had—but one of the more entrepreneurial kids told me he could probably find some for me if I made it worth his while. I told him that if he could make it happen, I'd buy heroin from him every day from now until forever if it was decent quality.

So, this youngster—who went by the name of "King"—decided to diversify his line of income. King became my heroin dealer, and although he wasn't very good at it, he was my only option since I had robbed my other dealer in Queens.

I did this—believe it or not—in an attempt to quit the drug once and for all. My logic was that If I robbed my dealer, I'd have to avoid him and thus be unable to acquire heroin. This was, of course, problematic logic, but I got two free grams out of the poor decision. Rich, the dealer, had refused to stop selling me dope after numerous requests by me. And given that he was a fragile old man, I figured that robbing him would not only be easy, but it would also convince him to finally honor my request. Robbing him worked in terms of his refusal to sell to me again, but it didn't take care of my total physical and mental dependence on opiates. I knew this beforehand in the back of my head, of course, but utilizing such knowledge would have required me to think beyond the scope of a few hours—something that junkies aren't exactly known for.

One afternoon while visiting King to score some H, he informed me that he didn't have any and wouldn't be able to get it until later that evening. This angered me, in part because he hadn't told me this prior to my hour-long subway journey, but mostly because I was getting sick and needed to get high.

King did, however, have some crack—not something I had much desire for at the moment, but I was accompanied by Kevin, who had more of a taste for the stuff. He wanted to buy some, and I figured it would help kill some time while we waited for the heroin to arrive.

When a heroin addict starts smoking crack, this is often how the ball gets rolling: "Fuck it, man…let's just smoke a little bit. Maybe it'll wake us up." It usually doesn't start with a solid amount of planning or weighing the pros and cons. It's almost like a casual act out of boredom and humor for a junkie; irony meets nihilism. How much worse could it really get? You've heard horror stories about where it leads, but the naïveté of how it starts is usually trite.

We loitered around a piss-soaked stairwell in a public housing project, and unlike most pairs of best friends, shared some crack. We weren't the only people in that stairwell smoking crack either. How cordial. Running into like-minded individuals while inhaling the fumes from their urine wasn't how I wanted to spend my Friday evening, but I remained impartial to this because smoking crack, as it turned out, was pretty damn fun. I couldn't believe I'd overlooked this drug for so many years, but after Kevin showed me how to properly smoke it to maximize its effects, my opinion had forever changed. I had become pro-crack.

Time went by, and in part because no heroin had become available, we bought and smoked more crack. Even though it should have been obvious, I was bewildered at the outcome: I couldn't stop smoking the stuff. I mean I literally couldn't stop until I'd spent my entire week's paycheck in a matter of a couple of hours. It was that compelling.

This, I would come to learn, was how crack operated. I would also come to learn that I *really* enjoyed smoking crack. Crack was the answer to at least some of my problems, notably the fact that methamphetamine was hard to come by in the big city. Besides, I had all but outgrown the volatility of a heroin addiction garnished with meth. The paranoia strewn from meth was far too complex, whereas crack produced a paranoia that was playfully manageable.

That's not to say that when you smoke crack you get less paranoid than meth, but you only get paranoid about one thing: the police. This one-dimensional fear is exceptionally more workable than the atrocities endured through a bout of meth psychosis. Not only was it easier to manage, but it could also be quite the adventure if you had the right mindset. Essentially every time I took a hit of crack, the resulting delusion would resemble something out of a Jason Bourne film—unlike meth, which typically resembled a three-day loop of a Nine Inch Nails music video.

Crack was quick, exhilarating, and most importantly, it always had the same, simple ending: I wanted more. Now, heroin feels really, *really* good. No one can argue that. But feeling really, really good can actually get *really* boring. Crack, on the other hand, makes you feel an array of emotions, and you're going to feel every single one of them within a ten-minute period. Crack shakes up the mundanity of heroin for a brief moment here and there, but unlike meth it never tries to be the star of the show. Sure, you'll wind up spending most of your money on it, but the bottom line is that the high only lasts a quarter of an hour. Once the monologue is over, it humbly steps to the side and welcomes heroin back onto the stage.

By summertime I had a decent routine ironed out. I worked all week (usually with about ten hours of overtime) and didn't use heroin. Instead, I used Subutex, which Kevin was bountifully prescribed. Subutex quelled withdrawals and allowed me to go to work and earn the paycheck that fueled my weekend gluttony. Daily heroin use would have been preferred, of course, but I couldn't afford it. I could easily do a hundred dollars' worth in a single evening, and now with my new fondness for crack cocaine, getting high everyday would be impossible without resorting to crime.

This was a line I attempted not to cross and, therefore, to justify my addiction as being "controlled and responsible." My meager paycheck rarely made the cut, however, so selling fake pain pills remained an occasional side gig.

On paper I was going to work every day and paying my rent. Therefore, in my unripened opinion at the time, my life was manageable and I was successfully using drugs. Of course, these two things wouldn't have been possible without my access to Subutex, but even so, I was a terrible employee, an even worse tenant, and I was so broke that I usually had to steal every meal. I was making fifteen dollars an hour and working about fifty hours a week, so after taxes I usually took home about $600 every Friday. One-fifty of that went to rent, and the four-fifty that remained was usually gone by Sunday.

This was the most miserable and lonely period of my life up until that point, although it was one of the most successful runs I'd ever have with drugs. Completely monotonous, day in and day out, experiencing nothing noteworthy or memorable. No hospital visits, no suitcases, no fearing for my life as I slept alone in the gutter. Several times I got "stopped and frisked" (an oddly unconstitutional practice of the NYPD at the time) and wound up doing a night in jail for heroin possession. Another time I did a night in jail for hopping the subway turnstile (apparently this was an arrestable offense after several warnings) and like the previous arrests, it was nothing to write home about.

Life could have gone on like this forever, scraping by just enough to get a little high here and there. But for Kevin, this was no way to live so recently after his major scholastic achievements.

I'll be the first to admit that Kevin was the better man between the two of us. Even with his own sizable demons, he was much more capable of shaking off addiction than I was. His desire was there, but I was most definitely weighing him down. He knew that he had to get clean, but he also knew that any effort was futile while being held hostage by his codependent leech of a best friend, so on the brink of winter he made the decision to move back to California.

The day he was to fly home, we got high one last time, then I accompanied him to the airport. I then went home to my rented room, filled two trash bags with clothes, and hopped on the subway to Penn Station, exactly where my New York journey had launched. I couldn't bear the mental anguish of having to be my own person. Sure, I could have kept my system going for years: work and take Subutex during the week, get high and spend all my money every weekend. But I'd have to do it alone.

Kevin made me feel worthy of companionship; he provided the only evidence that I was remotely human. Without Kevin—whom I was emotionally dependent upon—suicide seemed imminent if I stayed in New York. Void of identity, self-value, strong familial connection, or hope, I had sustained myself through Kevin—like a parasite. With no more host to burrow into, my existence in New York was unmerited, so once again, I found myself riding on a Greyhound bus destined for Florida.

The twenty-four-hour bus ride between New York City and Fort Lauderdale was a ride I was familiar with, but I expected that this one would be very different: this time, I was anticipating a bout of heroin withdrawals unrivaled to any prior kick. Firstly, I was strung out on East Coast powder (ECP), which was more potent than the black tar I was used to kicking. Secondly, it would be the first time I'd quit an intravenous habit. In drug circles, quitting the needle is known as a more intense but quicker process than quitting a tin-foil habit, but the added variable of my intermittent Subutex use was daunting. Subutex—like methadone—delivers a much more drawn-out withdrawal process than heroin, which begs the question: If the cure is worse than the illness, what exactly does it fix? Contentious debate topic aside, I was sailing into unknown waters: withdrawals from a year of the Subutex/heroin shuffle.

I stayed in Florida at my dad's sober living for ten months, and to be honest, I wasted most of it. I was miserable, I kicked heroin, I was still miserable, I got a job, I paid my rent, I didn't get high, and I remained insane. Heroin muted the self-hatred, so when I wasn't using, my imagination took advantage of this fact. With everlasting patterns of negative thoughts, I was left dispirited, knowing that the only medicine I had found seemed to always leave me broke and homeless. This was my great dilemma.

Dad, on the other hand, was experiencing a complete psychic change and flourishing. He had surrendered entirely and, unlike me, was willing to humble himself and accept a new way of life.

Using had brought me to my knees once again, but at the same time I wasn't ready to permanently give it up. This is the stage of addiction that can be best summed up as, "I can't live with drugs, but I also can't live without them"—the middle act of narcotically induced self-destruction. You stop using for a period and find yourself to be twice as crazy without the drugs as you were when you had them. At the same time, you're completely unwilling to do any type of work on yourself and refuse to accept that sobriety is even possible. I was "terminally unique," or at least I still thought I was. Nothing makes relapse more inevitable than thinking you're exceptionally afflicted. Thinking you're more fucked up than everyone else can sometimes be the worst form of egotism.

The economy had still not fully recovered from the recession, but I was able to pick up labor gigs through various sources. Sometimes me and a housemate would go to the gas station in the morning and wait to get picked up for an under-the-table day of work. Most of the time we got paid, but occasionally we'd get stiffed one way or another.

Once again, I found myself seeking temporary relief through hard labor. Still, I couldn't seem to convince myself of having an ounce of hope career-wise. White-collar success seemed abstract and mostly connection-based—which I had none of—whereas learning a trade seemed like a more simplistic route to one day achieving a decent income. I continued to follow in my dad's footsteps and pursue carpentry. I imagined it would not only bring us closer but also garner his respect. It didn't occur to me that simply getting my shit together any which way would achieve this, regardless of how many times he told me.

My first official job this go-around was at a small cabinet shop in Pompano Beach. I started at ten dollars an hour, but I quit after a month or so after not receiving pay for any of my overtime. This sort of wage-robbing seemed to be a common theme within the ethos of Southern Florida business practice.

After fibbing a bit about my skill level, I found a job at a much larger company assembling cabinets and running CNC machinery for fifteen dollars an hour. I was the only white person on the production floor—which I again took no issue with—and got along great with my mostly Cuban and Nicaraguan co-workers. Most of them didn't speak much English, which worked out to all our advantages, seeing that my personality was a negative hellscape at the time. Regardless, I was a good worker, and no task was beneath me. I'd clean the toilets when there was nothing else left to do. If it made the clock pass time, I was happy to do it. When things were slow, my co-workers would graciously teach me a thing or two, but in general they were confused at why I was working there.

"Why you work here, Guerito? Why you not go work at the bank? You young, white, American-born…there is opportunity out there," Zuniga said to me one day at lunch.

I told him I liked working with my hands, but I knew in my mind that I was still much too insane to maneuver the social minefield of an office job. Labor was labor. If you did your job well, nobody bothered you. White-collar work seemed frivolously abstract; it was much more dependent on social skills and office politics—two things I couldn't dream of being able to navigate without drugs. I felt comfortable in a workshop, wearing dirty clothes and covered in sawdust, sweating through my jeans. The more arduous the labor, the more I felt that I belonged.

I did enjoy seeing my father stay sober, though my general toxicity took a toll on the rebuilding of our relationship. During this time, I was a complete emotional drain on the man. As he was thriving through his second year of sobriety, I was constantly attempting to write the next chapter of his life. I wanted him but I didn't want Florida, and I did everything I could to coerce him into leaving with me. No matter how many people told me that the real problem was inside me, I couldn't rid myself of the concept that the solution was physical. I needed a home in California with a dad that was willing to enable my septic attitude from now until the end of time. That was my only imaginable solution.

With two years of sobriety under his belt, Dad knew this was utter bullshit, but I refused to consider it false. As a result, I wallowed in self-pity for ten months while he did nothing of the sort, leaving our relationship as crippled as it had been upon my arrival. He, along with everyone else, was powerless over my toxicity, which only alienated me further from the one community willing to take me in: fellow addicts.

Thoughts of suicide were increasingly making their way into all potential future plans, regardless of my location. Realizing that leaving Florida might not actually fix me, I set my sights on going home and having one last hurrah in California. Getting obliterated and going out on a high note was possible there, whereas a relapse in Florida was subject to various hiccups. I was unfamiliar with the drug world of Florida, and although I knew the state was bountiful with drugs, the underbelly of California was my comfort zone. That's where my final goodbye would be guaranteed to go off without a hitch.

I reached out to a few high school friends and found one with a room available to rent in his Oakland house, and after wiring him a month's worth of rent with a deposit, I had about $1,500 left in my bank account. This was intended to get my run started, and would hopefully be enough to bring it to a terminal conclusion.

My plan was this: move to California and try to use just alcohol and marijuana to quell the suicidal ideations. If that didn't fix the issue, I would get back on heroin and use it to kill myself. This was an actual plan. Alcohol was cheaper and more socially acceptable, so if I could harness it medicinally, I could live a somewhat orderly life as a pure alcoholic. Alcohol had potential. I hadn't drank heavily since I'd found heroin, but it had worked wonders in my adolescent years. Hopefully it still did. Or hopefully it didn't. One way or another, I just wanted everlasting repose.

My cream white 1998 Acura RL, which at the time of purchase had a broken odometer stuck around 176,000 miles, was in good enough shape that a cross-country trip with no car trouble wasn't out of the question. I intended to drive the three thousand miles from Fort Lauderdale to Oakland in about four days, spending nights in cheap hotels and doing a bit of sightseeing during the day. After all, this would have been my last opportunity for any sort of vacation (assuming Oakland was my *final* destination).

To avoid any glitches in my plan, I was to stay sober for the duration of my travels, waiting until my arrival in the Bay Area to officially relapse. I also planned on staying sober during the trip in case I had some sort of spiritual breakthrough. Maybe driving through the Texas desert for fourteen hours would induce a divinely inspired epiphany. Chances were slim, but any sort of inebriation could taint the results. I wanted to want to live.

The morning I planned to leave, I discovered that my car had a flat tire. Some would suggest that *that* should have been the wakeup call, and in a way it was, only I was too weak to listen to it. Nothing about my decision to move felt right, but this was an exceptionally blunt omen. The fact of the matter was that I intended on killing myself within the month, and any harbinger of bad news was irrelevant. Nothing could be worse than my already corrupt intentions. Nevertheless, a spiritual awakening would have been welcomed during my journey, but no such thing occurred. A mere warning sign as obvious and cliché as a flat tire was humorous, but not nearly motivating enough to make me question my itinerary. I was to meet God either by way of phenomenon or death.

I drove across the country. That's the long and short of it. I saw New Orleans, San Antonio, Houston, El Paso, and Tucson. Upon entering New Orleans, I tried to purchase heroin from what appeared to be a child driving a Ford Explorer. After making several phone calls, he apologized and informed me that he wouldn't be able to get any for several hours. As opposed to waiting and hoping this child would deliver on his word, I opted to push onwards and recommit to my original plan of staying sober until I got to Oakland.

How quick I was to abandon the plan was as pathetic as it was expected, but as you may have already learned from reading this book, the fact that there was a plan in the first place was somewhat commendable.

Entire days of cruise control passed, radio stations came in and out, truck stops were visited, and shanty motels in the middle of nowhere were utilized. By the time I was driving through Phoenix, my pulse started pounding. I'd soon be driving through Los Angeles en route to Oakland, and what made this significant was that I knew where to *easily* get heroin in that city. Several hours outside of Los Angeles, this fact was hot on my mind, leaving the back of my throat dry, and was accompanied by a rippling through my bowels. Several emergency stops were made at gas station bathrooms on this last leg of the drive.

Heroin is not easy to get your hands on in a new city with no connections, but it's not impossible. However, this difficulty in seeking it out, as well as the threat of getting arrested or robbed during its pursuit, can be enough to suppress the desire momentarily. This was not the case with a city like Los Angeles. Anyone can find any drug in no time at all with no connections. Skid Row is practically a drug flea market, and the possibility of making it through that city without making a pit stop was becoming less certain with each mile.

Getting loaded right before arriving at my new home in Oakland was more than a bad idea. My friend and I agreed that he would have to kick me out of his house (and keep my rent/deposit) if he discovered any hard-drug use, and although he supported the idea of me trying out some controlled drinking, his radar would be on full alert for signs of heroin use. He was already cynical about moving me in, so his suspicions would be most acute upon my initial arrival. Of course, the threat of being homeless had never stopped me from getting high in the past, so as the distance between me and Los Angeles lessened, so did my confidence in not sabotaging the entire mission.

Remember: this was the longest time I'd ever been sober. Well, physically sober. Mentally I wasn't exactly sound of mind. Apart from this malignance, I hadn't ingested a drink or a drug in nearly ten months, leaving my tolerance for such things at an all-time low. Because of this I knew that if I used any drugs once I arrived in LA, I'd have to be extremely careful. Sure, the end goal was eventual death—but not before giving regular alcoholism a fair shake.

After yet another pit stop incited by digestive peril—this time in a Palm Springs gas station—I filled up my tank and rolled into the depths of outer Los Angeles County. Just for fun I typed "Skid Row" into my Google Maps, and to my surprise it recognized this as an actual destination: fifty-six miles and counting.

Without making the final decision to get high yet, I elected to at least visit my old stomping grounds and brood over some prior cadavery. "I'll play it by ear," I thought, but beneath the thin veil of self-deception, I knew *exactly* what was about to play out—a mutiny welcomed with open arms. Following this verdict, a most peculiar stage of junkiedom unfolds that features a wide array of extreme human emotion. The highest highs of excitement sans chemicals mixed with such utter defeat that self-pity reverberates from the testicles up into the spinal column until you lose yourself in a third-person narrative. You feel the camera staring down at the back of your uninhabited skull, maybe to forgo responsibility over the script, or maybe in an attempt to dissociate completely. Either way, you're five steps past fucked with one of your shoes untied. By now you might as well pull the shoestring loose and wrap it around your arm, because inevitably you're going to need something to tie off with.

Upon exiting the freeway into the neighborhood of Boyle Heights (Skid Row adjacent), I stopped at the first liquor store I could find and bought a roll of aluminum foil. This action was in response to the first of many times I would tell myself the same lie: If you smoke it instead of shoot it, you won't get sucked in. You won't get too high; you won't crave more; you won't get caught; you won't go to jail…. The list goes on.

This is when the flood gates open. My plan was beguiling enough to trick me into giving it the green light (as always), and it didn't hurt that I had abandoned all sense of logic back at the gas station. It went like so: I would go to Skid Row and buy a ten-dollar balloon of heroin. I'd smoke it on foil, enjoy a mild buzz, and once my nerves were settled, I'd get back on the road. If I stuck to the plan and got back on the freeway as soon as possible, there would be no potential for escalation. This was actually not a bad plan. In fact, it was nearly foolproof. What my plan didn't account for, however, was that once I introduce a drug into my system, I have a 100 percent chance of not following the original plan.

Lurking past the epicenter, I parked my car on a less-traveled side street and wiped the sweat from my brow. The air was sweltering enough that the smell of hot trash and flesh-rot barged into my car the moment I cracked the door, but most of my perspiration was a result of shot nerves. With guaranteed temporary relief comes probable annihilation, hence the restless state of excitement.

Within a block of my parking spot, I was able to purchase that single balloon of heroin. Within seconds I was back in the driver's seat, foil in hand with a rolled-up dollar bill in lieu of a hollowed-out pen. Ten months of sobriety was about to be thrown away in a split second as the flame from my lighter melted the tar and I inhaled the first plume. What a moment. You take in the smoke and nothing changes, yet everything changes. It's not until the third or fourth hit that I felt a change in brain chemistry, marked by a sense of alleviation that dripped down into my bowels.

Ten months of anguish dissipates instantly, and everything becomes OK. Not great, but perfectly alright. Pure neutrality.

That's it. That's what I've always burned everything down to the ground for: a moment of feeling *OK*. Just OK.

Heroin makes you drowsy, and therefore it wouldn't be safe to drive 350 miles after doing it for the first time in ten months, right? I think we can all agree on that. I was never one to abide by any safety standards, but if the solution to such concerns was smoking a little bit of meth, then I was going to put safety first. It would be irresponsible to *not* smoke meth in this situation, I thought to myself. Just one little teensy-weensy ten-dollar bag of meth. I wouldn't even smoke it in a pipe. I'd just throw a little chunk on the foil and be on my way. This all happened—this actual thought process, roundabout justification, and eventual action.

I smoked that teensy-weensy ten-dollar bag of meth, and it worked like a charm. Except now I was too amped up, so I figured I'd smoke one more teensy-weensy ten-dollar bag of heroin to level out. The funny thing about it, though, is that it's cheaper to buy three balloons at a time, so I thought I might as well take advantage of the bulk deal and save five bucks. Might as well buy a needle and do a teensy-weensy shot as well, because after all, I couldn't relapse and *not* do at least one shot! That would be a tragedy. Almost as tragic as not smoking a little bit of crack. Just a five-dollar rock, I mean, if I'm going to relapse for one day and one day only, I might as well smoke a little crack, right? The answer is unequivocally yes to people like me.

Around and around I went, trip after trip to the ATM, hit after hit, and poke after poke. Somewhere around the third hour of this, everything went black, and over the next few days, nothing was recorded on the hard drive. Apart from a few images of trying to find my car, fighting off other drug addicts, and cooking up speedballs, I remember nothing. I'm sure there wasn't much worth remembering, but that's beside the point. This was a legitimate blackout lasting multiple days, not dissimilar from that of someone on an alcohol binge—a fact worth noting. As far as I knew, it was unchartered territory for a run-of-the-mill heroin addict, but I would come to learn that drug-induced blackouts would now join my repertoire of junkie stunts—with increasingly gruesome consequences.

I was awakened by the sound of a police officer knocking on my car window. Sprawled out across my backseat, I was just as confused as the cop.

A McDonald's sign sat directly beyond my field of vision through the back window, indicating that I must have fallen asleep in a fast-food parking lot. This wasn't unusual, so why the officer felt the need to wake me up was unclear. As I cracked the door open, I noticed that the inside of the car had a substantial amount of blood soaked into it, along with my clothing. This was an unfamiliar way for me to wake up, but unfortunately would become a much more common occurrence from that point on. Now I had a better understanding of what had piqued this cop's curiosity.

Within a few minutes there were more police officers, several paramedics, and a McDonald's manager circumnavigating my vehicle, which seemed like overkill until I saw all the blood on the exterior of my car.

Had I murdered somebody? Hope not. Was I stabbed? Seemed more likely. Still, I couldn't remember a damn thing. All I knew was that my face was in excruciating pain and seemed to be the focal point of where all the blood had come from. I had most likely gotten the shit kicked out of me, but the real mystery that the paramedics couldn't solve was what had happened to my lip. Given the unusual traits of the wound, they couldn't determine if I had been struck with a blunt object or slashed with a blade, but upon further inspection of my lip—and subsequently feeling it with my tongue—a snippet of a memory came to the forefront: I had been chewing on it at some point.

It was—up until that point—the worst thing I had ever done to myself. I would be left with very minor scarring across my bottom lip, but in comparison to my prior streaks of drug-induced picking, this was a new level of gore. I had—in my hyper-subjective opinion—destroyed my face and would never be able to look in a mirror again without being reminded of it. Blacking out and self-mutilation had now become part of the gig, and I was just getting started.

CHAPTER 9

RE-VAGRANCY

Four times in my life I've heard a doctor say, "I've never seen this before." This particular event marked the second time.

In addition to my lip damage and getting the shit kicked out of me, I also (once again) had a severe MRSA staph infection on multiple wounds, along with sepsis of the blood. This combo left me in a lot of pain, for which I was given intravenous Dilaudid (a relatively powerful synthetic opioid) many times a day, and I needed to remain in the hospital for about a week.

Out of embarrassment, I tried to lay low, but eventually I was contacted by all the people I didn't want to know what happened. This included Dad, who wasn't pleased but at least understood the insanity, as well as my friend whose house I had been scheduled to move into several days prior. I told my dad the truth, and I told my friend a made-up story about getting a staph infection from chipping my tooth on a cheeseburger at a truck stop.

Yes, this is really what I told him. This was the best story I could come up with after lying in a hospital bed for days with nothing better to do than craft a perfect lie. People that had grown accustomed to my bullshit knew to question every excuse I ever came up with, and this situation was no different. Nevertheless, people that care for you *want* to trust you, sometimes so badly that they knowingly eat the bullshit you feed them for years. It's quite unfortunate because those that love a drug addict the most are inversely victimized tenfold. Love is often blind to rational thought, and a good addict knows how to squeeze every drop out of this notion. We're familial terrorists.

After five days I was discharged from the hospital with a cane and a large bottle of Percocet—not a good recipe for someone with a penchant to abuse the fuck out of painkillers. During my debacle I had cut my leg somehow, which turned into a nasty staph infection—hence the need for a cane. Temporarily crippled with enough pills to kill the average person wasn't a springboard for success, especially when your goal was *not* to jump right back into opiate addiction, but those were the cards I was dealt. Trying out a life of manageable alcoholism was now completely shot.

I hailed a taxi to go find out whether my car had been towed or not. Miraculously and undeservedly, my car was still in the parking lot nearly a week later, blood smears and all. I went in to thank the manager for not having my car towed before indulging in a cone of soft-serve ice cream. Cane in one hand, cone in the other, I hobbled over to my car and prepared myself for the final stretch of my journey.

Oakland was about a six-and-a-half-hour drive from Los Angeles, but it took me a little longer because I had to pull over and rest just before I passed Bakersfield. This was because I had consumed about a third of my entire Percocet prescription in the taxi before I even got to my car, which in combination with just having been hospitalized, left me too groggy to keep my vehicle between the lines on the highway. Classic junkie hijinks.

After several more pit stops and another handful of Percocet, I made it to Oakland by nightfall to greet my now-apprehensive roommates. Mark— my old friend that hooked me up with the room—was more than skeptical about my late arrival, and given his reaction to seeing my scabbed-over mouth, I could tell he was disturbed about moving me in. My original story I'd told him wasn't adding up with what arrived on his doorstep that evening, but my rent was already paid, I appeared to be in good spirits (on account of the Percocet), and he was just drunk enough to not want to investigate any further.

On one of my several trips unpacking my car, a man in a wheelchair approached from the south side of the block. He was skinny, possibly addicted to drugs, and upon the gap narrowing between us, I could see that he was missing his right leg.

"Ay, bruh." He extended his hand to shake. "You new to the neighborhood?"

"Yeah, man, just moved back to town. I'm Jared."

"Cool, cool…my name's Kenny. I'm usually out and about so you'll be seein' me a lot, but listen…you ever need anything, just let me know," he said as he raised his eyebrows, giving me the universal junkie salute.

Pausing, I thought it couldn't hurt to verify the specifics. "What do you usually got?"

"You know…weed, coke; I can get pills…heroin—"

"I'm good right now, but…we'll talk later. I'm sure I'm gonna need somethin'." I interrupted, half relieved and half enraged that I had already found a local heroin dealer.

My original plan of just drinking in Oakland had been marred during the LA fiasco, but after having a few beers with Mark that night, I was still willing to give it another chance upon settling into my new home. However, having a heroin dealer camped out across the street was going to make this nearly impossible. Maybe it was just a coincidence, or maybe it was misinterpreted divine intervention, but by the next morning, I realized I was going to get back on heroin whether I wanted to or not. With no ability to lull the craving I had awoken in Los Angeles, I went and re-introduced myself to Kenny.

Whenever you first get back on heroin, the quality of the dope isn't of much importance. Heroin of low potency will still get you very high when you have no tolerance. Quickly—within a week—this changes, and a higher potency is required for any fun to be had. Kenny was convenient in that he sold heroin twenty feet away from my front door, but his dope wasn't going to hold up if I were to properly forget my problems. I would have to go out in the streets of a town I had become un-familiarized with and get the scoop. This is never fun. Before you find what you're really looking for, it's not unusual to get robbed or ripped off several times. This time was no different. Although I didn't get robbed per se, I couldn't manage to find anything stronger than what Kenny sold.

Twenty-Seventh and San Pablo, where there was a sprawling tent city, was a place of interest. It was close to the Social Services office, which is usually not far from where dope is sold in any city. I found Chris, a wiry white kid who looked like he'd been strung out for a good while, and asked him if he knew where to get any good dope.

I'd succumbed to commissioning a middleman. A junkie middleman can't help but always try to scam you, take some off the top, play games, and fuck you over an amount that's just shy of causing you to never come back. This is the business model. For some junkies, a middleman gig is their only way to financially support a habit. We've all done it at one point or another, but to make it a full-time hustle is not only lazy, it's gutless. A good drug addict always has more than one way to make quick cash, especially one that is on his own schedule. Middlemanning relies upon the schedule of others, and the return is usually a pittance in comparison to more advanced schemes.

I had no idea if this kid was a full-time middleman, but regardless I made it clear that I wasn't unversed in the trade. I proposed that we establish a transparent relationship. I wanted strong heroin, and Chris knew where to get it. Therefore, if he helped me get said heroin, I would buy him twenty dollars' worth of the stuff each time he helped me out. Not only that, but I would also let him get high in my car, and maybe even give him a ride somewhere if he needed it.

This *was* fair, and it worked out a few times until the kid, like any drug addict would, got greedy. It was in his best interest to keep this arrangement going, but a common issue addicts have is not having the discipline to value long-term stability over immediate gratification. Had he kept it going, he could have made twenty bucks a day with no hiccups, but he chose to risk it all for a quick ten-dollar skim off the top.

I confronted Chris when he tried to short me, but he played it off like he didn't understand what I was talking about. This was expected. I played dumb as well, and once he nodded off in my car, I got the dealer's number out of his phone. Having the number was not a sure shot of poaching the connect, on account of drug dealers rarely taking on a new customer who they weren't formally introduced to, but at this point there was nothing to lose. Besides, after stealing his dope and kicking him out of my car, I didn't have any other choice but to try.

He would have done the same. Any good junkie would.

The following day I called the number with no expectations. Chris had been scoring for us every day, and by this point there was no doubt that the dealer would have remembered my car. I explained I drove the white Acura that had been chauffeuring Chris for the past week, and that he had given me the phone number and said it was OK to call.

This was a major *faux pas* in the drug world. No one ever wants to give up their dealer's number because a dealer's number is power. Therefore, it's not only rare, but if it happens it's met with a high level of scrutiny. A dealer is never keen on his number being handed out without direct permission, and every time I'd come upon a dealer's number this way in the past, my attempt to make a purchase was rejected. Dealers are often more paranoid than the drug addicts, because with every new customer comes a higher chance of getting arrested. At least this was what it was like in the old days when people still got arrested in California for selling heroin. I'm sure the game is completely different now, and in some aspect, less exciting.

Lucky for me that day, this dealer was in a receptive mood.

His name was Ant. Some people called him Anthony, others called him A1, but I always just called him by the name he first introduced himself as. He drove a Buick Regal from the early nineties, which had miraculously broken down moments before I called him, and that's why he was glad to take me on as a customer. I not only had a car, but it was reliable and inconspicuous-looking, which was exactly what he needed in his life at that very moment.

Ant was probably in his late forties but could have been up to sixty years old—I'm not really sure—because years in prison can sometimes distort someone's visible age. Like heroin, prison is known as a human preservative. Around five foot ten and 260 pounds, Ant was on the thicker side of stout. He had the build of Tracy Morgan—in fact, he looked pretty much exactly like him—and acted a bit like him too, if Tracy was a sociopathic heroin dealer.

Within five minutes of meeting him, I knew he was hilarious, irritable, friendly, and very mentally unstable. I will *never* forget what he was wearing: a white wifebeater, a pair of boxer briefs, and *another* pair of boxer briefs slightly lower on his thighs than the first pair. That's it. Throw in a pair of shower shoes, and that's all that this man had on. Eventually I would come to learn that he wore this exact outfit more times than not.

I guess I should have seen the signs right away. I mean, who in their right mind would ever trust a man wearing two pairs of boxer briefs and no pants? This is the type of fellow who should clearly be avoided at all costs, but I couldn't stay away since he had some of the best heroin in Oakland. It was phenomenal, and in a town full of stepped-on garbage, he took pride in his stellar product. It really was so good that I, regardless of all the bullshit that this man would put me through (and the bullshit I would put him through), would come to develop a close relationship with him and spend many a day at his side.

Ant was carless, I had a car, and so our journey together began that first day of meeting each other. He needed to re-up on his supply every other day or so in East Oakland, so I began to work as his driver and got paid in small amounts of heroin. On top of this, he had four kids and was dating a woman named Jasmine, who had three of her own. His sons lived in East Oakland with their mother, while Ant, Jasmine, and Jasmine's three small children lived in a single hotel room on McArthur Boulevard.

I felt horrible for the kids, who were always on the verge of homelessness, because Ant and Jasmine's relationship was far from healthy. I could tell she was sick of him but needed a place for her and her kids to live, so she put up with his violent outbursts and slept with him so her kids could have a roof over their heads. She also loved crack, which Ant always had a lot of, so that also encouraged her to stick around as well.

Sometimes I'd stop by their semi-permanent hotel room to pick up some dope, and Ant would tell me to wait outside in my car. He would send one of Jasmine's kids out with a bag of heroin, sometimes even the six-year-old, and I'd literally buy drugs from a child. As uncomfortable as this made me feel, I never complained. I needed drugs, and would *never* put my morals ahead of attaining them.

I didn't have the greatest childhood, but buying heroin from a six-year-old made me realize how good it was in comparison. These kids lived from hotel to hotel, didn't really go to school, and had to pretend to sleep while their mom fucked a deranged man in the bed next to them just to keep their room and board. They were good kids. I can only hope they've been able to process and utilize the trauma to make good lives for themselves, but unfortunately, the odds were heavily stacked against them. One person's addiction was gravely affecting three completely innocent lives. Like me and many thousands of others, those kids were robbed of their childhoods, so please consider this when evaluating whether recovery should be the *main* component of how we fight addiction. Since then, a billion-dollar infrastructure has been built in the Bay Area to maintain people like Jasmine's addictions, as opposed to resources that could have helped her get off drugs and be the mother her children deserved. You can't save the childhoods of three innocents with free crack pipes and Narcan alone. That's not to say that Narcan shouldn't be widely available and free. For if Narcan were around when my mother overdosed, she'd possibly still be alive today. We need a multipronged approach that includes overdose prevention, but wide access to recovery treatment is how people like Jasmine's kids and me get a chance at a healthy childhood.

I lived with Mark on Tenth and Wood for a few months, working under-the-table construction to support my habit and pay the rent. I was getting paid fifteen dollars an hour, and combined with my savings and working as a driver for Ant, I was able to make ends meet. Ant kept me high as long as I picked up and delivered dope, took Jasmine to get her hair done, ran various errands, and babysat the kids. Regardless, Ant never had enough work for me to satisfy my habit, so I still spent hundreds of dollars with him a week.

Keep in mind that although I did all of this for Ant, he really didn't care for me too much. In fact, he didn't really get along with anyone. We almost had physical altercations on a regular basis, but he had a bad knee from a trucking accident that left him nearly handicapped. Because of this, every one of his threats was equally empty as it was hilarious. He acted like he couldn't stand me, but then again, he never wanted me to leave, like I was a punching bag on retainer. On top of this, he was completely unhinged; always paranoid, always angry, and always willing to start a quarrel with *anyone* he encountered. He'd gotten out of prison just a few months prior to the day we met, and given his short fuse and erratic behavior, I figured that any day he would be locked up yet again.

Still, he was my only real friend during this time. Mark was too normal, along with my other high school friends that still lived in town, but Ant was fucked up enough to make me feel the slightest bit comfortable. We were both mentally unstable, nearly incapable of feeling empathy, and completely dishonorable. Despite hating everyone around us, we were both fundamentally weak and couldn't handle being alone. Ant would often run bogus errands with me all day and feed me heroin, just to get out of the hotel room and away from Jasmine. He'd never admit it, but I knew in my heart that sometimes he just wanted a friend. I was no different.

By then Mark and my other roommates knew without a shadow of a doubt that I was back on drugs. However, it wasn't so much the fact that I was on drugs that they were concerned about, but the escalation of shitty side effects it was having on *their* lives. I was stealing their food, inviting shady characters over, and generally being a terrible roommate by all accounts. After telling me I had to start making plans to move out, they were nice enough to give me a week to find another place. Given that all of my income was once again devoted to dope and I had no money, that place would undoubtedly be my car.

And I was totally OK with it. Having to pay rent had become quite the nuisance to my drug habit anyway. Even though I was relieved to finally get kicked out, I never skipped out on an opportunity to catch a resentment. I wished Mark to hell as I packed my car with my belongings and drove off.

This was prime junkiedom: causing someone who cares for you massive discomfort, and then resenting them for removing themselves from your life. This was nothing new; it was merely business as usual for an emotionally and mentally deficient scumbag like me. A drug addict can play chess in their head until all the pieces align perfectly, showing that absolutely nothing was their fault. It's truly an art form.

I lived in my car, went to work when there was work, showered when there was an available shower, and ate whatever I could steal. When I wasn't working for Ant, I smoked crack, shot dope, and spent most of the time nodded out in my back seat listening to talk radio.

Occasionally an old college friend who had gotten sober would reach out to me, and they'd bring me to an AA meeting. If I couldn't steal from the donation jar, I'd try to borrow money, but this was usually rejected. Nevertheless, I would capitalize on the free coffee, socialize for a few minutes, then disappear back into the streets of West Oakland. Any verbiage directed at me regarding sobriety was met with contempt. I was different. To call my affliction something as simple as "alcoholism" or "addiction" was an insult, I thought. These people weren't suffering from the same thing as me. I was far outside of the herd, just like I'd been my whole life—the only thing I didn't realize was that it was all by choice.

Pushed to the limit by Ant's abuse, Jasmine and her children finally escaped and moved in with her extended family. Although I was happy for the kids, selfishly I was more interested in the opportunity this presented. I needed a place to sleep, and Ant needed someone to degrade, so this was nothing less than a match made in heaven.

Despite his many flaws, Ant made me laugh harder than any drug dealer I'd ever known. In fact, he made me laugh more than most people I've encountered to this day. He was utterly hilarious, a human quality that's allowed me to look past many people's defects, Ant being no exception. When he wasn't cracking jokes, he took pleasure in letting me know how much of a worthless piece of shit I was, and would dangle bags of heroin like a carrot just to watch me squirm. It was pathetic—the both of us—two men completely lost in a loveless pit of selfishness. He despised my beggarly junkie ways, but unbeknownst to him, he was very much a junkie too.

Ant snorted heroin; he snorted it all the time, but believed it wasn't addictive if it went up his nose. He'd drop a piece of black tar in an empty aspirin bottle, sprinkle in a half gram of lactose powder, and add several pennies to mix. He'd shake this concoction for a few minutes, with the pennies presumably breaking down the heroin, resulting in an odorous tan powder. I'd never seen someone consume heroin like this—turning black tar into something snortable—nor did I enjoy it whenever Ant offered me a line.

I shot drugs. I took a chance at death every time I got high, and although we were both physically addicted to the substance, Ant thought there was a world of separation between the styles of our habits. He was wrong about this, but I didn't see any great need to express this thought. When I was agreeable, Ant was generous with my pay, and therefore he was right about everything.

"Damn, Jay. People really think I'm out here ballin' an' shit. Mofuckas always tryin' to get one over, get fronts, borrow money an' shit. Like, If I was ballin'…why the fuck am I kickin' it witchyo sorry ass? A nigga be ballin', kickin' it with some junkie-ass white boy in a motel? Shit! A ballin'-ass nigga be drivin' around in yo fucked-up car? Runnin' outta gas on the freeway, ridin' on a spare tire an' shit? These grimy-ass niggas think I'm somethin'. Well, if I was somethin', I wouldn't be chillin' with yo mofuckin' ass, that's for damn sure."

"You ain't wrong," I'd say in agreement, after cackling at the belittlement directed at myself. Despite my tendency to agree with anything Ant said, this was one statement that certainly rang true.

Molly, my good friend from college, came to the Bay Area to visit a mutual friend. She had gotten addicted to heroin in Santa Cruz, as mentioned earlier, but had now cleaned up her act and had a few years sober under her belt. We had communicated on social media over the years, updating each other on how our lives were going, and as her life seemed to improve with time, mine just sunk deeper into a pit of despair. Her prosperity coincided with her sobriety, while my increase in suffering was equally congruent with the length of my addiction. This was obviously no coincidence.

What made Molly different from the people I ran into at AA meetings was that I had actually witnessed her transformation. She was once as pitiful as I, not to be trusted around anything that wasn't bolted down, and yet had figured out how to become a decent member of society. This was an inkling of proof that I had a chance in hell of getting my shit together.

Once in town, she reached out to me and offered to buy me lunch. Lately I had been shooting more cocaine than usual, leaving me significantly more haggard and sleep deprived, but an opportunity for the first decent meal in months was enough to pique my interest. I could see in her somber stare that she was deeply saddened by my appearance. My greenish hue was accented by the layer of grease across my face, and my hair hadn't breathed from underneath my sweat-stained Raiders cap for quite some time. Unquestionably homeless in behavior and appearance, cocaine provided just enough arrogance to quash reality.

Molly, on the other hand, was of sound and sober mind, as she delicately tried to convey the truth.

"You should really just come to LA. There's good recovery, good people. You could do really well. I could probably get you into the rehab I went to…. I mean, you don't look good right now. Like, in a close-to-dying kind of way. You understand that, right?"

I responded, while still chewing my sandwich, "Well, I just started a new carpentry job, and I'm learning a ton of shit, and like, this could really be it for me…like this could be a really good career path for me, I can't just…like, leave. I have no money, Molly, or health insurance, I should just… hold onto the job, I think."

"How important of a job could it be if they let you show up to work looking like a homeless person? I mean, you're literally homeless."

"Yeah, I'm, well…pretty fucking homeless, I guess. That's true. Been livin' in my car at least. They know it too, I mean, I don't think they know for sure that I'm on drugs. But I told them I'm couch surfing at the moment."

"Jared, you're gonna die soon if you don't get clean, so fuck the job. Just get your paycheck on Friday, cash it, do what you need to do, and drive to my house. I'm gonna help you get clean."

Something told me to trust Molly in that moment. In an act of rarity, I listened for once. And although her efforts wouldn't take hold (yet), getting down to LA was necessary in the overall journey. It was one step closer to the perfect disaster that would ultimately save my life.

The following Friday I cashed my check, bought enough heroin and crack for the ride down, and made sure that I had enough money left over for gas. I made it to her place with zero dollars to my name and an empty tank.

Molly lived in a three-bedroom apartment in the middle of the San Fernando Valley. Sherman Oaks to be precise, and it was delightful in comparison to the LA neighborhoods I was familiar with. She had a few roommates—all sober and around the same age as me—and from my first impression, they seemed like good people to be around. Nothing makes change look more possible than meeting those who have actually done it, and these people had seemingly escaped hell and made it through to the other side.

I was "different," though—according to myself—on account of the extremity of my consequences. I had chewed a small chunk of my face off, for Christ's sake. There was no doubt in my mind that I was fundamentally defective, which is a high hurdle to jump when conforming to a group seems to be the only cure to the madness. These people were genuinely happy. They smiled a lot, laughed hard, hugged each other, dated, had casual sex, went bowling on Tuesday nights, played in sober softball leagues, obeyed the law, had good jobs, went to the gym, loved themselves, and loved each other. A laundry list of shit I just couldn't fathom. I was a gravely sick individual, who needed nothing more than a few bad thoughts to wind up defeated at the hands of his own mind. Terminally unique. Self-obsessed to the core.

This kind of attitude doesn't go over well when you're trying to get off drugs, although most addicts find themselves in such a predicament when they're bottomed out. One thing that helps is going to a long-term, inpatient rehabilitation program. Being locked down for three to six months is long enough to develop some intimate relationships with other broken souls. You're practically forced not to feel unique or alone, whereas twenty-eight days at a medical spa isn't enough to form such a surrogate family. This was what happened to Molly and her entire group of new friends, and now she was trying to make it happen for me.

Molly got me into a detox that her friend worked at, and I stayed a week. I left early, got on the six-month waiting list for the rehab Molly went to, got high a few times, got kicked out of Molly's, moved back into my car, got back into that same detox, left early again with two other patients, and then we all moved into my car. If only I could have somehow monetized converting opportunities into setbacks, I'd have made millions.

I lived out of my car in the valley for about a month, mostly begging for change. Occasionally I'd break into garages or do some light thievery if I got some crack in me, but most days I was only getting enough money to maintain my heroin habit. I'd drive around the Valley and set up shop at various gas stations, and with my car parked at one of the pumps, I'd approach customers and tell them a sob story about how I was broke and out of gas.

Depending on how strung-out you look, this typically works on one out of five people. A dollar here, a handful of change there, and you can wind up with forty bucks in as little as an hour. Some people would say, "I won't give you cash, but I'll put some gas in your car with my credit card." That works too. A junkie driving on a full tank is an oxymoron, so an offer of actual gasoline was always welcomed. My main goal was to get cash, obviously, but I was never one to turn anything down. Forty dollars was my general target, but anything hovering close to twenty was good enough if business was slow. The old gasoline hustle always worked in a pinch, and although it was never consistently fruitful, it required a limited amount of effort.

A thirst for a sugary beverage raged inside me one night (junkies can't usually go twelve hours without a soda), so with the leftover change from my earlier scheme, I started my car and drove to the nearest market. After buying a large fountain drink, a man approached me in the parking lot and pointed towards an early-nineties-model Jeep, which appeared to not only be his vehicle but also his home. As I glanced at the disheveled car, he said, "Hey, man, my battery's dead. Think you could give me a jump?"

Without hesitation, I obliged. I was always willing to help someone, as long as it didn't cost me any money, get in the way of me getting high, and had a potential payout. Anything can be an opportunity when you're getting loaded, even so-called acts of kindness. We hooked our cars up with his set of jumper cables and talked for a moment while we waited for his battery to charge.

"Thanks, bud." The man took out a pack of Sheriff brand cigarettes from his shirt pocket, offered me one, then continued, "I owe you one. You get high at all?"

I accepted the cheap cigarette, lit it with my own lighter, then said, "Usually...depends on what."

"I just do speed. You want a bump for the road? It's pretty good shit."

"Fuck...I been kinda tryna stay away from crystal. I don't make great decisions on that shit," I griped.

"Naw, man, this is good shit...some old school shit. Not that new shit that makes you start talkin' to yourself. Take an issue."

"Damn," I chuckled, "alright, fuck it. I'll try a bit."

He went to his car for a moment and returned with a folded-up receipt that he placed in my hand. Inside were several small chunks of meth, which I promptly smoked on a piece of aluminum foil after we parted ways.

I had largely avoided meth since my lip incident about nine months prior, out of fear that meth was solely responsible for the grim result. Heroin didn't seem like the kind of drug that would make someone bite a little bit of their face off, and let's be honest, meth does. Therefore, I was scared as hell of the stuff from then on out. This left me in an uncomfortable predicament because, well, I'd just been handed free meth.

Was it a sign from the powers that be? Anything is if you want it bad enough.

I ran around the Valley's crevices like a sewer rat all night long, perusing dumpsters and alleyways, but soon found myself bored and in need of a comedown. I needed heroin. The problem was, as it usually was, I had no money. I was too tweaked out to convincingly beg at the gas station, so my standard emergency plan was out the window. I needed a real caper. Meth can induce a sense of grandeur and make you reach for goals that you normally wouldn't attempt. This sounds like a somewhat positive side effect, and it could have been if my goals didn't always revolve around robbing, scheming, and stealing. Somehow meth never inspires anyone to find a cure for cancer, but rather only a quick buck.

With anxieties rising for a shot of heroin, the Rolodex of bad ideas fluttered through my broken mind. After minimal effort I arrived at the all-too-familiar scam: selling fake pills on Craigslist. Oh, how I hated this one. It hadn't been tried in Los Angeles yet, and for all I knew could yield disastrous results. Still, I flirted with the idea. With my phone charging on the twelve-volt outlet, I checked Craigslist to see if anyone was posting about needing painkillers. After plugging in a few code words in the search bar, I found a post that included a contact number. I called.

"Hello?"

"Hi, uh…I'm responding to your Craigslist post. About *pain management*," I said in the commonly accepted lingo.

"Oh, yeah…yeah, I'm lookin' for something to help with that. Preferably oxy or Norcos, but I'm open to whatever you got."

"OK, well, I gotta bunch of Norcos right now," I lied. "Ten milligrams, that work?"

"Yeah, definitely…those would work. I need a lot though."

"How much is a lot?" My paranoia started to rise.

"I dunno…maybe fifty? I'm doin' a movie shoot downtown for a few weeks, and I'm gonna need enough to last me."

"A movie shoot, huh? What do you do?" I needed to grill him on a few details to make sure he was telling the truth. If he was a cop, he was going to have to make up one hell of a story to convince me he wasn't. I figured if I put him on the spot with a couple of specified questions, I'd be able to suss him out quick.

"Uh, I'm a grip. Like for the studios."

"OK, well, what kind of tools do you use?" I didn't even know what a grip was.

"Well, we don't really use a lot of tools…mostly work gloves, a utility knife, maybe some tape here and there."

"Alright…well, what movie are you working on?"

"What? I can't say…. We like, sign non-disclosure agreements and shit…. Why does it matter?"

I paused—this guy brought up a non-disclosure agreement? He couldn't be police. That was way too specific of a detail for some dumb cop to come up with. "Never mind with that. Just listen, I'm gonna be wearing a green plaid shirt and a black hat. What are you wearing?"

"Well, I'm at work, so just…work stuff. Black Slayer shirt, black work shorts; I have a long beard; I'm pretty recognizable. I'm a big dude; I stick out." This guy sounded legit.

"OK, well, where do you want to meet?" I asked, already giddy with sweat dripping down my forehead, knowing that I was about to make a few hundred bucks.

"Uh…how about Starbucks downtown, on Sixth and Spring? How much money should I bring?"

"Fifty Norcos—I can do it for two hundred bucks. I'll be there in forty minutes, and I'll call you when I'm close by, but listen, you need to put the cash in an empty cigarette box or somethin' similar, and then I'm gonna hand you a book, and inside the book is gonna be a cut-out section with the pills. OK? Once we do the hand-off, we separate. And remember, I'm wearing a green flannel and a black hat."

"Alright, um…OK, I can do all that. Call me when you're down here."

The deal was set. Of course, I'd arrive early, not wearing the clothes I said I would. This way, I could scan the scene and make sure everything was kosher. I didn't have fifty Norcos, nor could I get any, but I did steal a bottle of off-brand Tylenol from a local pharmacy on my way. I bagged them up, cut a section out of one of the books in my trunk, and placed the pills inside. It was foolproof.

I emerged on the scene hatless in just a wifebeater and unwashed Levis. Boy, did I think I was slick. After taking a seat at a countertop—with the book hidden between my legs—I texted my customer and told him I had arrived. He replied that he'd be there in five minutes.

Shortly after, a large man—about six foot two—walked into the Starbucks wearing what had been described to me on the phone. He even had a toolbelt with a tape gun on it.

"What kind of cop would dress this well for a sting operation?" I thought. None. No cop would, and therefore I knew I was golden. Eyes beaming, I checked the street through the windows to make sure there was no suspicious activity. No undercover cops lingering in obscurity. Nothing. Everything was coming up roses.

Taking a seat, the man looked around, presumably for me, but was thrown off by the lack of green flannel in the coffee shop. My senses confirmed that this was 100 percent legit, so I approached the man and took a seat next to him on a stool.

"I'm the guy. You're the other guy, right?" I tried to act tough.

"Yeah, I'm the…I'm the other guy. Do you smoke?" He awkwardly asked as he handed me an entire box of Newport cigarettes. This guy knew how to operate.

I smiled, "I do smoke, thank you. Anyway, here's that book I was tellin' you about. You're gonna love it." I said as I handed the book off to him and stood up from the stool in one motion. The deal was done, and it was time for me to get the fuck out of there. Two hundred dollars in the blink of an eye! Easy. No one does it better than me, I thought.

The purest of joy consumes a junkie when he's completed a mission, knowing that he can now stay high for another day. This feeling *never* gets old, and practically surpasses the feeling of getting high itself. It's tangibly fulfilling in comparison to the artificial pleasure of injecting yourself with poison. This time was no different, as I strolled away from the coffee shop like the gangster that I thought I was. Smiling from ear to ear as sweat poured down the small of my back, I was floating on a cloud destined for junkie heaven. And just as fast as that dopamine hit, everything retracted down my spinal cord and sunk me into junkie hell.

Not thirty seconds after the hand-off, I was tackled by several police officers. Unbeknownst to me, they had barreled out of a maintenance van just prior to crushing me into the concrete. With one cheek compressed into the sidewalk, I went limp and witnessed every drip of prospect seep out into the gutter. I wasn't going to get high that day. Probably not the next day either. In fact, I was going to jail. Maybe for a long time. Selling a large amount of supposed painkillers to a police officer wasn't exactly a misdemeanor back then. It wasn't going to be a "sit in jail overnight and get a slap on the wrist in the morning" kind of thing either. I was possibly going to do time, but the only thing I cared about was the impending dopesickness. Take my freedom, impound my car, give me a felony, send me to prison, put me on probation, do whatever you want. Just don't make me kick cold turkey in a jail cell.

Busted and on the brink of heroin withdrawal, I was brought to a single-man holding cell to await my fate. The drugs I sold weren't real, so my only hope was that on account of this, they would throw the case out. I let them know that the pills were fake upon getting cuffed, but the cops didn't seem to consider this a good enough reason to let me go. They did, however, consider it a reason to laugh while arresting me, which I couldn't fault them for. It was relatively funny.

Something about jail is so inexplicably relaxing. Not if you're there for years, I'd imagine, but when you're running around the streets on the hamster wheel, there's nothing quite like being forcibly removed from the situation for a few days. Baloney sandwiches, cold AC, and a place to rest your head; it's not always the worst alternative. Nothing scares a heroin addict more than the thought of having to detox in jail, but once you're there and you know there's nothing you can do about it, there's something ironically freeing about the ordeal. It's like an unmedicated spiritual cleanse of sorts.

Several hours passed after my initial arrest before I was taken to the detective's office for a chat. There sat a plainclothes officer, and of course, the bearded man that I sold the pills to.

"How you feelin', scarface?" The bearded cop started out snide.

"Fuck, man," I shook my head, "You got me. You fuckin' got me, man. You were good too, toolbelt and everything."

"Yeah, well, that's our job," the other cop chimed in. "We do this every day, one after another."

"Well I'm not gonna try and defend what I did. It was dumb…but I'm a fuckin' drug addict, guys. We do stupid things—I do stupid shit to get drugs."

Other Cop got right down to business. "Yeah, well, you fucked up, alright. I mean, drug sales to a cop? That's a felony, brother. You're gonna do time…real time, maybe even go to prison for this, but if you help us and remain cooperative, well, I'm not promising anything, but I'm just sayin', we're the only ones that can help you from here on out."

"Uh, OK…yeah, I mean, I know what I did, and I'm not gonna fuck around with you guys. So yeah, I'll do anything you want. What do you guys wanna know?"

"Well, first off, where'd you get the pills?" The bearded cop asked.

"Oh, the pills…uh, CVS, I think?" I had forgotten which drug store I stole them from.

"Listen, man, we're not fuckin' around with you." Other Cop raised his tone. "No bullshit games, alright? Just tell us who you got the pills from. Names and phone numbers are the only thing that are gonna save you right now."

"What? No, I mean…there was no guy, there *is* no guy. The pills aren't real, man…they're over-the-counter aspirin or Tylenol or somethin'. I got them at the drugstore, remember? I told you this when you arrested me."

"What?" Other Cop said as Bearded Cop interrupted and told his partner, "Fuck. Yeah, OK, I forgot about that. Jesus, this fuckin' idiot sold me fake pills." He then turned back to me, "Which is still a crime. In fact, it's *basically* the same crime, because you *said* they were Norcos. We got it recorded from the phone call."

"Well, fuck. Yeah, I definitely said that."

"Yeah, you did say that; you texted it too—which we have screenshots of—and also, the money that you took was marked, so you're pretty much fucked. Plain and simple. You're gonna have a court date in about two weeks from now, where you're gonna be convicted, no question 'bout that, but we can put some notes in the file that you were cooperative…if you cooperate."

"OK, well I'm cooperating, I think. Right? I mean…I haven't lied to you yet." I certainly hadn't.

"Yeah, well…we need some names." Other Cop was now fucking me with his eyes.

"What? There's no names. CVS? I don't know what you guys want—"

"Well, you're a fucking junkie, aren't you? So you must buy your dope from someone…. We need names, kid. We need a fuckin' name!" As his partner pounded the desk, Bearded Cop nodded in agreement.

"That's…that's like…a whole different thing." I twisted my head in confusion. "What would that have to do with any of this?"

Before my sentence wrapped, Other Cop opened a manila envelope labeled "Evidence." Upon reaching in, he removed a large blue book—the book that I had placed the fake Norcos in—and slammed it onto the desk. "We got you red fuckin' handed, tryin' to sell dope to a cop, and you're gonna sit here and play games?"

Once again, my spinal cord collapsed. The book that I was staring at—the book that I had hollowed out with a razor blade and shoved fake pain pills into—was the fucking Big Book of Alcoholics Anonymous.

If irony could be defined by a single moment throughout my entire life, this was it. A sign—if you will—that I had majorly fucked up and turned my back on a solution once again.

"Fuck! Fuckin' Goddammit! That's my *Goddamned* Big Book!" My sweaty forehead fell into my outstretched fingers.

"What the hell's a Big Book?" Bearded Cop inquired.

"It's like the main book of Alcoholics Anonymous. Like the fuckin' instruction manual on how to stop being a dumb asshole."

Both cops paused, looked at each other for a moment, then let out an assault of laughter. "Jesus Christ, how can I say this…you're, well—" The laughter started up again. "You're fucked on this one. But you'll, you know, get a public defender, and, well, who knows what'll happen. But my best recommendation would be to try and stay off the dope when they let you outta here, so this can be the *last* time you fuck yourself. Cuz this'll be your first felony, and lemme tell you somethin': once you get one of those, and you don't clean your shit up, you start to get a lot more, quick."

He was right. But the unfortunate part was that my punishment wouldn't do much in the way of alleviating my core problem. I was a drug addict, and I committed this absurd and victimless crime to procure some cash to buy more of the drugs I was addicted to. I should have been mandated to detox and treatment right then and there, but instead I'd end up getting a permanent and debilitating charge on my criminal record. Nowadays I wouldn't have even been arrested, let alone convicted, but that's not a viable solution either. The solution to drug addicts committing crimes to support their habits isn't the decriminalization of said crimes. It's building an infrastructure for treatment of that addiction, so addicts can get clean and establish a foundation for a life worth living. That's how addiction *and* the crime that stems from addiction gets addressed with a single humane remedy. Both the addicts and society win.

Instead of that solution, I spent about five days in a single-man cell, writhing with dopesickness and sleeping no more than a few hours my entire stay. I wasn't directed towards treatment, but I did get a permanent criminal record with too short of a jail sentence to even finish the detox. The problem with being in jail for only five days is that it isn't enough time to completely kick dope, so when you finally get out, you're too sick to enjoy freedom. After that amount of time in withdrawals you might as well just wait it out and stick the landing, but when you're that sick and have no one stopping you, it's basically impossible to not get high.

Damp with mostly evaporated sweat and bones aching to high heaven, I was finally called to see the judge on my last day. I talked with a public defender for all of three minutes, who didn't have much to say other than that I was fucked. Not fucked in the sense that I was going to prison per se but fucked as in I was stone-cold guilty. Dazed with withdrawals, I did exactly what he told me to do: I plead out.

The worst part of getting convicted wasn't the three years of informal probation. It was the fact that I would now be a convicted felon for the remainder of my life. I figured my life wouldn't last much longer, however, so this particular consequence wasn't of much importance to me in the moment. Boy, was I wrong about that. I took the lifelong scarlet letter of a felonious criminal record and three years' probation, and there wasn't a single word uttered about my addiction. The proper deal should have been the option of no felony charge after a mandatory year-long program with job placement. That would have been the truly progressive approach that I hope the rest of society is on the brink of discovering, but it might take a few more years of utter failure to convince the more stubborn. I'm not talking about drug court, and I'm not talking about a twenty-eight-day human warehouse facility. I'm talking about comprehensive, publicly funded long-term treatment centers that equip the formerly addicted with a reasonable shot at prosperity. Psychiatric services, permanent care for those that are mentally unfit, and specified skill-training that feeds people directly into the trades and labor-lacking fields of industry. Some of you probably think I'm dreaming, but you may be in for a surprise before the end of the decade. It all depends on how many more dead bodies those in power are willing to ignore.

A car is the lifeblood of someone who, well, lives in their car. The cops impounded mine when I was arrested, and unless I found a thousand dollars on the ground, the chances of me getting it back were slim. My car was not only my residence, but also the tool in which I made my living. With a car you can middleman, beg for "gas money" at a gas station, drive to different stores and steal things worth stealing, or even just do errands for drug dealers. Being carless doesn't make hustling impossible, it's just a lot more difficult—especially when you're five days into heroin withdrawals. I was most likely done for.

On foot and without a phone (because it was kept by the police for evidence), I begged for money at a train station until I could jostle eight dollars' worth of change in my pocket. Fortunately for me the competition on Skid Row was fierce, so despite being two dollars short for a dime bag, I knew that someone in that godforsaken place would eventually give me a bargain.

I dragged myself down to the main strip and bought a dime, but was too sick to shoot up. Dehydrated and suffering from gooseflesh, my veins were hiding deep within, so I had no choice but to smoke it. This got me feeling OK—not high, but well enough to take a deep breath and think for a moment about a plan of action.

First step was to acquire a government phone—or what is colloquially known as an Obama phone—from one of the vendors outside of the social services office. These things were a godsend. All you had to do was find a vendor (they usually congregated around hospitals, train stations, and anywhere else derelicts frequented), show them proof that you were on food stamps or government assistance, and *bam*: you got a free smartphone. Now, it was never anything fancy, but they always got the job done. Absolutely perfect for a deadbeat like myself.

I called Molly, expecting that she would help me, but what could she really do? She had attempted to help me enough times to no avail, so what was going to make this time any different? She knew that all I wanted was a place to stay where I could plan my next failure (whether I knew that myself or not) so she put her foot down and said there was nothing *she* could do. It was the right move.

Molly did, however, suggest that I call the Midnight Mission, which was a notorious homeless shelter/free rehab in the heart of Skid Row—literally the last house on the block for bums and drug addicts of all persuasions.

I thought that the mere suggestion was obscene and promptly shut it down. I wasn't at that level of desperation yet—in my head—but let's face it: I absolutely was. How a homeless drug addict could be this arrogant and delusional, I'll never quite understand. Our ability to blur the state of our own reality is exceptionally profound.

Los Angeles has a winter, and yes, it's nothing like an East Coast snowstorm, but it's still not fun to sleep on the street in just a wifebeater while you're kicking heroin. I used a cardboard box as an impromptu blanket for the first night, until I found a homeless shelter on Seventy-Ninth and Western in South Central.

They gave me a cot, fed me some spaghetti, and even showed the movie *Troy* on a flat-screen TV for us homeless folk. I presumed this was my life now. I spent the next few days trying to scrounge money and was usually able to get a dime bag before nightfall. I'd return to the shelter, eat spaghetti, watch another sub-par movie, and sleep on my cot before waking up and doing it all over again.

Unable to get enough money to ever truly get high, but at the same time only prolonging my withdrawal process, I was not happy with the way things were going. Being stuck in junkie limbo and getting nowhere fast, the thought of going to the Midnight Mission laid heavy on my mind. Maybe I'd give it a try until I got through my lingering withdrawals—a few weeks, tops. Then I'd be able to get my shit together and figure out a better plan. After finally making my first good decision in what seemed like years, I went to sleep on that cot for the last time.

CHAPTER 10

SKID ROW ROUND TWO

The Midnight Mission was ground zero for all the debauchery that plagued Downtown Los Angeles, compressed within a single city block. The actual building was still standing, but it was the impoverished masses and absolute horror that circumvented the structure that made it resemble the aftermath of a terrorist attack. It looked like a refugee crisis, and in a way it was, only most of the refugees were fleeing the demons in their own heads. Up to a thousand hopeless souls could be surrounding the Mission at any time, and that's not even counting the ones lucky enough to live within its walls. It doubled as a soup kitchen and homeless resource center, which attracted people down on their luck from around the entire county. Coming within ten feet of the courtyard entrance, one quickly realized that lunacy and addiction were at the forefront of the Los Angeles homeless epidemic.

Of course, it wasn't merely laziness, like some of our more conservative brethren have argued time and again, but rather the correlating factors of drug abuse and psychological disorders. No one would live in such a state of decay from mere sloth. Whether it was from the smell of feces and decaying flesh, or the sound of schizophrenic howls directed at invisible ears, the presence of mental illness was so overbearing it was practically contagious.

I arrived the next morning just in time to get a quick bowl of breakfast grits from the soup kitchen. After buying what would be my last bag of heroin for a while, I shot it in the courtyard bathroom, then proceeded inside the building.

Approaching the front desk, I saw several disheveled men sitting in folding chairs to the right of the entrance, and I asked them how I could get into the drug program. They instructed me to take a seat and told me that the intake counselor would come and meet with those seeking treatment around eight in the morning. I shuffled over to the row of chairs, where several other men with similar looks of desperation sat. One of them explained that depending on how many open beds the Mission had, people would be accepted based on whether they'd been in the program before. If you'd never been—which I hadn't—you'd get chosen first. From this, I figured I had a decent chance of getting off the streets that morning, and I was correct.

The intake counselor and I entered a large room that resembled a jail dorm, with roughly 120 bunk beds. People were up and about, slamming dominoes, working out, chatting, laughing, screaming, blasting music through Bluetooth speakers, and anything else that you would associate with general chaos. I still had to spend a few days in the "pre-admit" area before being accepted into the program, so we bypassed the main living quarters, and I was assigned a bed in a room off to the side.

This section of the dorm was partitioned off from the general population, where you were essentially quarantined until you were no longer high. At that point they would evaluate you, see if you were willing and capable to meet the requirements, and if you were, you got assigned a permanent bunk and began the program.

What became clear within a matter of hours was that this place was essentially a prison, except if you misbehaved, your punishment was that you had to leave the prison instead of having to stay for longer. There were no doors on the bathroom stalls, you showered amongst everyone together with dicks on full display, and you slept in a room with nearly 150 men.

I kicked bad the first week—worse than I thought I would have, given that I had only used a small amount of heroin each day after getting out of jail. What made it worse was that an abscess had formed on my right ass cheek from doing a muscle shot a few weeks prior, which needed medical attention a few days into my detox. After getting the abscess lanced (along with a nice shot of Dilaudid for the pain), I ate a chicken salad sandwich at the hospital and got food poisoning. This made for the worst kick I'd ever gone through stomach-wise, and sitting on the toilet with a lanced abscess didn't exactly make things any easier. Still, I persevered (with the help of reading about a dozen books), and after a little over a week I became an official client of the Midnight Mission program.

Calling this place a shitshow would be an understatement, but then again, that goes for most any rehab. This one, however, was quite different in that practically every client was in some state of homelessness prior to entry. Rehabs that take insurance have many amenities like hot tubs, yoga classes, and five-star chefs. This place had prison showers and daily rations of toilet paper. Honestly, it was the way a rehab should be. Who's going to quit smoking crack if the punishment is tri-tip sandwiches and swimming pools? Including the "graduate dorm," there were over two hundred clients in the building, making it the largest rehab I'd ever heard of, and since they didn't take insurance, the clients had to work and make the place run. Everyone had a job and was required to work at least four hours a day, five days a week. This made for a communal atmosphere that I highly enjoyed right away.

I was assigned to the building maintenance department, which mostly consisted of outdoor upkeep. In addition, twice a week we pressure-washed the sidewalk that surrounded the building—which happened to be home to about a thousand homeless people. We'd ask them to move their tents and belongings—which they always did eventually, but only after throwing trash and insults at us. Sometimes someone would say, "Hey, I took a shit in the corner over there. Have fun cleaning it up, cracker," which for some reason didn't bother me too much. After all, I was eating three square meals a day and sleeping in a real bed, which I was grateful for, regardless of the harassment.

Eventually I got a kick out of it every morning, and within a month it went from, "Pick up my shit, white boy," to, "Mornin', Jared." That's usually how it works out. Repetition is the mother of all skills, followed by the ability to not take yourself too seriously. I've found that when you fight fire with humility and humor, a lot of arsonists will eventually dump water on the flames.

I felt comfortable at the Midnight, perhaps for the first time in my life (without drugs or alcohol). It wasn't a cakewalk; the Midnight was not for the faint of heart. There was bad food, hard labor, cramped living quarters, and zero privacy. But I felt a part of. Suffering—on a group level—was invigorating. My ability to connect with other humans had never been stronger, halfway convincing me that I may have had a shot of making it in the world. To my surprise, I socially thrived in the hardship of living at the Midnight and established genuine human connection with the fellow outcasts of society. I was finally amongst a group of people in which I didn't feel completely alone.

Most men that didn't get an SSI check at the Mission were dead broke, and in order to keep up a cigarette-and-instant-coffee habit, we all had a hustle. Some cleaned shoes, others ironed clothes, and a few even made a living renting out their portable DVD players. However, most people figured out a way to turn their assigned job into a profitable trade. If you worked in the laundry department, you could charge people a few bucks to cut to the front of the laundry list, or if you worked in the security department, you could smuggle in goods from the outside. The cigarettes and coffee had to get in somehow, and that's where someone from security would skim off the top. Some "security guards" smuggled in contraband as well, such as porn, drugs, alcohol, and steroids. The vast majority of clients weren't getting high, but enough were that there was a small market for it.

The Midnight was one of the most successful rehabilitation programs for homeless people in the country before SB1380 passed in 2016. This measure ended all funding for housing programs that held sobriety requirements, and in order to keep the doors open, the Midnight had no choice but to eventually give in. Prior to SB1380, The Midnight's success came mostly from the fact that it was a long-term program. As you stayed there and continued to better yourself, you were rewarded with increasingly more independent living quarters. You moved from the prison dorm to your own cubicle after about six months, and then after twelve months you went to the third floor where you got a shared apartment. You could look for a job once you moved to the cubicle dorm and save money while you lived there, and this way you could have a big enough nest egg to ensure a proper foundation once you left. There were therapists, social workers, and teachers all working together to design an individualized path for each client. The goal was to permanently get you off drugs and out of homelessness and lead you on an incremental path of self-sufficiency—if you were mentally and physically capable. Some people qualified for permanent housing because of psychiatric issues, and those people were guided on that path. Others needed legal help, or maybe some schooling to obtain a GED to ensure better employment opportunities, and they were guided down that route. Even with all its flaws, the Midnight Mission was a miracle factory. And if I could have it my way, I'd build programs across the country modeled off the *old* Midnight. It would certainly be better than what we have going on right now.

After a month of working in building services, I transferred to a warehouse job, which had some of the best hustle-capability of any department. I was now working with the plethora of donations, which gave me access to the top-quality toiletries, clothing, and non-perishable food. I was living good, staying sober, and taking advantage of going to AA meetings via the Midnight vans every night. Around this time a new client named Jay arrived in my section of the dorm.

Judging by everything from his attire to his hairstyle, he looked like a genuine artifact from the early aughts. Complete with an outdated leather jacket, a pair of Banana Republic cargo khakis, and a Von Dutch trucker hat slumped over a greasy head of brown hair, Jay had apparently been unconscious since the year 2004.

We hit it off immediately over our shared interest in movie trivia. Apparently, he had been involved in the movie business as a writer and a director on some small projects, before he fell on hard times from an opioid addiction stemming from a motorcycle accident. I didn't believe most of what he told me, until we got ahold of a smuggled-in Obama phone and he showed me his Facebook page. The guy had pictures with everyone from O. J. Simpson to Dustin Hoffman. He even showed me his IMDb page displaying all the credits he had in the business. Nonetheless, Jay's dynamic flair for storytelling sparked a desire within me. If this guy sitting next to me in a homeless shelter had an IMDb page, it wasn't that far-fetched to think that I could write something myself.

One afternoon on the smoke deck, I asked Jay how to really become a writer. He took a long drag from his cigarette, blew the smoke out aimlessly, and said, "Well, the way to become a writer is to write."

Sounds stupid, but here we are.

The only place where we butted heads was on our sobriety. I had thought I'd met my match with consequences after getting a felony conviction, and I was trying to stay focused and really clean up my act—at least until my probation was over.

Jay was just trying to "take a break" from the hard stuff. In fact, he pretty much recreationally used drugs the entire time we were in the Mission, somehow slipping under the radar. The Mission drug tested us semi-regularly, but Jay was able to dodge anything in his path when it came to getting caught. I stayed sober, whereas Jay would sneak a Vicodin or a Xanax here and there, but we both played the game and manipulated the Midnight system to our own advantage. We'd sign out for overnight passes and say we were going to stay at our sponsor's house, but actually go out to nightclubs and try to pick up girls. Jay constantly lied about who we really were, most often coming up with a story that we worked as documentary filmmakers that were making a movie about Skid Row.

After some time and reflection, I'm not even sure if Jay thought he was lying. I think he truly thought he was an undercover client that was simply gathering experience to base his break-out film on. He certainly didn't think he was a drug addict, and maybe he wasn't, given the fact that he could casually take pills without immediately destroying his life. Down the line he'd eventually succumb to utter defeat multiple times over and finally sober up for good. But somehow while he was at the Midnight, he had seemingly un-pickled himself.

Six months had passed, and Jay still had not suffered one negative consequence of his covert drug use in the program. This stunned me to the point that I started to question the entire concept of drug addiction. This is always the beginning of the end for a real drug addict: when you start thinking about shit like you're some kind of philosopher. I've done it too many times to count, and the philosophy always ends up at the same place: I think it's time I try to responsibly use drugs.

That day came on a Friday, when I thought it would be a good idea to take one Vicodin with Jay while we were out on the town. It went swimmingly. I felt wonderful and didn't go off the rails in the slightest. I promised myself I'd only take one, and not only did I stick to my guns, but I also woke up the next morning and had no desire to get high again.

Come Sunday, I thought I'd reward myself for my good behavior with another Vicodin, and by Tuesday, I was back in jail.

Just five days after my initial relapse I got nabbed trying to score heroin, and since I hadn't made the buy yet, I was lucky enough to just get charged with loitering. The next morning I was released, and since my arrest paperwork only said "loitering," I actually convinced the Midnight to let me back in.

Using a bit of deceit and humor, I told them a funny story about how the cops didn't believe I was at the Mission because I was white, and since I wasn't doing anything illegal, they took me in on the bullshit charge.

It worked. They breathalyzed me for safe measure (but skipped a drug test) and let me go back to my bunk. Regardless, the whole thing aroused some suspicion in my counselor, and although the event got lost in the bureaucratic mess of a two-hundred-bed shelter, within a week I was kicked out when I failed a random urine test.

Even after having a brush up with the law and making it back into the Midnight by the skin of my teeth, I found myself completely unable to keep a needle out of my arm. I knew I would eventually get caught and lose my bed, but it didn't matter. Once an addict has had a taste after a lengthy bout of sobriety, heroin always trumps any potential consequence. This fact was as true as it was easy to forget. And although I did relatively well at first and half-heartedly worked a program, my ultimate mistake was not sticking with the winners. I love Jay to this day and I'm glad he's now sober, but he'd be the first to admit he wasn't a good influence back then in the realm of recovery. I was repeatedly told by my counselors, and even other clients, to stay away from him. Unfortunately, it would be years before I'd be lucky enough to get back in a program and utilize such wisdom.

With nothing to do and nowhere to go, I did what all good drug addicts do in such a predicament: I walked down to the social services office and signed up for food stamps and cash relief. Within a few hours I had enough money to get high for a solid two days, which wasn't much, but it was enough to find my footing.

This was not an unfamiliar road for me. Skid Row. Homeless, carless, jobless, loveless, lifeless. I'd traveled down it several years earlier during the Occupy Wall Street protests, so I knew the ropes, but in no way was

I prepared to step back into the shit. I was twenty-six years old with the emotional intelligence of an adolescent child and had nothing to show for myself besides a few good stories and a facial scar. Although I had nothing worth losing, the mere fact of going from square one to square zero was somehow more defeating. I anticipated that no amount of fun would be had during this second interlude.

Peppered with various tales of adventure and amusement, my first go-around on Skid Row hadn't been all that bad. I had been younger, less weathered, and unjaded by the lechery of newfound destitution. When you lose everything, the sheer magnitude of such an event can manically keep your gumption alive. But when you had nothing to begin with and find yourself back in the gutter, the banality of your suffering drains you of any enthusiasm. In my case, apathy defined my final stage of moral bankruptcy. I embarked on a run of drug abuse built upon a foundation of sand. In no way was I enthused, so much so that this time I didn't even try to acquire a tent. I simply un-stashed hidden pieces of cardboard every night and sprawled out on whichever segment of concrete I fancied. A tent implies semi-permanence, whereas cardboard implies "just kill me and throw my body in the river."

After several attempts were made on my backpack while I was sleeping, I moved west into downtown and found a more solitary place to lay my head at night. Now with my backpack tied to my belt loop, I slept with a metal pipe in between my legs to fight off any mid-slumber threats. I'd be lying if I said I never used that metal pipe, and I'd be lying if I said I didn't enjoy every skull-crushing swipe. Although gutless, self-hatred is easily soothed by hurting those that share your peril. I'm not proud of what I did, but you must understand: a man that has lost any desire to live usually finds his moral compass broken.

When you're homeless in Los Angeles, you can apply for a hotel voucher from the social services office. When I caught wind of this, I did what I needed to do to make it happen. It sounds nice: *hotel* voucher. I figured I'd watch cable television, go for a swim, and maybe even take a steam if they had the appropriate amenities.

Upon receiving the voucher, however, I realized that the wording was somewhat misleading. The voucher worked at one place: the Weingart Center, which was more of a fancy homeless shelter than a hotel. You got your own room for an entire two weeks, with a shared bathroom at the end of the hall on each floor. To my dismay, there was no television, no air conditioning, and not even a private shower. Even in the direst of circumstances, I could still find a way to be an ungrateful piece of shit. That's really the universal crux of a drug addict.

I broke into cars and the occasional construction site and stole what I could to get by. At night I'd head back to the Weingart and self-induce a state of temporary schizophrenia. By now I was sometimes shooting crack cocaine—which sounds extreme, but let's face it: just *smoking* the stuff isn't exactly a walk in the park. Mainlining drugs was more industrious, and although smoking crack was quite an enticing ritual in itself, nothing satisfied me more than hacking into my own bloodstream and spiking the well. Sitting naked in the musk of my own extinction, I couldn't help but replicate my parents during that last year that I lived with them. Various crackhead tropes ensued: climbing out onto the window ledge to avoid the FBI hearing me through the electrical outlets, peering under the door for shadows of footsteps that didn't exist, shooting up random pills I found on the sidewalk from earlier in the day, and smoking any little thing from the floor that resembled a piece of crack. This was my heritage, I thought. This was how I was always meant to finally disappear. This was my namesake. This was how everyone around me had known it would end since I was twelve years old.

Within a week of my two-week voucher, The Weingart hotel promptly asked me to leave. Apparently, I had made a mess in the shared bathroom with my own blood. I didn't remember doing this, but given my track record, I took their word for it. The trail of stale blood between the bathroom and my room I discovered upon leaving convinced me that they were probably right.

Like any gentleman that just got kicked out of a crack motel, I promptly overdosed right outside the front lobby and got a free ride to the hospital. It wasn't exactly planned, but talk about good timing. Door-to-door freeloading on the government's dime had officially become an amateur profession of mine, and apparently, I was so good at it that I could still get a grift in sans pulse.

Upon revitalizing me at the hospital and doing some bloodwork, I evidently had a MRSA infection accompanied by sepsis of the blood, which helped formulate the greatest homeless tip I've ever given: if you're dying for a hot shower and a bed to sleep in (free of charge), just pick at an open wound until it turns into a staph infection. With the right amount of determination, they're pretty easy to catch. When you show up at the hospital, not only do you get to skip the line, but they give you your own master suite so you don't infect any of the other patients. You'll be eating Jell-O and watching *The Price Is Right* in no time.

I went to the hospital a lot over the next couple of months. Sometimes they were mental hospitals, and sometimes they were just the normal boring ones. I also went to jail a lot, but LA County was so full that they never held onto me for more than a few days.

I'd frequently run into a guy I knew from the Midnight Mission named Richie, who like me, was running around downtown and doing similarly irresponsible things. Although tall, Richie slinked down enough that his head was no higher than mine, and he had the appearance of someone that had once been a member of an early 2000s pop-punk band. Thin as a toothpick with no front teeth, Richie had a slick aura that probably could have gotten him any chick outside of a Good Charlotte concert. We looked similar in age, but he was probably around thirty-five years old, and I could tell that he was a noble veteran when it came to getting high. He was all about the business of staying loaded, and business always appeared to be good. He boosted, which is a term for professional shoplifting, and this was a street trade that I wasn't all that well versed in. I saw that he made wads of cash day after day, while I was scrounging around trying to steal bikes and winding up little more than empty handed. This man had the secret—the secret to eternal highness—so I made it my mission to fall under his wing.

As a street hustler, it's wise for some to work alone with no one in the way to mess things up. Some people work better in teams, but in Richie's case, he had a decent solo routine that "paid the bills," so to speak. Why would he take a chance and let me into the operation? In what way was I going to be a positive addition to his business model? One night I stole a purse with multiple credit cards in it, and in the morning, I went to find Richie and let him join in on the loot.

I often stole credit and debit cards, which aren't worth anything unless you know what to do with them. I knew a guy in Chinatown that ran a liquor store, and he'd sell me cartons of cigarettes with any credit card and no ID. A pack of Newports was selling in the stores for about nine bucks at the time, so I could go downtown and sell packs for five dollars like hot cakes. No matter how many cartons of cigarettes I showed up with, I'd sell out within half an hour.

I told Richie to come along with me and he could take the day off from boosting. Although being known as a fast-cash hustle, boosting was extremely stressful and time consuming as a full-time gig back then. There was still *some* risk involved, unlike now where it seems to be a free-for-all in many cities. He obliged, and we spent a few hours together shooting dope and lounging in an alley, discussing life on the streets and what we did to keep it going. I was just your average street junkie—stealing what I could, scamming social services, and middle-manning dope to suburban kids that were too scared to cold-cop on Skid Row.

But Richie had what I liked to call a junkie trade. He woke up and went to work every day, doing the same thing, and made good money doing it. He told me that he was making over $250 a day (tax-free, mind you). The junkie American dream.

"Yeah, man, I got a good thing goin'. Been doin' it off and on since like, 2010 or somethin', but things have definitely gotten a lot harder recently. They're locking a lot of things up now, and not only that, most of these drugstores in LA know me at this point and call the police the second I step in the parking lot. I've been havin' to bus out further and further just to hit stores that don't recognize me. That's ninety percent of the job, just fuckin' traveling." Richie explained, as we sunk deeper into a back-alley couch and chain-smoked cigarettes.

"Well, it sounds like a good gig, shit…it sounds a lot better than what I do." I took a drag from my hand-rolled cigarette and continued, "I mean, I steal shit too, but I'm barely making any cash some days. I steal stupid shit."

"You gotta start boostin', my boy. You'd make a killin' right off the bat cuz none of these stores recognize you. You'd go unnoticed anywhere for months. Shit, maybe years." Richie croaked.

"Yeah, but I don't know how to do it. I mean it sounds pretty straight-forward, but I don't know the ins and outs of it...like you, you know?" I paused. "But what if I went with you and kinda learned how to do it? Like you took me in as an apprentice, you know? I'd split the payout with you, and that way it would take a li'l stress off your back."

"Fuck...well, listen, man. I usually run solo, almost always have...but you seem, you seem like a chill dude. And we get high on the same shit. I like that. None of that meth shit, just crack and dope. I guess if we worked together, there'd be less chance of getting jumped or busted by the cops." Richie was starting to nod his head in acceptance.

"But wait, hold up. What about this?" I was inspired. "You walk into the drug stores, and they follow you immediately, right?" A lightbulb went off above my empty skull. "Well, what if we had a system where you walked in and got everyone followin' your ass, and then I come in like a minute later, unguarded and unwatched. All the focus is on you, while I rob the fuckin' place blind. You just kinda take all the heat to some other aisle while I hit the ones that actually have the good shit. That's, like...maybe a really good idea, right?"

"Fuck.... Yeah, man, that *is* a good idea."

And that was it. Richie and I were partners from then on out.

Any part of LA that could be reached by train or bus, we went. We went, and we stole. Then we went back and stole some more. We hit every drug-store we could think of and bled it dry. We stole razors, teeth whitener, skin products, Rogaine, makeup, and over-the-counter heartburn medication; anything our fence was willing to buy, we were willing to steal. We had sev-eral main fences (a professional recipient of stolen property), all of whom gave us lists of items that they needed, and we always delivered.

Nessa, who was our go-to, would front us a hundred bucks every morning to get the necessary drugs needed to function, and we'd pay him back before lunchtime. We'd go on one run in the late morning and one later in the day and make anywhere from fifty to three hundred dollars a run. Sometimes you showed up to a store and someone had just boosted everything right before you, and sometimes you made hundreds of dollars in five minutes. The real work was getting to the stores. Some of them took hours to get to by bus, but when you're boosting every day, it's a must to diversify the areas that you boost in.

I got along exceptionally well with Richie. Most of the homeless folk running around our area were strictly tweakers, but neither Richie nor I used crystal meth. He didn't like the way it made him feel, and I had lost my taste for it. I knew that when I did meth, I got weird, and when I got weird, I wound up getting put in a suitcase or a jail cell. I was able to put the meth down for good, and I couldn't have done it without the help of crack. I grew to absolutely adore the stuff because of this fact. So much so that I smoked it around the clock. We both loved crack so much that even if we made $500 in a day, we'd be broke by the late evening and have to do a nighttime boost. Out of the year I spent on the streets with Richie, only a handful of times did we wake up with a spare twenty-dollar bill.

Heroin and crack, although a magnificent combination, loses its punch as your tolerance rises. This is when you need a third player to join the game. Klonopin, which is a benzodiazepine like Xanax, became that third player for me. It's a drug that I don't find all that much fun to ingest on its own, but taking five at a time with some heroin really brings out the best in both substances. After a while, even swallowing *ten* at a time becomes lackluster, so then you have no choice but to bring out the big guns. I found myself shooting Klonopin with heroin at the same time, and let me tell you something: I'm not trying to brag. I'm really not. But shooting benzos and heroin at the same time is literally a death wish. It's pretty much the most hardcore shit you can do drug-wise, and we were doing it for breakfast. Sometimes we'd break down crack with lemon juice, and shoot crack, Klonopin, and heroin all at once. We were indestructible. For two guys that wanted nothing more than to fall asleep and never wake up, we just couldn't die. We even had a golden rule: if one of us overdosed, the other one took an oath to walk away without calling the paramedics. Both of us wanted to die, but neither one of us had the balls to actually follow through with a plan. Instead of jumping off a bridge or hanging ourselves with a makeshift noose, we were both too weak to take charge of our desire. We figured with the amount of drugs we were doing that death was just around the corner, and like the cowards that we were, all responsibility would fall on our maker.

Above all else, there was complete transparency and honesty between the two of us. We absolutely never stole from each other or ripped each other off. When we bought heroin, we cooked the entire bag, sucked it up with one syringe, counted the milliliters, and squirted half of the liquid into another syringe. I held the drugs while Richie held the cash, until he got too high on Klonopin one day and dropped over $200. After that, we switched.

On Fourth and Flower, there was an exceptional hotel called the Bonaventure. It had about half a dozen glass elevators that granted its passengers one of the best views in Los Angeles. Being decrepit drug addicts, Richie and I never actually stayed at the Bonaventure, but we did set up camp right next to it under a freeway off ramp. We had sleeping bags and pillows stashed, which we retrieved every night and set up on a flat segment of walkway. Sleeping next to another person was much safer, in that a fellow homeless on the prowl seemed less likely to fuck with two men as opposed to one. Still, logic and reasoning are not always at the forefront of a pilferer's mind, so we did experience the occasional attempted backpack thievery. Heavily armed with weapons of melee, we rarely entered an altercation that didn't result in our victory. We were the "crazy white boys" of Skid Row that could out-steal you, out-smoke you, and if push came to shove, stab someone that got in our way.

These were the most reprehensible days of my life, yet I felt vindicated with the purest feelings of glory. I was homeless, mentally ill, malnourished, infected, unwashed, and enslaved to constant injection of poison into my bloodstream. I was a nameless cadaver like the ones under any overpass that you drive by every single day. But I was finally good at it.

We made more money than most of the normal citizens that brushed past us in disgust, yet we laid our decomposing bodies on concrete every night. Once every few weeks we'd sneak into a hotel pool and rinse off, but besides that, we were layered in whatever chemicals were excreted through our drug-soaked pores. Shasta Cola and Little Debbie pastries were the only food we consumed, despite making over $2000 a week in untaxed revenue. On rare occasions we'd splurge and get a bacon-wrapped hot dog from a street vendor. When our socks would start meshing into the flesh of our feet, we'd peel them off and go steal a pack of fresh ones. Changing our underwear was a similar process. With pockets full of twenty-dollar bills, we bought loose cigarettes one at a time, never paid for public transportation, and God forbid if we ever splurged on a forty-dollar-a-night Skid Row motel room. Every dollar went to maintaining our drug habit. A minimum of one hundred dollars each a day for heroin, and the rest on crack and Klonopin.

Eventually we both ran out of veins in our arms and had to resort to less desirable body parts to poke. We often helped one another by shooting each other up in our necks. If a car side mirror was available, I could inject my neck myself, but we usually had to rely on teamwork. We taunted strangers, punched security guards, urinated wherever we pleased, and mugged anyone drunk enough or alone enough when the bars closed. Pardon me for stealing an antiquated phrase, but we were a complete and utter menace to society. Scum of the earth, freefalling straight into an early grave or a lengthy prison term: whichever happened to come first.

Although generally rotten, Richie was at least intriguing. Born in Wisconsin to a couple that would eventually divorce, he went through some tribulations as a child, but for the most part was raised in a normal home. He excelled at dirt biking, eventually making his way into the professional racing circuit. This led to motocross, and by the time he was sixteen he was sponsored by numerous companies and traveling across the country. Not too long into his motocross career, he had a terrible accident (which is how he lost all his front teeth the first time) and was hospitalized for many months. Like most people that sustained critical injuries in the early 2000s, Richie was prescribed copious amounts of Oxycontin, and, well, you know the rest of the story. From oxy, he moved to heroin (which happens to most of us), and with the exception of a short prison sentence, he had been getting high for over a decade. For a guy with no front teeth, he was relatively handsome, but he was a thirty-five-year-old man with the attitude of an angsty teenager. Not exactly a persona that had a draw with high-quality women. He was absolutely the most bitter and negative person I'd ever met, yet his companionship was thoroughly comforting. It shouldn't have been, but then again, his social toxicity was only soothing to someone like myself who shared his hatred for reality. We were brats. Sociopathic, delusional man-children that would have jumped at any chance to be coddled by the society that we loathed.

Being top notch in the loyalty department, Richie made me feel safe—both physically and emotionally. In a brotherly way we loved each other, and it wasn't just for the fact that our shoplifting operation required such a harmony. We simply had no one else. This was a sort of medieval brand of comradery. We literally fought for our lives amongst each other as brothers in arms. If one of us was taking a hit off a crack pipe, the other one was always on the lookout for an oncoming threat—be it a police cruiser or an envious crackhead looking for fisticuffs. Getting sucker-punched while smoking crack wasn't exactly a rare occurrence for a skinny white kid on Skid Row. In fact, we got sucker-punched all the time. If one of us got sucker-punched, the other would swing a chain, thrust a knife, or crack a skull with whatever weapon was available, and eventually our reputation outweighed most people's desire to give us trouble. Our drug dealers always came to our aid as well because we happened to be some of the greatest customers on Skid Row.

Months went by, seasons changed, and the routine continued like clockwork; all the while I still couldn't get high enough to drown out the shame of who I'd become. One of us would go to jail for a quick slap on the wrist here and there, while the other would hold down the fort, which was much more difficult emotionally than it was operationally. Being a complete piece of shit is a lot easier when you have a partner in crime. Still, these were also hard times since our shoplifting system worked much better with two people, but we always survived. We'd always be there for each other when we got out of jail, welcomed back to freedom with a nice big shot of heroin.

Our shenanigans continued into the winter, when the environment started to get the best of us. Our bodies had deteriorated from months of horrendous drug consumption, which only became more apparent when the temperature started to drop. The December rain didn't help either, exacerbating the rotting of our feet. With our ability to walk long distances diminished, work became harder to get done. The lack of operable veins in my body made getting high a near impossible chore as well. Things hadn't necessarily been going well during the warmer months prior, but when making enough money to stay obliterated became more difficult than ever, I started to want out.

There was no family to save me, or detox to check into, which left me with two options: die or go to jail. Obviously, death was the preferred solution, but when you really get close to ending your own life—I'm talking "leaning over a bridge" close—the idea of God weighs heavy on your mind. What if I was wrong and there really was an afterlife? It sounds completely absurd, but I'm telling you: on the brink of committing suicide, you become a lot more open-minded to such a notion.

Richie and I would often stand on the Figueroa walking bridge and discuss the possibility of Hell. We'd contemplate when it would be time to throw in the towel and cook up one final hot shot (a purposeful injection of a lethal dose of heroin). A major issue develops, however, when your heroin tolerance grows to astronomical proportions. You're strung out to the point that you want to die, but your tolerance has gotten so out of hand that you might not be able to fit enough heroin in a needle to kill yourself. At this point our veins were so haggard that shooting up was our biggest source of stress, sometimes taking up to an hour of digging to finally hit something still connected to our circulatory systems. Streams of dried blood covered every article of our clothing as if getting high had become a literal battle.

Malnutrition and dehydration weren't helping the fact that I was always struggling to find an exploitable vein. I found myself one night on an external cement staircase on Fourth and Flower outside of the Bonaventure Hotel. Stripped down to just my boxer briefs, I was dripping blood from every appendage after dozens of failed attempts at intravenous injection. At my wits' end, screaming out of pure defeat, I poked around every visible vein in both my ankles to no avail. I could hear city workers pressure washing the lower part of the staircase, making their way up to the blood-soaked steps that I was perched on.

I started bawling. Tears poured down my face in the same direction that blood streaked down my lifeless arms and legs. The city workers turned the corner and found me lying nearly naked in the fetal position, loaded needle in hand, crying like an abandoned child. I *was* abandoned. Heroin was the warm embrace of a mother that I hadn't had in nearly two decades, and in that moment, it was rejecting me from an arm's length away. Richie approached seconds later, who was also unable to hit a vein, and we cried in each other's arms. Two hardened men covered in their own blood, weeping away and grasping one another in an attempt to fill the maternal void.

Shortly after, Richie and I broke the cardinal rule and bought a ten-dollar bag of meth. Although undesirable, smoking a little speed could be used strictly as a tool to raise our blood pressure and expose some new veins. We knew that getting tweaked would be bad for business, but if we were going to successfully shoot heroin that night, it was our only hope. The plan worked and we got our shots off, but I still couldn't stop crying.

A two-week stint in jail wasn't going to save me; I needed to do a small prison term to truly remove myself from the grip of dope. Prison wasn't the best solution imaginable, but unfortunately, it was the best solution available to people like me at the time. In order to live long enough to see my thirties, I needed long-term *forced intervention*. Many don't like to hear that, but it's my honest opinion. I was too strung out to go back *and stay* at the Midnight without a medical detox, of which none were easily accessible for people like me with no resources. And even if there were, I was too mastered by my addiction to voluntarily complete that kick. On my knees, palms clasped together, I prayed, "Kill me or put me in prison. Please, God. I can't do this anymore. You must help put an end to this.... Kill me or lock me up. Amen."

Whether God is real, or whether it was just the result of a self-fulfilling prophecy, my prayer was answered in haste. Something must have had its eye on me, because I was fighting a prison sentence not twenty-four hours later.

CHAPTER 11

5300

The next morning I was hungry and in need of an outlet to charge my Obama phone, so I wandered towards the public library and left Richie alone at camp. The downtown public library, although glorious in its book catalog, was little more than a place for the mentally ill to take bird baths and escape the rain. I usually only went there for brief moments to use the electricity.

Still incensed by the revelation of the night prior, I charged my phone for a moment so I could call Molly. She had never lost total contact with me throughout my LA journey, even visiting me on Skid Row from time to time to give me a hug and buy me a meal. Over five years sober at that point, Molly was a resource of hope and possible solutions, although there wasn't much that could be done for a drug addict with no agency, let alone health insurance, at the time. I needed to go to rehab—which was out of Molly's control—but I figured that if I called and made it apparent that I was on the brink of death, she'd let me sleep at her place and maybe start a methadone program. Thank God she didn't.

Unlike any library I'd ever been to, this library had a food court. It featured a Panda Express—a homeless gem, in that everything comes in a Styrofoam container, so digging through one of their trash cans usually produced a half-eaten, garbage-free meal. I figured that I'd head over and try my luck while chatting with Molly. With one hand occupied holding my phone, I wasn't in the greatest position to sift through garbage, so instead I vultured over to the dining area to pick off abandoned trays.

A woman stood up and left several pieces of orange chicken on her tray, tempting me to make a move. All while still talking to Molly, I approached the tray and began plucking pieces into my mouth, when out of nowhere, I received a jab to the side of my skull. Someone fucking punched me. Was it the lady? Who would assault someone over a few pieces of orange chicken?

Completely stunned, I dropped my phone mid-conversation and watched it bounce on the tile floor. I then put my hands up and turned towards my attacker. To my surprise, it wasn't the rightful owner of the orange chicken, but instead I was staring straight into the eyes of a fellow crackhead.

"Mothafucka, getchyo nasty-ass fingers out my chicken. The hell's wrong witchu, boy!" yelled an older gentleman whose words were accompanied by flying spit.

"What the fuck are you talkin' about!? This ain't your food, motherfucker!" I rebutted.

"That *is* my food! And you best be payin' me for it after you stuck yo dirty-ass hands in my shit!" This man was making a bold statement that we both knew was a complete lie.

"Bitch, I'm not payin' you shit! You're lyin' through your fuckin' teeth right now. You punched me in the face for that shit? Fuckin' orange chicken! Are you fuckin' crazy?" I screamed as the employees made their way from behind the counter.

"Listen up, you li'l punk-ass bitch, you're gonna pay me for that food, or I'm callin' the police!" This guy was bold as hell. I was fucking impressed.

"Listen, man, you nutty motherfucker—I ain't payin' for shit. We're two crackheads fighting over leftovers. What the fuck are the police gonna do?!" I screamed as library patrons started to migrate towards the altercation. "They're gonna take *your* ass to jail if anything, cuz you fuckin' punched me. Over Goddamn orange chicken!"

"Yeah, well"—he bent down and extended his hand over my phone—"I'm takin' this shit and ain't givin' it back until you pay me my ten dollas. How 'bout dat?"

This man now had my property in his hands. Punching me in the face while I was eating was one thing, but holding my phone hostage was a level of disrespect that warranted a physical reaction. In no way could I let this guy punk me for my phone, but how could I stop him? I could start a fist fight in a Panda Express like a gentleman, or I could turn up the burners and dump gas on this fire. I had a knife in my back pocket, which I carried for moments like this—so from a meth-induced perspective, it seemed like the most appropriate time to utilize it.

Now wielding a blade in front of an uneasy fast-food restaurant staff, I had crossed the point of no return.

My foe laughed, then said, "Man, are you serious? You gonna stab my ass? Let me tell you somethin', bitch: you pull a knife on me, you better use it."

I looked at the knife, then him, then the patrons, who—although startled—were enraptured along with the Panda Express staff. I realized he was right. If you pull a knife on someone, *you better use it*, or else you might look like a bitch. This is not sound logic, but I was running on nothing but a few bites of orange chicken and low-grade speed, so this was the best I could come up with. An awkward amount of time passed before—like a casual loon—I lunged forward, he lurched back, and my attempt at stabbing was foiled. How anticlimactic. Fortunately, my less-than-heroic moment was swept under the rug for the time being. Security guards arrived directly after the failed barrage and promptly restrained both me and my opponent.

The cops that arrived on the scene were not pleased with what probably wasn't their first crackhead kerfuffle of the day. I lied and said that I hadn't tried to stab anyone, and even though I believed I was *legally* in the right, I figured the truth would only complicate things. All I did, according to my lyin' self, was pull the knife out. My assaulter disagreed, along with a few witnesses, and their claim was confirmed once the police looked over the surveillance footage. Still, the guy sucker-punched me, so I took a knife out and tried to stab him. Doesn't that somehow level out?

Can't we just call that a draw? The short answer was no.

What this is called in the state of California is "assault with a deadly weapon." Not exactly a small deal in the eyes of the law. In fact, it's a violent felony, and when you're already on felony probation, this isn't a good combo. I was going to jail, but I wasn't necessarily going to stay there. I was probably going to prison, which if you don't remember, was exactly where I had wanted to get sent to the night before. Coincidence? Maybe. None of us will ever know for sure, but nonetheless, I was relieved that my wish was granted.

I could have gone for just a regular felony—a violent felony was a bit harsh in my opinion—but all I needed was a sentence, and a sentence is what I would finally get. The only glimmer of hope I could see was through the bars of a jail cell, which is tragically ironic, but a truth that I had to accept. I needed to be locked away from the captivity of my hijacked mind, or I would surely die.

Richie had done time in prison, so on account of the prospect that I would inevitably get pinched, he had coached me thoroughly on what to expect. He told me that I'd need to join a gang based on my race, which I wasn't thrilled about—but apparently this was my only option. Being a Jew, it didn't seem like I would mesh well in a white power gang, but he assured me to just play it cool. "Don't go in there with a fuckin' yarmulke on, just be casual and don't tell anyone," he'd explained to me. Alright, I could do that. I could pass for a non-Jew if need be.

I sat in a holding cell for a few days until they transferred me to Men's Central Jail (MCJ) to be put in a medical pod. I was kicking heroin harder than ever before—and they knew it—so I'd have to stay under medical supervision for a week before they'd put me in General Population.

I spent a lot of time throwing up, shaking in my bed, sweating through my crusty mattress pad, and hallucinating from the inability to sleep. Standard junkie routine. Even though it was the worst kick I'd ever experienced, jail was the perfect place to get it over with. No rent needed to be paid, no job needed to be gone to, and most importantly, I couldn't fucking leave and get high. That simplified the process. With the exception of the occasional bout of diarrhea and vomiting, I hibernated in the fetal position and tried to stay stagnant.

After a few days of this, I could finally hold down a peanut butter and jelly sandwich and occasionally left my bunk to chat with the other inmates. Someone came into the pod with a deck of cards, and a couple of younger Black guys asked if anyone wanted to play spades. I figured it might be good if I played and tried to get my mind off the kick for a few minutes, so I obliged. As I took a seat and the cards got dealt out, two white guys approached me with concern.

One of them said, "Hey, brother, why don't you step over here, we need to talk to you about something."

"Alright…like, before I play?" I asked.

"Yeah, you're gonna have to sit this one out," said the younger, shorter one as he gestured for me to stand up from the table. This guy was probably in his late twenties, didn't stand taller than five foot five, and if it weren't for his array of swastika tattoos, he could have passed for Latino. Both men took me to a corner, shook my hand, and introduced themselves. The younger, shorter one went by Crash, and the older one's name was Cliff.

"First time locked up, brother?" Cliff asked.

"Well…I mean, I've been to jail before. No longer than a few weeks though." I paused. "This is my first time in Men's Central; I've never made it out of the Glass House on Temple Street."

"Is this your first time in blues?" Crash was referring to the blue jumpsuit we were all given in exchange for our street clothes.

"Yeah, first time in blues."

"Alright, well MCJ ain't the Glass House. This the real deal, my boy, and we're all goin' to general pop or prison from here on out," Cliff said as he put his arm on my shoulder, "and there's a lot of rules, big dog, a lot of 'em, and you just broke a cardinal one."

Trying to mask my panic, I emphasized my naïveté and said, "Ah, shit. I'm sorry man…I really don't know what's goin' on; I mean no disrespect."

"It's all good, brother. It's just politics, and they don't really apply here in the medical pod…but if someone caught wind that you were playing cards with some niggers and we *didn't* do nothin' to stop it, well, then, that ain't good for us down the road, you feel me?" Crash explained, not holding back with the slur. This was discomforting. Here I was, a Jew, taking advice from a man with multiple swastika tattoos, casually dropping N-bombs. This was not good.

"OK, OK…I get it, so rule number one: don't play cards with the Blacks. Alright, anything else I shouldn't do with them?" I asked.

"Well, yeah." Cliff scratched his handlebar moustache and continued, "You shouldn't do *anything* with them. Why would you wanna?"

"Um…yeah, yeah, you're right. I don't know what I was thinkin'. Sorry, guys, I'm just kickin' dope real hard right now—not thinkin' straight." I tried to sound agreeable.

"It's alright, my boy, just know that if it ain't white, then it ain't right." Crash pointed at the skin on his arm then continued, "There's a lot more to this politics shit, but you'll get the hang of it. Wherever you end up, whether it's a dorm or a tier, the white boys will come up to you right away and go over the rules of the pad. But shit, you might get out before you even make it to a dorm, though. What're you in for?"

"Uh…assault with a deadly weapon."

"Oh yeah, you ain't leavin' anytime soon. You got a good case?" Cliff asked.

"Well…it happened in a Panda Express, and there's video footage—"

Crash interrupted, "I'm just gonna be honest with you, big dog. You're probably headin' to prison…but it's all good, prison's where boys become men. And the food's way better. Shit, if it's your first offense, you ain't doin' more than eighteen months."

"Cool. Good to know." Good to fucking know.

Prison culture was apparently much more racist than I had anticipated. This was unsettling both because I wasn't a racist myself and because I was in fact half Jewish by blood. I may not have looked like Mel Brooks, but I was bar mitzvahed—which pretty much made me a card-carrying member of the tribe. I knew I could get by on my Anglo-esque appearance, but my last name was probably going to become an issue. *Klickstein.* I mean, it's no Goldberg or Cohen—but it doesn't exactly scream white power. Also, I wasn't excited to pretend I was something that I wasn't. It was cowardly, but I was in no shape to cause a ruckus. In the moment I didn't care about what was morally right, I just wanted to do my time and avoid any hardships at all costs—minus the cost of my dignity. I just didn't know how possible it was to hide my true identity for eighteen months, and more importantly, to be potentially dealing with the consequence of getting called out. Could I pretend to be a white supremacist for a year and a half? Probably not well, but I was willing to give it a try if it meant I wouldn't have to spend my whole term fighting for my life.

Shortly after my riveting conversation with Cliff and Crash, I went to see a jail doctor, who prescribed me ibuprofen and weighed me. I clocked in at 131 pounds, and I'd already been in custody for a week, so I figured at the time of my arrest I was no more than a buck twenty-five. The ibuprofen—a nice gesture—was going to do little in the way of helping me with my withdrawals, but I couldn't complain. Time was the only healer, and I was about to have a lot of it at my disposal.

After my visit with the doctor, I graduated to the next level of processing. I was moved from my medical pod to the 2100 block of the jail. There I was housed in a single-man cell with open bars, cropped in a row with about twenty other inmates. This was hell. Something about being locked alone in a cage yet being able to hear the deafening chatter of nineteen other nameless and faceless prisoners was even lonelier than simply being alone. This went on for nearly ten days until a CO announced that bunks had become available in one of the school dorms. I didn't know what a school dorm was, but it sounded less torturous than a single-man cell, so I immediately volunteered.

The next day a guard let me out of my cell and escorted me to dorm 5300. He waved to the pod commander who sat on the other side of a tinted-glass window, and as the steel door unlocked and creaked open, it revealed a room smaller than a tennis court with a hundred men living in it. Fifty bunk beds, about ten chairs, three tables, and one flat-screen TV. Within seconds of entering, a shirtless, husky white man approached and extended his tattooed hand for a shake. "Hey, brother, you run Wood?" he asked.

"Um, yeah, I'm a Wood." I tried to sound like I knew what I was talking about.

"Good shit, brother. My name's Jon Jon; welcome to the pad." Now I noticed that the tattoo on his hand was a swastika.

"Well, thanks, my name's Jared. This is actually my first time in a dorm." I replied.

"Well, you're lucky, cuz we got a pretty tight-knit crew in here. Shit runs smooth—races are getting along—you got in the right dorm, brother." Jon Jon motioned for me to follow him towards the back of the room, then continued, "Come meet our rep, Ian. Real solid white boy, naps a lot, but let's see if he's awake."

As we walked through the pathway in between the rows of bunk beds, I waded through a sea of convicts in various states of leisure. Some were playing cards, others were chatting amongst each other, and through all the initial chaos, there seemed to be some order. I was immediately reminded of my first moment at the Midnight Mission. An overwhelming smell of testosterone made the room feel even more cramped than it already was, but unlike the powder keg that you'd expect, it was more a semblance of inter-connected suffering. One hundred men confined to the same shithole, counting away the days and trudging the path of least resistance.

"Hey, Jared—you said Jared, right? Let me see your paperwork. Gotta make sure you ain't no snitch or kiddie-toucher or nothin'. Just protocol, brother. We check every Wood that comes through that door," Jon Jon said as I handed him my crumpled rap sheet. He looked over it as we closed in on Ian's bunk. "*Hmmm*, last name Klickstein, huh?"

"…Yup." I froze for a second, then gutlessly repeated my surname with a bit of German flair: "…Klickschtein."

"Sounds German. You German, my boy?" Jon Jon lowered his brow and stared straight down at me.

"Um, yeah," I lied. "I mean, I was born here, but yeah, my lineage is…German."

Jon Jon smirked, looked down at Ian, who was lying awake in his bunk, then pounded his chest and gave out a mighty Sieg Heil salute. "We got a purebred!"

"Shut the fuck up with that Nazi shit! You're gonna scare the kid." Ian sat up now from his bunk and shook my hand. "We're not Nazis; we're Peckerwoods. Well, Jon Jon's a Nazi, and Jimmy over there's a Nazi too… but most of us just plain ol' Woods. Welcome to Fifty-Three Hundred, my boy, I'm Ian, your shotcaller."

Ian, who was covered in crudely done prison tattoos, had a large head with a slightly bloated yet handsome face that looked roughly thirty-five years old. He stood a couple inches taller than me, about five foot ten, with a conventional frame that sported a bit more muscle than flab. He wasn't physically intimidating because of his build—which was rather average—

but more so because of the volatility that emitted from his feral eyes. Within moments of first conversing, Ian displayed several tics that some would associate with a mild case of Tourette's syndrome but were most likely a result of long-term meth abuse. Either way, they only added to the distress of his persona. His verbal cadence was maniacally choppy, leaving little room for his cutting wit to be caught by anyone with a slow mind. Out of everyone I met during my entire imprisonment, Ian had the sharpest sense of humor, yet in most arenas of thought, he was an absolute moron. The case for his intellect wasn't helped by the fact that he ended almost every sentence with an ironically emphasized "Mahhhhh boyyyyyy!" Regardless, I was captivated by his high-strung energy and peculiarity.

"So listen, big dog, take a seat here, on my bunk, don't worry, you can always sit on my bunk, just ask, any white boy's welcome, but make sure your pants are clean! No doo-doo stains, or we're gonna have *major* problems, we clear, mah boy!?" Ian rattled off while laying out his secondary bedding and gesturing for me to sit down. Jon Jon shortly followed and took a seat to my right.

"Now if it's your first time dealin' with politics, it's gonna seem like a lot to take in. There's a lot of rules, so many fuckin' rules, and you'll definitely wind up breakin' a few." Ian paused to take a seat to the left of me, then continued, "It's all good though, my boy. There ain't a Wood in here that hasn't slipped up at some point. Shit, ask Jon Jon what happened to him last week! We beat the brakes off 'im, but we did it with love."

"That's right!" Jon Jon piped up.

"But the important thing is that we take our consequences like men. It's just a part of this kind of life that…well, you're now a part of, my boy. Do you like to fight?"

"Do I like it, I mean, I…am willing to fight. I just came in off Skid Row, where it's not exactly peaceful." I didn't know how to answer. The truth was that I didn't like to fight at all, but I was in jail now. I had to be careful with how I presented myself.

"Well, I'm gonna be honest with you. Ya look like dog shit right now, like you're dying from cancer or some shit." Ian looked me up and down. "What I mean is that you don't look like you'd take well to a punch at the moment—which is OK, some of us come in rough. I've been there myself, my boy. But after a few weeks, you'll get your weight back up, but right now if I were you, I'd *really* try to not break any rules."

Embarrassed, but knowing he wasn't wrong, I responded, "Yeah, I've been on a sick one the past year or so. And I'm still pretty fuckin' dopesick, but I'll level out in a week or two. So what're the rules?"

"Well, it's pretty simple. You don't share food with the Blacks, you don't shower with 'em, trade with 'em, sit on their bunks, over-associate with 'em, I mean, you can talk to 'em and be friendly…but keep it short and sweet, my boy." Ian continued, "It's a respect thing. It's to maintain the peace between the races. The more you associate with them, the higher the chance that somethin' kicks off, then all of a sudden, *boom*: we got a race riot, and if somehow *you* kick off a race riot, I'll personally make sure that you'll be leavin' this dorm in a stretcher. Nothin' personal. That's just how shit works in here."

"OK, makes sense," I said with my best straight face. "What about the Southsiders?"

"The homies? that's different. We run with 'em, so we can eat together, shower together, all that shit. But you gotta maintain the highest level of respect with those fuckers. Just cuz the whites and the Mexicans get along, doesn't mean shit can't go down, so if you ever have a problem with a Southsider, you come talk to me first before you do any dumb shit. Cuz if you somehow start a race riot with the *Mexicans*, my boy, I'll personally make sure you leave here in a body bag. I ain't tryin' to fight sixty Mexicans in this tiny-ass dorm, and I'm sure you don't want that either, my boy."

Jon Jon threw in his worthless two cents: "Just think of it like the Mexicans got straight hair like us, so we're not all that different, you know? They're sorta white, just…browner."

"…OK, copy that. So what happens if I do accidently break a rule?" I asked, assuming there was some kind of graduated warning system.

"My boy,"—Ian smirked—"you'll find out soon enough. Depends on the rule, though. If it's small, you might just have to do a hundred and twenty-three burpees. But if it's anything involvin' the other races or cleanliness, it's a three-on-one beat down for twenty-three seconds. I'll throw you in the next boo-bop, let you get a feel for it. They happen on the daily, my boy."

Jesus Christ. I was in no shape to fight a small child, let alone three grown convicts. My bones were so brittle from malnourishment that a standard body punch would have collapsed my ribcage. In all honesty, this moment was the most terrified I'd ever felt in my life. Ian made it clear that violence was going to be an integral part of this experience—that it was essentially unavoidable—and given my withdrawal-induced frailty, I felt like I wouldn't make it out of my first fight alive.

Even when I was in peak physical shape, I had always been one to avoid violence. As a young child, I was prone to fighting, but from a lack of siblings I was never primed to handle physical conflict from adolescence onward. In addition to this, I was on the smaller side of an average full-grown man, although seeing the way Youngster and Shadow fought back in my Occupy LA days made me realize that size didn't always matter. Still, I was nearly forty pounds underweight, but more importantly, I didn't have the fortitude for violence when sober. I was either going to have to change this or figure out a way to garner respect without the use of my fists.

Still brain-fogged from the withdrawals, it seemed impossible that I wouldn't slip up. Not sharing food with Black inmates, although racist and stupid, seemed relatively easy to obey. It was the laundry list of miscellaneous rules that had me distraught. There were a dozen rules pertaining to appropriate shoe wear in the showers alone, never mind the endless number of rules of how and where to properly use a toilet. If you didn't wash your hands after taking a piss and someone saw you, you had to go to the back and get the shit kicked out of you for twenty-three seconds. If you saw someone not wash their hands after taking a piss and you didn't tell on him, and then someone saw that you witnessed it and didn't tattle, you had to go to the back for twenty-three seconds. The whole system ironically relied on the act of snitching.

By chance I ended up on a top bunk above the Southsider rep. He, unlike Ian, was relatively sane, mild-mannered, and commanded a great amount of respect from everyone in the dorm. Cito was in his mid-forties, had spent his entire life in and out of custody, and besides his crippling meth addiction that spawned his criminality, I grew to believe that he was a decent man. The Southsiders were ultimately in charge of LA county jail, so Cito being the head honcho of the dorm made him the puppet master of 5300.

Contrary to the way Ian held power, Cito ruled with grace. There was often a line of Mexicans—both gangbangers and normal citizens—that waited for their chance to sit down with Cito and behold his institutionalized enlightenment. Showered regularly with gifts—mostly commissary snack food—Cito saw that I was underweight and fed me generously.

Regularly he'd confide in me his distaste for the newer generation of Southsiders. "Back when I was a youngster startin' to get locked up, we'd read, play chess, shoot heroin, talk about philosophy and shit. You know, try to better ourselves with our time. These youngsters nowadays…half these homies don't even know how to fuckin' read. They just politic and fight, puff their chests out like they're an OG before they even touch down on a prison yard for the first time. You know what I'm sayin', Jared? This new generation…they're just fucked up."

As for the Peckerwoods, there was Ian, Chucky, Psycho, Tex, Mike, Fred, Knuckles, John, Jon Jon, Jonny Boy, and Jonny Rotten. Aside from a few senior citizens and random vagrants, this was the gang. A motley crew of standard idiots, varying from habitual bad decision-makers to legitimate psychopaths. There was a lot of "keeping up with the Joneses"—the Joneses being the Southsiders—which was difficult both because of our thin numbers and limited amount of cumulative brain cells. Working out for at least an hour a day was mandatory, mostly because Ian wanted the Mexicans to think we were a reliable ally. We weren't, but by golly did we half-heartedly try. I personally didn't give a shit about any of the race stuff or politics, but to survive in there (or at least have a semi-enjoyable social life) you had to pretend to some degree. In fact, I came to find that anyone with an IQ higher than the temperature didn't really give a shit either. Before I came to this realization, however, I attempted to pretend that it was a concern of mine because I thought my life depended on it.

This came to light during our first "race meeting." When a certain issue arose in the dorm, a particular race would call a meeting, and the other races would allow them privacy in the shower area to discuss the matter at hand. In an effort to fit in and not blow my Jew cover, I made a failed attempt at conformity. After Ian announced that all the Woods were required to meet in the shower area over a dorm dispute, I joined the caravan of confused white guys and obeyed the order.

"So, what are we meetin' about? The fact that we're superior to these other motherfuckers? I'm gettin' tired of being cooped up with these animals," I said with great regret. Although I didn't actually believe a word I said, I thought pretending that I was a racist was the only way to safely integrate.

With his swastika tattoo glistening in the awful fluorescent light, Jon Jon put his mitt on my shoulder and said, "Hey, big dog, why don't you pump the fuckin' brakes on that race shit. No need for negativity right now." A man—a self-proclaimed Nazi—just scolded me for saying something racially insensitive.

"Sorry, Jon Jon." I shook my head "Just pissed off. Still feel like shit from the withdrawals."

"Another thing, you better knock it off with that withdrawal shit. You've been in here for fuckin' weeks now. Ain't no way you're still kickin'." I wish he was right, but it would take me yet another few weeks to get a full night of sleep. The Klonopin/heroin withdrawal combination was a killer, and the excessive malnutrition and brain damage from the crack didn't make it any easier.

Jon Jon continued, "We're white boys, and it's OK to be proud of that, but you start talkin' like that out there, and we're gonna have a fuckin' race war on our hands, so keep that shit to yourself. As long as they don't fuck our women and make any mixed babies…fuck it, I got no issues with 'em." Although incredibly insensitive, this was a rather tame statement from a man that Sieg Heiled on a daily basis.

Several court dates passed, and a verdict in my case still hadn't been finalized. Panda Express had been requested several times to provide the security footage, but had yet to do so. None of it really mattered to me because I wasn't having all that bad of a time. What seemed like the standard punishment was an eighteen-month prison sentence—of which I would serve half on good behavior—along with a violent strike on my criminal record. Nine months seemed like the perfect amount of time to get my head right, especially if it was in prison instead of jail, but I didn't want the violent felony. With the way things were going, however, it was looking like my case was going to be dropped altogether. This would be a dream to most people, but for me it sounded like a premature release right back into hell, so I told my public defender that I didn't mind doing more time. In fact, I *wanted* time. What I also really wanted was for my probation to be terminated so I could leave the state and go back to Florida. She talked with the DA, told them my plan to get out of California's hair, and struck up a deal: a sentence of six months on violation, all charges dropped, and my probation to be terminated after serving my time. It couldn't have been more perfect.

Now knowing that I was going to be locked up for a while, I needed to figure out a way to make some money. Everyone either had family that sent them money or had to figure out a way to make a few bucks in order to buy some higher-quality commissary food. Some people made jewelry out of plastic bags and string, and others provided services like doing people's laundry or giving haircuts. If you had no money on your books, you could get two stamped envelopes and two razors a week for free, which I could then trade for two soups. A soup was the equivalent of a dollar, and one dollar could buy you three bagged lunches. Two dollars a week wasn't enough to get by, so I'd play cards and gamble my two dollars and usually be able to double my money. This still wasn't enough—especially for a guy that came in forty pounds underweight—so I needed to figure out something more lucrative than the baseline envelope hustle.

Depending on a few criteria, some people got special diets. This included vegetarian, low sodium, and high protein/low carb. Inmates that received a special diet lined up at the front door before everyone else and collected a tray that didn't look much different than those that were on a regular diet. The exceptions were a few Muslims—who received a prepackaged halal meal—and a guy named Louis who received a prepackaged blue box.

Louis was a Peckerwood who looked to be in his late fifties and mostly kept to himself but also seemed to command a bit of respect from all the races. He had given me a few soups early on in my stay when he saw that I was down and out. Being a locksmith for some three decades, Louis told me that he developed a habit of breaking into private residences. Not only was it easy for someone with his trade skills, but when combined with an addiction to crack, Louis had a hard time giving it up before he was caught.

Whatever Louis was getting in that mysterious blue box at chow time was worth a pretty penny. I often saw him sell the blue box for what looked like a handful of soups, so whatever his special diet was must have been pretty damn special. Out of any edible item in the dorm, it appeared to have the highest resale value, which meant that it was outside of my budget, but not my interest.

I waited one day for Louis to finish his lunch and throw it in the trash. Upon examining the remnants inside the trash can, I spotted the blue box and couldn't believe what I saw: Hebrew lettering. I nearly threw up in the trash can from a mixture of anxiety and bewilderment. Louis, who was respected by everyone from the Blacks to the Nazis, received a special Jewish diet. Could this be? Could a Jew be allowed to live amongst the white supremacists? Whether Lou was faking or not, one thing was certain: the mythological "special kosher diet" turned out to be no myth at all.

I approached Louis the next day at lunch and said, "Hey, Lou, how you been?"

Louis, who looked like Santa Claus with a cocaine problem, looked up from his shawarma and responded, "Just another day in paradise."

"Can I ask you a quick question, Lou?"

"Sure thing."

"Well, I noticed your special diet—looked like there was Hebrew writing on the box or somethin', is that some sort of special *Jewish* diet?" I asked.

"Yeah, kosher diet. It's the best damn thing in here; I'll give you a box sometime. You like ravioli?" Louis inquired as he took another bite of pilaf.

Astonished, I continued my questioning. "So…are you…Jewish?"

"Well, yeah, of course. That's how I got it."

"And that's OK with everybody? No disrespect, Lou, I'm just curious. I see that you and Jon Jon get along great—he doesn't have a problem with it?"

"I've been in and out of prison for twenty years. Once upon a time it was a bit of an issue, but things are just different now. The whites, well… they don't have as much power as they used to, too low in numbers to give a shit about details, so about a decade ago, the Peckerwoods decided that the Jews were OK. Sure, the skinheads weren't happy with it, but they never outnumber the Woods, so they sorta just had to take that one on the chin," Louis explained nonchalantly. I'd hidden my identity for nothing, it seemed.

"Well, damn, I sorta just assumed that, you know, the white gangs didn't take too kindly to Jews…that's why I haven't told anyone this, but," I crouched in closer to Louis's ear and whispered, "I'm actually a Jew too."

"Really? Well fuckin' get on the kosher diet, make up to ten dollars a day if you want. Sometimes I just eat it, but if I need the money, plenty of people always want it. Easiest money in county," Louis said.

"But, Louis…" I looked around to make sure no one was ear-hustling. "If I try to get the kosher meal, everyone will know I'm Jewish…and I told the guys when I came in that I was German."

"Oh…. Yeah, that might be a problem. You'll be punished, for sure, not for being Jewish, but for lying." Louis gestured an offer to sip his coffee then continued, "Oh yeah, they'll beat you good…but it'll be worth it. Just take the beatin', rest up for a few days, then put in a diet change request. You gotta pass the test, though. You can pass the test, right? You were bar mitzvahed and all that?"

"Yeah, I mean, technically I'm half Jewish, but I know enough about the holidays and traditions and all that shit. You think I'll probably get twenty-three seconds?" I was questioning whether it would be worth it.

"Yeah, you could get more, I really don't know. Ian isn't known for being light with the boo-bops, but he does love the kosher chicken meat-balls that I get on Tuesdays and Thursdays. Maybe try and cut a deal."

Anxious but committed to bettering my life in jail, I asked Louis what I'd need to know to pass the kosher test. It was the most desired special diet in the whole jail, so they didn't just hand it out to anyone that claimed they were Jewish. Not only did you have to go over your family history, but you had to answer a few random questions about lesser-known holidays and customs. It wouldn't be a cakewalk, but I certainly had a better chance than most at passing.

What I was more worried about was coming clean to Ian and the boys.

Later on in the day after hours of restless thought, I found the justifi-cation to approach Ian and reveal my secret. I figured the income I could generate from selling the kosher meal outweighed any temporary pain I would receive from a reprimanding. With no alternative way to provide for myself, this was my only conceivable option. Pain was guaranteed, permanent damage was possible but not likely, and perhaps I also stood to gain a bit of respect. Despite surviving for years on the street, I was now uncomfortably sober and out of my element in jail. I was a coward, I thought. Maybe getting an ass-whooping would not only knock the fear out of me, but help me find more acceptance amongst my brethren. I didn't exactly fit in where I was—nor did I know if I'd want to—but what I did want was to prove to myself that I wasn't as weak as I imagined.

Ian, who was laying back with a John Grisham book when I approached his bunk, honored my request when I asked if we could talk privately.

"What's goin' on, my boy?" Ian asked as he slid his bookmark into the trite novel.

"Well, Ian, honestly…I've gotta come clean about somethin'. I figured it would be better to just tell the truth as soon as possible."

This sparked Ian's attention. "Well, you ain't wrong about that. It's better I'm hearing it from you and not someone else, that's for damn sure."

I paused, took a down-reaching breath to cleanse my gut, and thought about the dozens of kicks and punches I would shortly receive. Seconds of silence passed as Ian's eyes only grew wider and more diabolical, culminating with his lip quivering in anticipation of causing a verbal scene. Before he got the chance to let out a sound I muttered, "Ian…I'm…I'm Jewish. Well, half Jewish if you wanna get technical about it."

To my amazement Ian's eyes compressed and took on a relaxed position. "This is…an interesting development, my boy. Cuz I remember you saying you were of German descent…but it sounds like that was a lie. You lied. Is this correct?"

"Well, sorta…more so omitted the whole truth, I mean, I do have a German last name, or Yiddish, but that's pretty similar? Someone in my family was in Germany at some point, they were just…Jewish. And I'm biologically Irish on my mom's side, if that helps my case at all," I rambled on.

Ian silently boiled for a few seconds, angrily contemplating the situation before saying, "This ain't an issue of how Jewish you are…. I'm fuckin' half Armenian; I could give two shits about that. This is about honesty. I get that you haven't dealt with the race politics before…probably thought if we found out we'd stick you in a fuckin' oven!" Ian laughed at his own hack joke before returning to a severe tone. "Even so, there's gonna have to be consequences."

"Yeah…that's understandable." I tried to sound nonchalant, but in actuality I was more frightened than I'd ever been on the streets. No one should ever take issue with you not disclosing that you're a Jew upon introduction. Ninety-nine percent of the time, no one would. However, this wasn't real life; this was LA county jail, where making problems out of nothing was the number one pastime. Inmates thrived on the drama like middle-school girls and turned any delusion into racial division with great efficiency. It wasn't a charming world that I'd entered, but it was the world that I temporarily *had* to call home, and if I were to survive in it, I'd have to play ball. This was a world where sometimes you had to take a beating by three racists just to make a few ramen soups to get by.

"Alright, here's what's gonna happen: you're not gonna talk about this conversation, and if anyone has anything to say about how this went, you tell 'em to keep it movin' or take it up with me. Understand?" I nodded before Ian continued, "You lied about bein' a Jew, and that's OK…as long as you get that kosher diet. You *must* get the kosher diet. If you don't, this shit you pulled ain't gonna go off without you gettin' roughed up, we clear? So once a week, you're gonna give me the chicken meatballs, and besides that, you're free to eat or sell anything else. White boys get first dibs on purchasing, of course. Then the Mexicans, then the Blacks. You follow that, my boy?"

"That's…that's it?" I was dumbfounded. "That sounds…good, Ian. I can do that. I can definitely do that. And I can pass the kosher test. I'll put in a diet-change request right now and nail that shit, I promise."

Now methodically stamping his foot in typical OCD fashion, Ian briefly cackled then said at a hushed volume, "This is gonna be a good thing, my Jewish friend. Chicken meatballs, mushroom rice pilaf, shawarma, brisket, my boy…good days are comin' for you."

Having avoided violence I was somewhat thrilled, but couldn't help but feel a bit disenchanted by Ian's clemency. Was the reputation of LA county jail just one big farce? I'd somehow sidestepped any boo-bops up until that point during my stay, and frankly, I had been looking forward to one as an opportunity to develop some grit.

On Skid Row I was skirmishing almost daily, but when both parties were malnourished and strung out on crack, it wasn't exactly a training ground for the art of combat. Most of the violence I encountered was sucker-punches and failed muggings, other than the occasional beating someone half to death with Richie. The difference was that I had been numbingly high and not alone. I had a partner in Richie, and to an even further extent, heroin. In jail I had no such partners.

Although I hadn't received any beatings yet, I was on the other side of a few. Due to my smaller build, I was often used as an abatement in three-on-one fights, especially when the offender was older or of smaller size. My first one involved a middle-aged man who was being punished for sharing beans with a Black inmate. Did he deserve to be punished? Absolutely not, but Ian informed me that if I didn't participate in the beating, I would get beat for twice as long myself. After about ten seconds of punching this old man lightly in the body, Ian grabbed me, and told me he'd knock my teeth out if I didn't start aiming my punches at the man's wincing face. I punched the man repeatedly until he dropped to his knees and a small pool of blood had formed below on the concrete floor, then helped him right up after Ian told me to stop. We shook hands, then Ian hugged us both and said, "You see, this brings us together. We punish our own as we love our own." I was disgusted with myself for weeks.

It took a few days before I got called out of the dorm to interview for the kosher meal. As opposed to requesting a low-carb or vegetarian special diet, the kosher meal was not given to you at the discretion of a doctor. You had to interview with an officer who was well versed in Judaism (with the help of a volunteer rabbi), and after an allotment of questions, he either approved or denied the request. This officer was also in charge of approving halal diet requests, so I was escorted to a room along with several Muslim men.

A middle-aged Black man sitting next to me asked, "Hey, man, you Muslim?"

Confused, I replied, "Uh…no. I'm applying for the kosher diet. You know, the Jewish one."

"Oh, shit! That's the one I'm applyin' for too!" he exclaimed.

"Nice…are you Jewish?" I asked, suspecting I already knew the answer.

"Naw, but I studied a bit. Asked some guys in my dorm a few questions. Hanukkah's the one with the candles, right? You get gifts 'n' shit?"

"Yeah, it's the one with the gifts. And the candles, but listen, man…I don't think the test is gonna be that easy. Hanukkah is sorta like a beginner question. There's gonna be way harder shit than that."

"How many candles, though? Eight, right? Eight nights, eight candles, eight gifts." The guy was dead set.

I couldn't help but chuckle before explaining, "Well, it's actually nine candles, cuz there's an extra candle that lights the other eight candles…but honestly, and I mean no disrespect, I'd suggest that you try and get the halal meal. It's just, you know, way more believable."

"What's the halal meal?" he asked.

"Oh, it's the *Muslim* special diet, and you could pass for a Muslim way easier than a Jew."

"Naw, man, I already failed the Muslim test. Gotta try this Jew shit out."

"Well, shit. All I can say is that there's nine candles, so you definitely got that question in the bag. Good luck, man."

My name was then called by a sheriff who had poked his head out of an office room. He summoned me, and I took a seat in the folding chair that sat across from his desk. Fortunately, my last name was relatively Jewish sounding, so I had a solid foundation for my plea. Through a series of questions about obscure holidays, I halfheartedly proved that I was indeed Jewish, but what I didn't realize was that this wasn't a Jewish test. It was a *kosher* test, which meant I needed to prove that I was a *practicing* Jew. Most American Jews aren't very devout, and associate *Curb Your Enthusiasm* with their culture much more than anything biblical. Being no different, I had zero desire to actually abide by kosher law, but just being born a Jew wasn't enough to qualify for the kosher meal.

I told the officer that I was a Skid Row junkie and wished to get back to my Judaic roots in order to turn my life around. This was nonsense, of course, and I can only assume that he smelled bullshit, but he approved the diet nonetheless. "I'm gonna sign off on this, but first, one word of advice: get your shit together, kid. Stay off the fuckin' dope when you get outta here."

And with that, there was no more gambling for bologna sandwiches.

The next day my diet approval was processed, and like both Ian and Louis foretold, jail life for me was immediately elevated. After a few days of savoring every bite of the new cuisine, I developed a sales regimen of selling at least one of my meals a day. For both lunch and dinner I received a kosher box, and depending on what entrée it was, I could sell it for three or four bucks. Sometimes I'd sell both, and other times I'd presell packages of meals at a discounted rate.

Three or four dollars doesn't sound all that life changing, but in jail it was enough to rise out of poverty. With a little bit of money in your pocket, jail becomes a lot more fun, and when jail becomes a lot more fun, time passes much more quickly. Four dollars a day adds up, and eventually I found myself able to play poker at the high-stakes table. In addition, many higher-ranking inmates wanted a chance to purchase one of my kosher meals, which aided in my popularity and sense of feeling respected. I bought excess orange juice from the trustees and sugar-potent candies from the commissary store, and with that combination we were able to make and sell pruno (jailhouse wine). Regardless of attending AA meetings in jail, I occasionally enjoyed a cocktail. When it was banana breakfast and PB&J lunch day, I'd buy twenty excess lunches from the trustees, and combined with a few treats off the commissary list, I'd make a large jailhouse cake and sell pieces at a profit. Not only was this a fun hobby, but it was also quite time-consuming, so it grew to become my main pastime while locked up.

Being confined to one room for months on end, the main objective becomes to make the clock run with ease. Just make it to the end of the day, every day. "One more day down and closer to freedom," as they would say. However, the idea of freedom was different for me than it was for my fellow inmates. Most of them had families and somewhere to go when they got out, whereas freedom for me meant being released back into the hellscape of homelessness in Downtown LA. I feared for the day I was released as being nothing more than an exchange of prison cells. One inside a physical building, and the other trapped by the inescapable fact that outside of jail I'd still be imprisoned in my own mind. I knew the best option would be to go to Florida as soon as possible, but I was scared that I wouldn't be able to get on that bus. Sure, I was no longer physically addicted to heroin, but would the mental obsession grab me the second I got out and trap me back on Skid Row?

Months went by, cakes got eaten, pruno got drunk, holidays passed, books got read, and blood got shed. One evening I was spreading (preparing a meal) with my normal crew of friends—who happened to be Southsiders—when a commotion in the back of the dorm grew apparent. Hurling bodies made their way down a corridor of bunk beds as I attempted to discern what was happening. Clearly it was violent and unplanned, which was extremely rare because of the known consequences.

Everyone knew that if you wanted to fight someone, you had to ask your rep and have it arranged in an organized fashion away from the vision of the guards. This way, there were no dorm-wide consequences such as the loss of TV privileges. What I was witnessing now, on the other hand, would most certainly catch the guards' attention and instigate a full lockdown.

As people observed in confusion, it eventually became clear that this was a fight between a Southsider and a Peckerwood, which meant one thing and one thing only: an oncoming race riot.

If any person of any race is fighting another race, every member of either race was required to join in. If anyone was seen not participating, they would undoubtedly receive a punishment of the greatest magnitude in the aftermath. I—who was surrounded by four of my Southsider friends— was not in an ideal position for a race riot. In fact, I had hung out with the Southsiders so much that we had quipped about this exact scenario playing out one day. My friend Chacho had joked, "Ay, homie, but if it ever does go down between the Woods and the Southsiders, just come find me. I'll give you a quick two-piece to the face and you can pretend to go down, just roll outta the way and shit. We only gonna wanna beat Ian's ass anyway."

How ironic that we'd discussed this exact situation, and now it was happening as I was eating dinner with Chacho and three other Mexicans. I made eye contact with Chacho, he gave me a nod, I nodded back, and then he punched me a few times in the face. After going down I rolled towards a wall and cradled my head. Eventually a few other Southsiders spotted me and stomped me out for a moment, but for the most part I was unscathed.

Ian, on the other hand, had a symbolic target on his head that every Southsider wanted a shot at. He got more than a few kicks to the skull before the guards came in and threatened to gas the dorm. We were ordered to lay face down on our bunks, while officers examined security footage to determine who were the main agitators. After they were removed and put into the SHU (special housing unit), we were told to remain on our bunks for another hour or so. The sheriffs turned the TV back on, cleared us to get off our bunks, and to my surprise, everything went back to normal.

Me and my Southsider friends continued where we'd left off, and simply laughed away the preceding events. This is how utterly dumb the social structure in jail is. Everyone's split up by race and must follow the gang rules to a T, but in reality, most people don't really give a shit. Everything is about keeping up appearances and avoiding punishment from the next level up.

Did Ian really care if I shared food with a Black guy? No. He told me this. He just enforced that rule because if word got out that he didn't, he might get stabbed down the line. Everyone was scared, wanted to be accepted, and most importantly, wanted to join a team. Was Jon Jon evil for being a self-proclaimed Nazi? Maybe, but maybe not. Maybe he was just a frightened moron that wanted to be a part of something. Maybe his parents smoked meth and neglected him to the point that when he first went to Juvenile Hall as a teenager, he finally felt loved when he mindlessly joined a white supremacist gang. I'm not trying to justify Jon Jon's distorted beliefs, but you have to understand that Jon Jon was a complete idiot who smoked away every last brain cell in his skull. He was too dumb to be capable of evil and was simply full of fear. Fear of being alone. Fear of being left out. Fear that he would never amount to anything, just like his father who spent most of *his* life in prison. He didn't know the first thing about the actual history of fascism, nor could he even define it. He simply found the wrong tribe in the wrong place at the wrong time. I can only hope that after getting to know me and relating to a Jew—a fellow human—locked in the same cage as him, maybe he's reconsidered the whole Nazi thing. He's still in prison at the time of me writing this, so I doubt it. However, I kept in touch with a few other people from my time in jail that have definitely adjusted their beliefs after befriending a Jew.

The night after the race riot, we got pretty drunk off of pruno and someone broke out a stick-and-poke tattoo rig. Ian suggested that some of the younger guys that participated in the brawl get a "23" tattooed on their fingers. This represented the twenty-third letter in the alphabet—W—for Wood.

Drunk and wanting to feel a part of, I obliged and let a young gentleman who went by the name of "Sickfuck" poke jailhouse ink into my flesh with a dull staple. I'm not proud of this tattoo, nor am I of the other tattoos I got while locked up, but they serve as a daily reminder of where I end up when I make bad decisions. I've since covered up the "23" (for obvious reasons; it's technically a gang tattoo, and I'm, well, not a gang member), but the other tattoos still remain.

Drunk and brandishing a fresh Peckerwood tattoo, I briefly flirted with the idea that maybe I'd finally found my people. Maybe Sickfuck, Ian, Jon Jon, Jonny Rotten, and Psycho were the best I'd ever get to feeling a part of a community. Given my recent track record, I was headed down a path of regular visits to jail and prison, so I wondered if the best plan of action was to fully adopt the Peckerwood identity. Upon sobering up the next morning, however, I was uncertain. This was no life to look forward to. In and out of prison and gambling for ramen soups with criminals wasn't a future that I wanted, yet it would be inescapable if I kept getting high. If I was able to find solace and comradery with these degenerates, maybe I could attempt to do the same with sober people when I got out. You are who you surround yourself with, I thought, and right now I was surrounded by shitheads. I knew I had to figure out how to never come back or I'd become one permanently.

Along with receiving the kosher meal, I also got to meet with the jail rabbi once a week as part of the kosher regiment. There weren't too many Jews in Men's Central Jail—maybe half a dozen—so he would only drop by for a couple of hours. He was a full-time rabbi at a temple in town but volunteered once a week to come meet with us, and he told me there were many times when months would pass and there would be no Jewish inmates at all. Playing into the game of being genuinely kosher, I had to pretend to some degree that I was attempting to be a practicing Jew. Because of this, he gave me a small prayer book and a yarmulke.

No one in my family ever wore a yarmulke outside of a once-in-a-decade visit to temple, so I wasn't much more familiar with the custom than any of my jail mates. I intended on hiding it away under my mattress in order to draw the least amount of attention to my Jewishness as possible, but despite my secrecy, several people were thoroughly intrigued by the small circular cap. The first to inquire was Cito, my Southsider shot-caller bunkie.

"Ay, homie, so what's the deal with the hat?"

Not sure how to answer, I responded, "Honestly, I don't really understand it myself. I wasn't really raised religious. It's some sort of sacred Jewish hat, that's all I really know about it."

"Shit, sacred Jewish hat? Does it bring good luck!?" Cito laughed. "Can I hold it?"

"Yeah, man. Shit, you can wear it if you want," I joked.

"*Fuckkkkk* I can wear it? You sure?" Cito placed it on his bald head.

"Of course. It looks good on you," I responded, charmed by his fascination.

"Damn, bro"—Cito grinned—"I like this thing. I can feel the power, my boy. Ay, you think I could wear this when I gamble?"

Flabbergasted at the request, I responded, "…Yeah, I guess…I mean I'm not sure what good it's gonna bring you, but sure. Take it for a spin."

This inspired several others to request the use of my yarmulke. I questioned whether I was disgracing my own culture by allowing this, but then again, my whole existence had pretty much disgraced the culture already.

Besides, everyone that asked to wear my yarmulke showed it the utmost respect, even if it stemmed from an absurd belief that it held some kind of financial magic. It was as if their prejudice about Jews inspired them to show *more* reverence for the yarmulke, somehow. They handled it as if it were a baby bird, gently cradling it with two hands and crowning themselves slowly to never damage it in any way. As the yarmulke started to make appearances at the poker table, people's curiosity flared about its supposed mysticism.

Soon after, I found myself consulting random inmates with legal advice. They believed that because I was Jewish, I could mentor them on a defense strategy in court. I always tried to explain to them that I was merely a crackhead who knew nothing about the law, but it didn't matter. I became a completely unqualified consultant of sorts and tried to help the best I could.

The madness culminated when Jon Jon requested if he could wear the yarmulke during his upcoming dice game. Despite looking like the kind of guy that would want to put me in a death camp, he assured both Ian and me that he would be unconditionally respectful, so I obliged. What followed was an absolute miracle: a man—a Nazi—shirtless with swastika tattoos on full display, coronated with none other than a Jewish headpiece while shooting dice, joyously winning soup after soup and belting out mazel tovs like it was the high holidays. A beautiful conundrum of dishonor and toxic solidarity. If there ever was a time that a camera was truly needed, it was this moment, but unfortunately the only image is within the minds of the inmates of 5300. We all got to witness a triumph of biblical proportions that day—a Nazi wearing a yarmulke, all the while gambling and hugging his Jewish friend—and in our minds is where that horridly charming image will forever stay.

After what felt much longer than half a year, my release day finally came. I was in no way excited. With no concrete plan other than I'd eventually go back to Florida at some point, disappointment and anxiety consumed me as a result of what should have been considered great news. I didn't know what was going to happen, but I did know that I couldn't go back to heroin. One shot and I'd be right back at it again, on a fast track towards fighting another prison term. Committed to abstinence from heroin, I tried to muster up the faith that everything would be alright as long as I stayed clean, and this gave me the courage to march into the release cell with some confidence.

I was a different man then when I walked into that jail six months prior. Seventy pounds heavier, head shaven, with a much-too-long jail goatee and an unrivaled chutzpah. I literally couldn't fit into the clothes I had been arrested in, so I was given a paper suit to change into. Although physically transformed, I hadn't changed much in the way of my thinking. Sure, I was scared straight to some extent, and I wasn't in the mood to seek out dope, but in no way had I gained the tools in that six months to be able to turn it down if it crossed my path.

There were about twenty of us being released at the same time, all packed into a cramped holding cell at the inconvenient hour of 2:00 AM. Not a great time to get released if your goal is to not smoke crack. I looked across the room and made eye contact with a fellow inmate who I recognized from the streets, and my heart sunk. A fellow junkie that used to drive to Skid Row from West LA and buy heroin through me on occasion.

"Jared! Whatsup, man? Goddamn, you look different, how long you been in here?"

"Hey, man, yeah, I know. I've been locked up for like six months. how long you been in here?" I asked.

"Just a few days, dumb possession charge. I'm sick as fuck right now. What're you doin' once they release us?" the kid said, trying to hold back the snot dripping from his nostrils. I could see that he was kicking hard.

"Man, I don't really know. I kicked dope months ago—sorta tryin' to stay away from it, you know? Besides, I got no money," I muttered, as the itch re-emerged after lying dormant for nearly half a year.

The kid heaved in a withdrawal sniffle, smiled, then said, "I got arrested with sixty bucks on me, don't worry about it. I got you."

I suffer from what we call the "ism": the malady within that drives us to still use drugs after a long period of abstinence. Jail did wonders in releasing me from the physical addiction to heroin but did nothing to quell the mental obsession. Despite never getting physically addicted to heroin ever again after that last kick, I still had several periodic short relapses where I managed to destroy everything. Solving the physical component is first and foremost, which jail did, but without a structured plan in preventing relapse, there's little chance at long-term success once released. Had I been sent straight to a year-long program that was abstinence-based and provided therapeutic services and job training, my chances of remaining clean would have been astronomically higher. Of course, this would have cost the taxpayer an arm and a leg, but housing me in jail for six months wasn't exactly cheap. Add in the long-term costs of perpetuating addiction and criminality, and my proposal starts to look like a bargain.

In the end, I still think jail saved my life. It was a terrifying consequence that in some ways changed my behavior, but as you can see it didn't give me the skills to stay off drugs for good. It did, however, detox me from heroin for the last time and give me a taste of the incarcerated life—a life I ultimately didn't want but knew would be unavoidable from then on out if I didn't change my ways. I believe I have the type of demeanor that greatly benefitted from getting locked up, but this isn't the case for everybody. And when realizing that most of the people I was locked up with were in there for crimes stemming from addiction, sometimes I wonder if turning San Quentin into one giant rehab might be a much better solution than the way it currently runs. There have to be consequences for bad behavior and rewards for good behavior—that's entrenched in the basis of human psychology—but drugs throw a wrench into the gears of our reward systems. The solution, however, isn't to do away with consequences outright. If you do a crime you should do the time, but we as a society need to rethink how we rehabilitate in that interval. This is the crux of how we really start putting a dent in the crisis we have on our hands, and ultimately save a ton of money and lives. It's not cheap keeping thousands of drug addicts' addictions on life support while repeatedly jailing and hospitalizing them for eternity.

Because this proposed solution wasn't in place, the best thing I had was jail. It helped me get off the streets, kick heroin, grow the fuck up, and stare the possibility of a terrifying future in the face. But ultimately it wasn't enough. I needed something exponentially more hideous to jostle my conscience awake from hibernation. Luckily enough, I'd get that something, but most addicts aren't so fortunate. That's why we *must* change our approach to the epidemic. The answer isn't sending everyone to prison, and it certainly isn't coddling them to an early grave at the cost of a functional society. We need long-term, on-demand treatment for all, and a system that actually incentivizes homeless drug addicts to utilize it. I can only hope that my story thus far has inspired some of you to agree.

After getting out and fucking up for a day, I bought a Greyhound ticket to Florida after selling my food stamps. I spent about five months in the same sober living I'd lived in before. In what amounted to little more than a metaphorical oil change, I detoxified myself from institutionalization, stayed clean, worked hard labor, saved money, and bought a plane ticket back "home." Molly rented me a room in her apartment, and I intended on remaining sober. How? I was hoping through osmosis. This lasted all of three days before I got into contact with Richie.

Since we had parted ways after my arrest, Richie had done good for himself. He'd linked up with the cartel and was running drugs from Los Angeles to Vegas. In fact, he had his own apartment in Chinatown and a fiancée. The key to his success, he told me, was that he had stopped smoking crack and shooting heroin. His wonderful fiancée had gotten him on a manageable regimen of *smoking* heroin and snorting meth instead. The result was that he was no longer homeless and was making a ton of easy money with his new "job." He had so much work that he needed help and asked if I'd like to come by and discuss a job opportunity.

In need of work, I obliged, although I knew deep down that I was only interested in getting high. The potential cartel job was exciting, but as I sat on the bus heading towards Chinatown, heroin was the only thing on my mind. Clean for months and living with sober friends, I willingly chose— once again—to throw it all away for a moment of opiate-induced serenity. After all, I felt uncomfortable around my new sober roommates. They all had years of sobriety, flourishing careers, and healed relationships with their families. I didn't, and used this fact to feel the furthest thing from fitting in. Richie was on my level; he was a fellow piece of shit in my eyes, and therefore I would be able to find solace in our connection. But in reality, heroin was what I was after in my desire to feel comfort. Richie would enable such behavior, whereas my good-hearted roommates wouldn't. This was the real reason I left Molly's apartment and went to see Richie that night.

After embracing and saying our hellos, I got down to business and asked Richie if he was holding. We got high, discussed our shallow plans of making tons of money with the cartel, and caught each other up to speed about our lives. Once his fiancée left to walk the dog, Richie broke out a needle that he hid from her, and we started shooting a mixture of heroin and meth. The last thing I remember was Richie giving me a tattoo before I blacked all the way out, and although I don't remember anything during the following eight hours, it wound up being the most important night of my life.

CHAPTER 12

BLOODBATH

On the morning in which it all changed, I woke up in a bathtub that was filled with lukewarm water and blood. This combination stretched across the floor, the sink, and the walls of the bathroom. In fact, there was so much of it that the gag-inducing smell of iron it produced made me vomit immediately. I quickly expelled this into the already-corrupted bathwater, took a labored breath, then splashed it back up towards my face to loosen my eyelashes. After several decelerated heartbeats, my other senses kicked into gear, revealing the sound of someone yelling from beyond the locked door.

They weren't yelling in English—maybe it was Mandarin or something similar—which in no way alleviated my confusion, but a situation this grotesque was probably best suited to remain ambiguous. Sometimes the truth is more sinister than any product of the imagination. This was one of those times.

I was tore up—beyond *just* high. Apoplectically lost and unhinged from any sense of reality. I had lost an incredible amount of blood (this was the only decipherable fact), which left me in a balancing act somewhere between a weak pulse and a death certificate. My face was in a substantial amount of pain and was percolating fluids down my chest into the water of the unkempt tub. I raised myself out of the basin, steadied myself by grabbing onto the sink, and put on my clothes without drying my torso off. At that point, I was ready to wake up and abandon whatever nightmare I was in, when in the moment of pinching my arm, I caught a glimpse of my face in the mirror.

I will never—ever—forget the *cadaver* I saw staring back at me. From my mustache up, my face appeared relatively normal, with the exception of a small open wound above my left eyebrow and some dried blood at the crown of my skull. This wound was small, and definitely not the source of blood that encrusted a generous portion of the bathroom. When I looked at my lower lip—or to be more explicit, where my lower lip *no longer was*—the source of where this onslaught of blood was coming from became obvious. Not only was my lower lip gone, but the flesh all the way down to the beginning of my chin was absent as well. I took a closer look in the mirror and discovered sinewy strands of flesh fastened in between my crooked lower front teeth. The only logical conjecture was that I *ate* a sizable portion of my face.

That's a terrifying sentence of civilian non-fiction if you hadn't already noticed. Possibly two ounces of human meat was digesting through my gut at that very moment. When self-cannibalism is the only *rational* conclusion you can come up with when you find yourself in a specific dilemma, you start to question whether you ever deserved to exist to begin with.

I've never heard of anyone doing anything like this before on drugs. Sure, some people take a liking to pulling out their hair when high on meth, or maybe biting the inside of their cheeks, but I made three square inches of my oral cavity vanish like a Donner Party–inspired parlor trick. Engorged with inflammation and delirious with blood loss, the image of my own teeth marks at the border of my chin could not be shaken. Visible fucking *teeth* marks, like that from a soft-baked chocolate chip cookie. There was an overwhelming metallic taste in every swallow, and I could feel the massive amount of blood I consumed start to clot all the way down my throat. Not an ideal experience.

Shit, it was far from an ideal *traumatizing* experience. I'd had countless self-inflicted mortifying incidents—mostly from past heroin/meth/cocaine blackouts—but this monstrosity was currently in first place for the worst thing I'd ever woken up to. Like any good drug addict, my only concern at that moment was returning to a state of unconsciousness as soon as possible.

Almost instantaneously, I felt the absolute necessity to kill myself. There was no doubt in my mind that any other option would be tolerable. My suicidal mindset was not a product of sadness, but merely a long-awaited acceptance of reality. It was a long time coming, and I actually felt fortunate that I finally felt inspired enough to really put an end to it all. This was my magnum opus of self-brutality. I could not go on living if I were to be reminded every time I looked in a mirror that I had mangled my face to this degree as a result of trying to catch a buzz. It's one thing if you become disfigured from taking a blast of shrapnel on the beaches of Normandy, like a hero—it's still a tragedy, and potentially much more disfiguring, but at least there was a noble reason for why it happened. I did this to myself in exchange for a quick high that I don't even remember; no amount of self-forgiveness could ever nullify the shame.

My drug addiction had perpetually left me in a catch-22 scenario. As I continued to get high over the years, the rate at which I was destroying my life escalated. The only way I could emotionally deal with this trap was by getting high. The cure to all my problems had become the source of all my problems as well.

My dad always told me that when a heroin addict was at the end of his rope, there were only two solutions. The first was to shoot too much heroin and get incredibly high (thus finding temporary relief from all your woes) or shoot too much heroin and die. I'd welcomed both outcomes for years, but the problem with the first option was that it only worked until you needed the next hit. The second option was permanent mitigation, which was the only acceptable solution after this.

I found myself slumped over the red-splattered sink, staring at my own unrecognizable face in the mirror. I made an executive decision at that moment: my life would come to an end that day. I was a complete nuisance to everyone around me, and a continuous enemy to my own physical safety and peace of mind. I was a junkie; a worthless dope fiend; a helpless baby of a man who only sucked at the teat of his friends, family, and various other victims within society. I had tried time and time again to change my ways, clean up my act, put down the needle, get a job, pay taxes, contribute, achieve financial and emotional stability, give back to those who had given so much to me, be a better son, nephew, employee—a better *anything*— but I just couldn't maintain a life free from dumb-fuckery. No matter how much better life got when I was sober, and no matter how bad I knew my life would be if I got back on dope, I could *not* control myself and stay away from heroin. The experiment was over.

I wrapped my undershirt around my face and haphazardly slipped my shoes back on. The yelling in Mandarin and pounding on the door was still a constant.

I yelled back, "Un secun! Ah ee out in un secun!" (it's not easy to pronounce certain consonants when you're missing half your mouth) and prepared myself to unlock the door.

This was the final stage of my addiction. Absolute mayhem. I emerged from the bathroom doused in blood from head to toe and aroused nothing short of the fear of God in the sweet old couple. The good news was that it was a shared bathroom on the floor of a boardinghouse, and therefore I was not technically committing a home invasion. This alleviated a bit of stress, given that it increased my odds that the police weren't already on their way. I discovered this as I made my way down a hallway of cracked doors, each with an Asian senior citizen peeking through to get a look at the commotion. Above all else, I feared the police. Not because I was scared of going to jail, but that if they were able to arrest me, I'd have a much harder time getting a chance to kill myself. I didn't have time for a police interrogation; I needed to die *now*.

I still had no solid memories of what happened the night before. That is, until I looked at my right forearm and noticed a never-before-seen tattoo. Despite being crudely drawn as if it had been done by a toddler, it took the silver medal in the "regrettable things I did last night" category. I couldn't make out what the tattoo was at first, but after a moment of observation, I concluded that it was Hebrew lettering. Why did I ask Richie to tattoo this on me? I didn't speak a word of Hebrew, which amplified the mystery, but I quickly realized that such a concern was futile. A bad tattoo that I didn't remember getting wasn't an issue for someone that intended on killing themself within the hour. I had bigger things to worry about, specifically dying as soon as possible. The tattoo did, however, manifest a few bits and pieces of memory from the night before: I suddenly saw images of myself in a cluttered room with Richie and his fiancée.

I must have done more heroin while Richie took a break from giving me the tattoo, then fallen out of consciousness. We all know that it's a very dangerous, potentially fatal drug. On a few occasions, however, if I'm significantly high on crystal meth, a typically fatal amount of heroin will send me into purgatory—walking zombie status, if you will. This didn't exactly explain how I ended up coating a stranger's bathroom with my DNA, but it did offer some building blocks to the previous evening's storyline.

Prior to this dreadful autumn night in Los Angeles, I had been totally sober for months. In a time span of about eight hours, I managed to relapse on heroin, get incredibly high on crystal meth, shoot more heroin, induce a blackout, get a strange tattoo, gnaw away at my face for hours, and nearly die from blood loss. Now, I've had some rough segments in life, but never had I caused so much damage in such a short amount of time. I've gone on drug benders that lasted months before any real consequences occurred, but if there's one fact that I know about my drug career, it's that the speed at which I create pain for myself has progressed exponentially. I had now reached a point where I wasn't good at getting high anymore. I was actually embarrassed. My ability to get high was once a source of pride and self-esteem, but what I didn't know was that it would eventually encompass everything I had to live for. Now that I could no longer do it with any success, it was time to do the world a favor and go into permanent retirement.

My equilibrium was severely skewed, and I was beyond weakened from the blood loss. I had about a mile walk before I got to Skid Row and could buy my last dose of heroin. There was about forty dollars in my pants pocket, so I decided the way I was going to end my life was with an intentional overdose. I wasn't jumping off a Goddamn bridge with leftover money to spend. I walked south, passing Union Station on my left, and began to make my way into Downtown Los Angeles.

Although not homeless at the time of this event, my appearance was the worst it had ever been during my career as a Skid Row regular. I could barely shuffle myself down tent-littered streets, but I was goal-driven. As I made my way to the intersection of Sixth and San Pedro, I was literally marking my path with the drippings from my open wound, which was offending some of the Skid Row inhabitants that I passed by.

I came upon the main drag of dope dealers—who would normally fight over getting my business—but due to my unsettling appearance at the time, they were reluctant to take my money. Two blood-soaked twenty-dollar bills that were nearly indistinguishable hung from my hand, as drug dealer after drug dealer refused me service. This predicament was completely foreign to me. I had bought dope in the past with food stamps, packs of cigarettes, power tools, checks, gift cards, stolen makeup, iPods, electric razors, all kinds of shit—you name it—but this was the first time that I'd experienced any resistance to actual legal tender.

I eventually found a drug dealer with standards low enough to accept my bloody payment, and I bought five balloons of heroin, along with a needle and a cooker. This was about three-fourths of a gram of mediocre downtown dope, which would normally not be a lethal dose to a junkie with any sort of habit, but having been dead-sober for months prior to the previous night, I had virtually no tolerance to opiates. When someone has *no* tolerance, one balloon of heroin could potentially kill them, let alone five. I didn't want to take any chances of survival, so I played it safe and planned to shoot all of them at once. After all, I wouldn't need to save any for later.

All the variables in my plan were accounted for, so I marched onward towards the Fifth-Street flea market and snuck into the public bathroom to cook up my final shot. I sat down on a toilet, shut the stall door, and loaded the cooker with all five balloons of heroin. Given that I was on the brink of death, this took me a few more minutes than usual, but what can I say? I was determined. I needed guaranteed closure.

After finalizing my decision, I briefly filibustered before accepting my fate; I pondered whether Heaven or Hell actually existed, said a prayer to my dead mother, apologized to my father, took a deep breath, hit a vein, stalled for a moment, mumbled something to God (or whatever), asked if he was real, didn't get an answer, cracked what must have been one hell of a crooked smile, and pushed the plunger down on the syringe.

It was the last thing I remembered before I died.

HOME
(CONCLUSION)

That was six years prior to the time of me writing these words.

As I stated in the introduction, I started writing this book as a suicide letter. That's what this whole thing was. I fully intended on killing myself eventually, but during the months of surgeries and healing, I figured I'd document my life to pass the time. On the off chance that the surgeries went well and I wouldn't look terribly disfigured for the rest of my life, I promised myself I'd wait to commit suicide until after the process was finished. I held onto a shred of faith that maybe it would all work out. Or maybe I was too much of a coward to pull it off. Either way, I couldn't be happier that I didn't off myself. My life has grown into something beyond my wildest dreams, and it's only in the toddler stage. I'm five years sober after twenty-nine years of broken thinking.

Many people selflessly came together to save my life after the incident, most notably Molly. I owe my life to that woman. She let me stay in her apartment for six months until she got me into a long-term rehab, as I healed from the accident and subsequent surgeries to fix what I'd done to myself. Secondly, I owe my life to the doctors that rebuilt my face. After being revived, I somehow wound up at a hospital with a plastic surgery training department. I agreed to let them "practice" on me, and guess what? Not only did they do it for free, but they also did a pretty damn good job. Is it perfect? It's as perfect as humanly possible. Did I deserve such a blessing? Absolutely not, but I'm eternally grateful. The way the pieces perfectly fell together makes this no less than a miracle, and there's no doubt that the chance of spoiling this opportunity of a lifetime played a role in helping me stay clean. After all, whoever aligned all the pieces perfectly together certainly wasn't going to do it twice. I figured you only get to eat your face and get it fixed once in this life.

The question arises of whether this all could have been avoided. As someone who for years had no money and no health insurance, yet was a danger to myself and society, sometimes I ask why wasn't I stopped? I don't mean locked up in jail forever; I mean forced into long-term treatment before I had the chance to mutilate myself this badly. Firstly, there really weren't a lot of options for long-term treatment even if I had genuinely wanted it. LA county alone only had a handful of non-profit rehabs for the destitute, all of which had unrealistically long waiting lists through my tenure. There were the missions on Skid Row, but they didn't have enough funding for medical detox, so they weren't always viable options for opiate addicts and alcoholics. The available detoxes usually had similar wait times, and you had to call every day in order to keep your spot in line. If you lost your phone or got arrested for a few days, the process started over. The fact that it's beyond difficult to access detox and treatment for those that need it the most, even when they're *willing*, is the crux of the problem.

The non-profit rehab I got into after the surgeries was only possible because Molly was an alumnus. Even so, she spent those months exhaustingly pulling strings to get me in. Years prior, I was on the waiting list for that same rehab for nearly a year until I wound up doing my stint in jail. Even though I half-heartedly wanted treatment, I still called every day, and sometimes I wonder, if I had gotten in, would I have ever had to wake up in that bathtub? It's not the rehab's fault; they only have so many beds and so many dollars for a growing population of addicts. The problem is that we've spent enough money to build one of these rehabs in every city within Los Angeles County, but instead we've squandered it on everything but. It's one of about four uncorrupted rehabs in LA proper, each with less than eighty beds, serving a region with tens of thousands of homeless addicts.

The politicians in charge of wasting those billions of dollars should be jailed for such incompetence, but the way things are going, it wouldn't surprise me if one of them became president someday. Hopefully books like this one may help prevent that from happening, but unfortunately there's no easier place to fail up than America. Take me for an example: I'm a published author solely because I have a ton of experience being an absolute parasite. Most authors toil to create three-dimensional characters and complex story arcs, and all I had to do was remember how much of an asshole I was. If that's not failing up, I don't know what is, but fortunately my background in being a degenerate has become uniquely valuable in recent years due to our leaders' ineptitude. I might have a leg up on these politicians when it comes to solving this problem, which I discovered through the process of writing out my story. Unbeknownst to me six years ago, that's not why I started this book, but it's why I *completed* it.

As a homeless drug addict who flirted with the idea of treatment in my heyday, I realize now that there's no excuse for why the infrastructure wasn't there. We're the richest country in the world and have spent millions on handing out needles and crack pipes alone, yet we're detrimentally lacking in legitimate, everlasting solutions. Frankly, the fact that detox and treatment is *still* barely accessible to those in need is an abomination by those that represent the areas most afflicted. They have no shame. And given how much money we've burned on alternative failed routes, I'm shocked they haven't been deposed. In the past decade they've tried handing out permanent housing to crackheads with deadly results, decriminalizing petty crimes so drug addicts could continue financing their habits, and withheld funding from any shelter or housing program that promoted sobriety with the passing of SB1380. Anyone with eyes can see that as a result, the problem has gotten exponentially worse. The focus, in my humble opinion, should be on creating *thousands* of available detox and treatment beds in California alone and building a mass shelter system for all as opposed to permanent housing for a few. Shelter these people, evaluate their needs—whether it be addiction treatment, mental health care, or employment—and proceed with individualized plans of action. Make the state a pilot program for the nation to follow suit. Get FEMA involved. Once the infrastructure is there, incentivize people to get clean instead of rewarding their bad behavior. It doesn't take a master's degree in psychology to figure this out, but sometimes the answer is too simple for the overeducated to grasp. Turn half the prisons into long-term treatment facilities for all I care; a large enough portion of the inmates are severe drug addicts anyway. Let's try a solution that helps them never have to get locked up again instead of enabling the source of their criminality.

Another issue is the question of mandated treatment. Understandably, this is a controversial topic. Mandating criminals to jail makes sense to most level-headed people, but the idea of mandating an addict to treatment is less palpable. Obviously all people that use drugs shouldn't be forced to go to rehab. In fact, most addicts shouldn't be either. But the extreme ones like I was, who have become a danger to themselves, a danger to others, and drain society with rampant crime and antisocial behavior, *need* repercussions at some point. When one's behavior affects the civil liberties of others, they can no longer be given free rein to do whatever they please. People that chronically behave this way because of drug addiction—specifically those that have become homeless as a result—should eventually be mandated to treatment in my opinion. We used to just send these people to prison, and although some reformed addicts claim that prison saved their lives, this generally has a negative outcome for most. Sending them to long-term treatment, however, could be the path forward. I say this as someone that's at least *willing* to discuss legalization and safe supply; I *don't* think it should be a crime for someone to simply use drugs. But when someone's drug abuse is affecting another person or society at large, this expands beyond the issue of personal freedom. And the dignified way to handle this isn't for the state to subsidize a deadly lifestyle. It's to subsidize the treatment of the illness.

Opponents of mandated treatment often say you can't force someone to recover; they have to want it. And I understand this notion. However, consequences tend to encourage people to want to change. Take away *all* consequences, and you're going to have a lot fewer drug addicts ever wanting to turn it around. The only other options are letting them kill themselves in the streets, letting them kill themselves in free studio apartments, or locking them away in a jail cell. Currently we're trying the "kill themselves in the streets" approach, and we all know how that's turning out. San Francisco tried the free-housing strategy, but in a study conducted starting in 2016, 25 percent of the residents died and 21 percent *voluntarily* went back to being homeless within five years[2]. That leaves us with the option of

---

2   Joaquin Palomino and Trisha Thadani, "Broken Homes," *San Francisco Chronicle*, April 26, 2022, www.sfchronicle.com/projects/2022/san-francisco-sros/.

sending them all to prison or sending them to treatment. Call me a bleeding heart, but I'd like to finally give the latter a shot.

This wouldn't be a punishment. It would be a second chance at life, complete with medical detox, alternative forms of therapy, opportunities at education, skill training, and job certification. Imagine arresting a homeless drug addict that committed a crime, and instead of sending him to prison, we taught him how to weld and fed him straight into a labor union after his treatment commenced. For those that are capable of self-sustainability, a personalized route will be designed within the treatment plan. For those plagued with debilitating mental illness or disability, a path to *permanent* supportive housing and medical treatment will be necessary. Sorry, but these people deserve to not die in the street. I'm sure if we refrain from funding a proxy war in the next ten years, we could afford to help these people for the next century.

Perhaps I'm being a bit idealistic, but these centers could be theoretical miracle factories. A self-sustaining system that employs those that graduate and relies upon recovered addicts helping others. Maybe I'm dreaming. Or maybe you are if you think we can free-crack-pipe our way out of this mess. The bottom line is that the radical harm-reductionists have had their hands on the wheel for ten years, and the only place it's gotten us is a glimpse of dystopia. It would only be fair to let someone else drive at this point, and if it turned out to be an utter failure, I'd humbly hand the reins back over. But I'd be lying if I said I wasn't confident about my proposal.

People have called me a proponent of "the War on Drugs 2.0." That's a catchy mudsling, but I prefer to call it the war on addiction. Furthermore, one of the most important components of the war on addiction would be addiction prevention. But how do you prevent addiction? With hope. With a bustling middle class. With affordable housing. With a way to be able to actually support a family. With a pharmaceutical and medical industry that doesn't overmedicate and get children strung out on speed for the sake of profit. With ex-military moms and dads not strung out on dope and traumatized from endless and pointless foreign wars. With a path to home ownership where you don't have to compete with multinational corporations and foreign investment. You know, the shit that people used to talk about when they were running for president thirty years ago before a candidate's stance on gender ideology determined the fate of our country. In other words, the shit that actually matters. It doesn't take a political scientist to know that America's seen better days, and with the country so divided and rife with economic and medical fraudulence, addiction couldn't be more comfortable. To fundamentally defeat this crisis, many things need to change beyond our approach to handling addiction. But I'm just a well-versed junkie, and many of these problems are over my head. Still, we must start somewhere, and there's no better place than molding drug policy to reflect the mechanisms of terminal addiction. Hopefully my detailed story, and testimonies from others like me, have given you a glimpse under the hood of what truly works for a down-and-out addict. But in the end, this issue is multi-faceted and reflective of most of our national maladies. Think about it next time you go to the polls, whether it be for your local council or the presidency.

I went to that non-profit rehab for about four months. Twice, back-to-back. No one's perfect, especially a severe drug addict of my variety, and after slipping up for a couple of weeks (and losing one of my toes in the process) they let me come back for what I hope was my final stay. Having been two for two in the "losing body parts during a relapse" department, I was extremely open-minded and willing. I did everything anyone with more clean time told me to do if they said it would help me stay sober. Most of the staff were alumni who were formerly homeless or imprisoned, which gave the clientele hope—living proof that change was possible right before our eyes. It wasn't some fancy Malibu rehab owned by a publicly traded corporation concerned with their bottom line, but rather started by ex-heroin addicts who couldn't have cared less about becoming millionaires. They made us cook, clean, and help make the place run in every which way, because it wasn't just a rehab, it was our home for four months. For some of us, it was our first home in many years. I made some of the closest friends I've ever had, friends that I would drop everything for and fly across the country in a heartbeat to help, and they would do the same.

I was essentially handed a lifelong family, and unlike jail, this family was actively trying to heal.

One of the most important components was that they let us go look for jobs after a few months. Never struggling to find employment, I quickly got a decent-paying carpentry gig and was able to save a few grand before graduating. This gave me the opportunity to buy a shitbox car and move straight into a sober living. Not much, but it was more than enough to give me a glimmer of hope. More importantly, I *earned* it. Restoring one's self-esteem is critical for recovery, and as it turns out, self-sufficiency feels pretty damn good. The ability to live at the rehab free of charge while earning a paycheck relieved just enough financial insecurity that I didn't burn it all down for once. Leaving that rehab after earning a measly few grand was enough for me to see a realistic path towards stability.

Furthermore, I moved to one of the several *affiliated* sober livings within a block radius of the treatment center, so it was like I never really left. We were encouraged to come back, volunteer, and help those just coming in off the streets. This further fed our sense of self-esteem and *usefulness*. I spent my first year of sobriety close within the orbit of my rehab community, with incremental steps towards full independence. I delicately learned, for the first time, how to functionally operate before jumping back into the deep end of life. A year sounded long at first, but it was nothing in comparison to the many decades my life expectancy has increased. This isn't a problem that can be fixed with a mere twenty-eight-day vacation at a medical resort and a prescription for Seroquel.

I did the group therapy, went to the meetings, got the sponsor, did the twelve steps, got the job, bought the car, got the girlfriend, lost the girlfriend, got the big screen TV, the friends, the roommates, the apartment, and the peace of mind. What got me to stay sober? I don't know anything for fact. No one really does when it comes to conquering addiction, but all the twelve-step stuff helped immensely. This book's intention isn't to advertise for AA, but I'd be lying to you if I said it wasn't the most integral part of my recovery. It gave me a *healthy* sense of community. That's really all it is; a vast network of people suffering from the same affliction who will selflessly love you until you can love yourself. Sounds stupid to some, but for a guy that had no family or loved ones left, it finally closed the void.

Am I happy? For the most part, yes, but life doesn't just become perfect once you figure out how to stop smoking crack. I used to have simple problems, like how am I going to sell this bag of stolen lip gloss for heroin money? Now I have more abstract problems, like what can I do to be a better son? Sure, life is more boring, but boring beats sleeping on a piss-soaked sidewalk with a tire iron tucked between your legs. Boring comes with lasting relationships, familial connection, and a sense of purpose. Without these three things, we're left with a hole that for some reason drugs seem to perfectly fill. Joining a recovery community temporarily filled this hole, until, through immense cognitive behavioral therapy in the form of working the twelve steps, my psyche was permanently altered. Now that hole is overflowing.

But of course, my past isn't forgotten. I will forever cherish the horror I got to experience in my twenties, because it allows me to appreciate the mundanity of my thirties. I couldn't be more grateful. I abused drugs so hard that I literally have a scarlet letter on my face for the rest of my life, so no matter how deep I dive into the abyss of normality, I'll never be able to avoid the daily reminder of where I once was. This is my failsafe of never forgetting how bad it can get.

Back before the incident when I was trying to get sober in Florida, Dad told me numerous times that I never smiled. Nowadays I'm rarely spotted without an imperfect grin on my face. Sure, from time to time I get sad and ashamed over what happened. Sometimes I wake up and can't believe it wasn't all a dream, thinking to myself, "You're really that guy, the guy that did this to himself." But more often than not, I live in complete acceptance of it. Listen, it really doesn't look that bad, and if anything, it finally scared me straight into a life worth living.

Thousands of hours of introspection went into this book, most of which was written at night after a ten-hour workday on a construction site. Whether or not this book gets read by no one or by a million people, the act of writing it was thoroughly worth it in itself. I'm sure it was more fun to read than to have actually lived it, but regardless, I'm not complaining. I couldn't imagine my life playing out any other way, and I'm more than alright with how it's turned out.

Was I born with a disease? Maybe. Were my parents? Same answer. What I do know is that all three of us had a substantial amount of trauma, and with our limited resources, heroin was the best band-aid we could find. I don't know every answer, and I'm not here to preach. All I know is that my immense experience has given me a more rational and informed opinion than most supposed experts. Dad and I, with tremendous consequences and the help from other reformed addicts, seemingly beat addiction. People like us have an education that couldn't be learned with a century of school-ing. Mom, like over a hundred thousand people in this country last year, wasn't able to beat it. If I can get anything of worth out of my many years of suffering, it would be to greatly reduce that number for good.

I'm literally just a junkie with a decent resume of chaos. No different than the junkie that's half dead sprawled out on the sidewalk who you step over on your way to work. No different than the crackhead who sleeps underneath the overpass by where your Pilates class is. No different than the tweaker who broke into your car and stole the change out of your cupholder. There are thousands of people across this country that are inca-pacitated by homelessness and addiction, and if given the chance, most of them could pump out a story not much different than mine. Don't believe me? Next time you drive by the bum asking for change at the freeway onramp, pull over and have a conversation. Ask him what his deal is. If you sobered him up and gave him a laptop, he'd probably write a better book than this one.

I'm an outright mental defective, and so are the drug addicts I just described. I was just fortunate enough to experience a seismic consequence that changed me on a cosmic level. This shift was so strong that it inspired a friend like Molly to sacrifice her sanity for half a year to help me back on my feet. And later on at rehab, my story inspired many in recovery to show me the utmost support and love. We need community to heal, as well as a helping hand at getting on our feet and preparing to live a productive life. Not everyone on the street can be as lucky as me and have a friend like Molly after waking up with part of their face missing. And that's why addicts without a Molly in their life need a vast infrastructure of *incentiv-ized* treatment.

Handing someone like my former self a free apartment and a welfare check would have only led to one less plot in a graveyard. Sure, a single mother of three that falls on hard times could use this sort of help, and I'm all for it. But for the tens of thousands of Americans that are homeless *because* of addiction, we need to address the root problem on a national level. We need state-facilitated detox, long-term rehabilitation, psychiatric care for those in need, and job training, but most importantly, we need to supply an incentive to change in the first place. Once the laws are re-enforced, avoiding jail with mandated *comprehensive* treatment and the potential to earn subsidized housing and job opportunities could actually work. This, along with being held up by a community of people in all stages of conquering addiction, is our best bet.

First it was fellow addicts that saved my life, and with time came my family. Uncle Neal and Aunt Suzanne eventually came around and agreed to meet me for dinner. Months passed, one thing led to another, and I was invited to their home to see my little cousins (who hadn't seen me since they were small children). A year passed and I was trusted to housesit, and a few years after that there's now no question that I'm a full member of the family. Recently Uncle Neal told me, "Hey, we love you. But not only that, we *like* you. We literally enjoy having you around. You're a positive influence on our children." From complete erasure to positive influence. Not to sound corny, but that's the sort of magic that makes this all worth it. Both of them, like Molly, played a major role in saving my life. From their refusal to enable me to their willingness to let me earn back their trust, I couldn't be more in debt for their role in my vibrant life today. I owe them, Molly, the non-profit rehab, and my trudging buddy Pierceon everything. Without Pierceon, my best friend and possibly the most stand-up person I've ever met, I don't know if I would have jumped in the middle of the herd like I did my first year. This book is dedicated to them, along with Aunt Ina and Uncle Bruce—the ultimate heroes of my story.

When I was about nine months sober, my little cousin asked me about the Hebrew tattoo I woke up with in the bathtub. Being able to read a little bit of Hebrew himself, he informed me that it translated to "home." I had no clue how to read Hebrew or why I'd requested such a tattoo in a blackout. Confused, I asked him how it was pronounced, and he responded, "Bite." ⬚⬚⬚⬚⬚⬚. Do with that information as you will, but for me, that was the moment I realized I had little understanding of this world, nor should I. Some things are better left unanswered.

ACKNOWLEDGMENTS

Thank you to Neal Tabachnick, Murray Weiss, Joel Gotler, Michael Shellenberger, and Adam Bellow for believing in me. Without any of them, none of this would be possible.

ABOUT THE AUTHOR

Jared Klickstein was born in Boston, Massachusetts in 1989 to heroin-addicted parents. He spent his teenage years outside of Oakland, California after being adopted by his aunt and uncle. He attended UC Santa Cruz where he got addicted to heroin himself, dropped out, and spent nearly ten years chronically homeless and addicted around the country. After a notorious run on Skid Row in Los Angeles and a subsequent jail sentence, he sobered up in 2018, wrote this book, and currently resides in Oakland, California. He works as an independent journalist.